Sewing

LAURENCE KING

Published in 2019 by Laurence King Publishing Ltd
361–373 City Road
London EC1V 1LR
United Kingdom
Tel: +44 20 7841 6900
Fax: +44 20 7841 6910
e-mail: enquiries@laurenceking.com
www.laurenceking.com

ISBN: 978-1-78627-198-3

Front cover photograph: Jumpsuit by Phillip Lim, New York Fashion Week 2016.
Photo by Peter White / Getty Images.

Book design by The Urban Ant Ltd.
Screengrab editors Chen Chen, Brad Dary
Contributing editor Barbara Arata-Gavere

Printed in China

Sewing

Techniques for Beginners

Francesca Sterlacci

Editor: Barbara Seggio

Instructors: Ruchira Amare, Barbara Arata-Gavere, Darlene Donohue, Tina Doyle, Corina Gheorghiu, Thao Minh Do, Martha Palaza, Barbara Seggio

LAURENCE KING PUBLISHING

Contents

Brief Contents

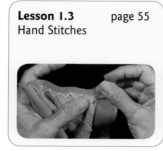

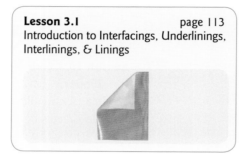
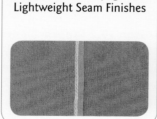

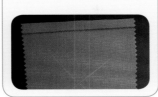

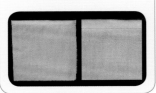
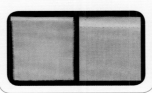
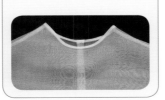

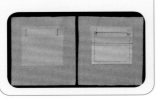
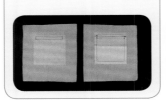

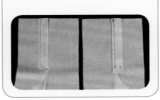

How this Book Works

You will find helpful Tip boxes throughout the book, highlighted in green

Each lesson begins with a set of Learning Objectives detailing key skills you will develop

Any fabrics and tools you need to complete the project are listed here

At the end of each chapter, you'll find a Self-evaluation checklist. Use this to measure your progress

The lesson is divided into key stages or Modules

Step-by-step photographic sequences guide you through each Module

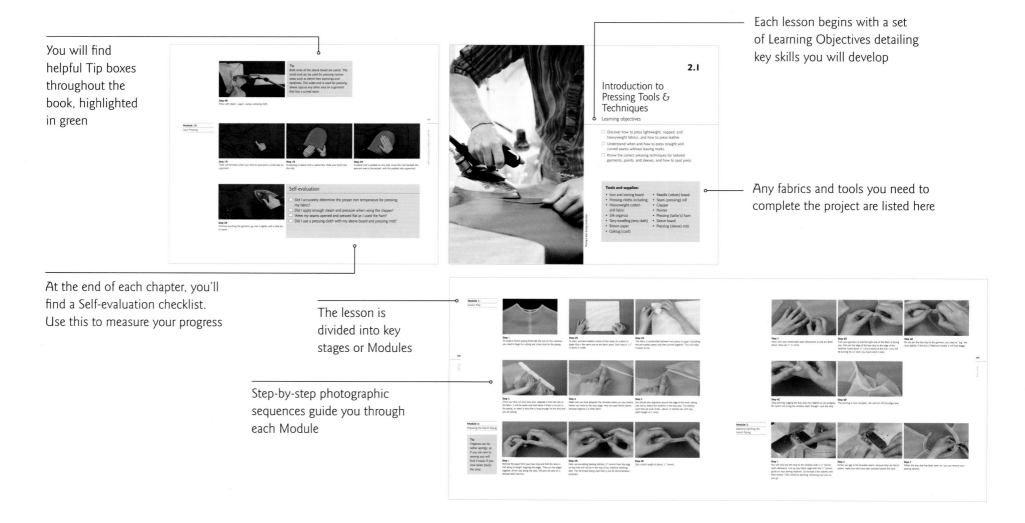

You can also view the video lessons from the University of Fashion—see **www.universityoffashion.com** to subscribe

Preface

The culmination of the design process ends with a sewn prototype. By learning industry-standard sewing techniques, designers are able to create professional-looking garments. The information in this book builds upon basic theory, from learning the types of sewing needles, threads, buttons, and hand stitches, to choosing the appropriate seam and hem finish for your fabric.

Learning how to press a garment while under construction is absolutely critical, as is knowing the various pressing tools and techniques used by experienced sewers in the fashion industry. Understanding knit fabrics, stretch percentages, and techniques used to sew knit seams, hems, and necklines demystifies the knit-fabric sewing process.

Understanding where and why garments require interfacing, lining, underlining, and lining, and learning about the various types and their application, is the difference between a garment that looks homemade and one sewn professionally.

Working with bias binding to create neck and armhole binding finishes, and learning how to sew a range of pockets and zipper treatments, provide the designer with many of the necessary skills to bring their designs to life.

As technology continues to impact the fashion industry, new paradigms and strategies have emerged in the field of fashion education. In 2008, the University of Fashion (UoF) identified a solution in addressing student learning needs in an Internet-dominated world. By creating an online video library with hundreds of lessons in key design disciplines, the UoF provides the perfect tools to teach fashion design to aspiring designers, fashion college students, home sewers, industry professionals looking to upgrade their skills, and the fashion-curious. To reinforce that learning further, the UoF has partnered with Laurence King Publishing to create *Sewing: Techniques for Beginners*, *Draping: Techniques for Beginners*, and *Pattern Making: Techniques for Beginners*. The books work on their own, with step-by-step sequences based on the videos. But they can be used in conjunction with the videos to create the ultimate learning experience.

We wish you every success with your sewing projects.

Francesca Sterlacci

Introduction to Sewing

SEWING is the process of constructing a garment, either by hand or machine. In the fashion industry, once a garment has been designed—either through the process of draping, or by creating a flat pattern—a muslin prototype known as a "toile" is sewn and tested for fit. Once the pattern has been adjusted to take in any necessary corrections revealed by the fitting process, a complete garment is cut out of the intended fabric. This is then also fitted, in case the fabric necessitates further corrections to the pattern and, if necessary, yet another prototype is made and fitted before the garment moves to the production stage.

Knowing how to sew will make you a better designer; it will teach you what can and cannot be accomplished. Designers who are familiar with sewing techniques are also often inspired by the design possibilities that these techniques can suggest. Learning how to sew, and understanding the tools and machines involved, will expand your dressmaking and tailoring techniques and make you an educated designer, able to communicate more effectively with your sample maker, technical designer, and your factory. To quote Christian Dior, "In a machine age, dressmaking is one of the last refuges of the human, the personal, the inimitable."

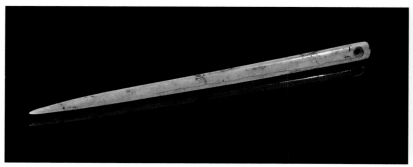

Above and right: Bone needles

The Oldest Art Form

Sewing dates back to the Paleolithic period, when prehistoric man would have created body coverings out of animal skins, sewing them together using needles carved from bone. Due to the thickness of the skins, they most likely created a kind of thumb guard to push their bone needles through, thus inventing the first thimble. They used animal sinew, the fibrous tissue that joins muscle to bone, as thread, and also laced garment pieces together using thin strips of animal skins. As man learned to use metals, needles gradually came to be made from copper (around 7000 BCE), then bronze (by 2500 BCE), and iron (from around 1200 BCE). Steel needles were being produced in Europe by the Middle Ages. It is hard to believe, but it was not until 1755 that the first patent was awarded for a needle with an eye.

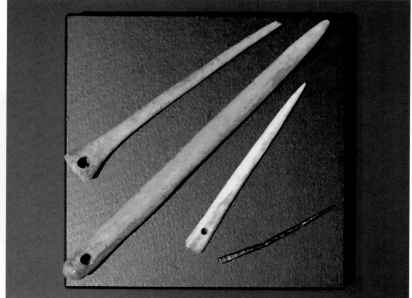

Right: Elias Howe's version of the lockstitch machine, patented in 1846.

Below right: An advertisement for an early Singer machine aimed at the domestic market.

By around 5500 BCE the Ancient Egyptians had learned to make thread from flax and cotton plant fibers, and from animal hair, which could then be spun onto spools, dyed, and woven into cloth. Then, around 2,500 years later, the Chinese had devised the technique of making thread from silkworm cocoons. Although China exported its silk, the method of its production (sericulture) remained a secret until it eventually spread to other countries in the region. Silk production began in Europe in the fifth century, established with a few silkworms smuggled out of China by two monks, who returned with them to Constantinople (today's Istanbul). In the mid-1700s, several inventions in England transformed the process of spinning and weaving cotton to make textiles, and cotton remained the fiber of choice for clothing until the invention of synthetic fibers some 100 years later (rayon viscose in 1855, followed by nylon in 1931, and polyester in 1941). Later, different thread blends would become popular.

For the Ancient Egyptians, and for the Ancient Greeks and Romans many millennia later, clothing had consisted of simple draped garments that were held together with pins (known as fibulae) or buttons, and required little to no sewing. Over the following centuries, however, fashion gradually shifted from wrapped and draped styles to form-fitting silhouettes requiring more complex construction techniques, and by the Middle Ages, sewing guilds had been established that taught both garment construction and pattern making.

The Industrial Revolution

The most significant changes, however, came with the Industrial Revolution. Innovations in England had allowed the establishment of mass-produced cotton, and the invention of the cotton gin by the American Eli Whitney in 1793, which automated the process of separating cotton fibers from their seeds, drastically reduced production costs.

The availability of mass-produced textiles went hand in hand with a newly industrialized system of garment manufacture. Until this point clothes had been made by hand, with a single garment taking weeks to construct, depending on the complexity of the design. Now garment production could take place on an industrial scale, and the invention of numerous machines would transform the process, for both industrial and domestic manufacture.

The Sewing Machine

In 1830, ten years after the invention of the tape measure, the Frenchman Barthélemy Thimmonier invented one of the earliest known sewing machines. However, pressure from tailors' guilds thwarted its success at the time. In 1833, the American Walter Hunt invented a lockstitch sewing machine that was then

perfected and patented by fellow American Elias Howe in 1845. This machine could only sew straight seams, but it greatly reduced sewing time compared to hand sewing. Then, in 1850, another American, Isaac Merritt Singer, created an improved version that could also sew curved seams, and was operated by a foot treadle. This left both hands free and, therefore, drastically sped up the process. In 1889, Singer invented the first electric sewing machine, and by the 1930s, factories and homes converted from using foot-pedal machines to motor-powered sewing machines, eventually equipped with special features.

The first computer-controlled sewing machine was introduced by Singer in 1978, and soon after, home sewing machines from manufacturers in Europe and Asia—Bernina, Brother, Juki, Necchi, and Pfaff—began to flood the market.

Today, the home sewing machine does much more than sew; it is capable of zigzagging, embroidering, serging (overlocking) seam edges, and making

Right: A 1964 electric Singer sewing machine.

Far right: A modern garment factory.

buttonholes. Some industrial models can also be programmed to sew seams and cut threads automatically.

Manufacturing Systems

From the nineteenth century, with the introduction of first electric sewing machines, factories employed machine operators to sew a specific section of a garment, a system known as "piecework." This proved to be a more efficient production model than having operators sew whole garments.

Then in the 1970s, a new manufacturing system called just-in-time (JIT) was developed in Japan. (In the West it also became known as the Toyota Production System—TPS.) Its aim was to increase efficiency and speed up response times. Among other innovations, this system groups garment-assembly processes into modules instead of dividing them into their smallest components.

Multifunctional operators work on machines that are arranged in a U-line and move from one machine to the next, taking the garment with them. The benefits are many: fewer operators are required; all of the operators in the group are responsible for the quality of each item produced in their line, which leads to an increase in quality; the operators report less fatigue than if they are sitting and sewing throughout a shift; and a substantial increase in productivity.

The garment factory of the future will see a major increase in the use of robotic sewing machines. Machines are already in use today that are capable of completing basic elements of the process.

Industry Standards

The Industrial Revolution also prompted a system of standardized sizing for mass-produced, ready-to-wear clothing. In the U.S., measurements taken from Civil War soldiers helped standardize men's sizes, while in 1863, the Butterick paper pattern company patented size specifications for women. Founded in 1898, the American Society for Testing Materials (now ASTM International) began issuing standards in 1941 that soon became universal. These standards included machinery standards, thread types, sizes, and classifications, as well as garment sizing and measurement-taking standards.

Dressmaking

Dressmaking refers to clothes made specifically for women. Originally, dressmakers created garments from a client's measurements. Then, in the mid-1800s, Charles Frederick Worth created the first "fashion house" in Paris, and from this point on the term "dressmaker" took on a new meaning; designers now did the designing, while dressmakers did the sewing.

At this made-to-measure end of the clothing market—the couture world—a designer's workroom (*atelier*) is where the designer designs and the garment samples and small production lots are sewn. Garment construction is overseen by skilled workers called *midinettes*, typically: a *première* (female head of workroom) or a *premier* (male head), who is responsible for putting the design into three-dimensional form; a *seconde* (assistant to the *premier*); *petites mains* (seamstresses); and *arpettes* (apprentices). The skilled sewers are divided into two areas: the *flou*, where dresses and gowns are made, and the *tailleur*, for jackets and suits. While sewing machines and irons are used for primary seams, the buttons and buttonholes, pleats, zippers, and embroidery are all done by hand. Couture garments can require three to ten fittings, and take anywhere from 100 to 1,000 hours to construct, depending on the garment. Today, couture garments range from US$15,000 to $150,000 each, depending on the fabric and amount of beading, embroidery, and other details.

For ready-to-wear and all mass-produced garments, the process is somewhat varied and depends on the company and whether they maintain a "design room," or manufacture their samples abroad. A design room is something of a luxury, since it involves employing one or more pattern makers/drapers and one or more sample

Sean Connery being fitted by Anthony Sinclair, creator of the Conduit Cut.

makers. The alternative is to employ technical designers and specification writers to interpret a design and create a "tech pack," a computer-generated blueprint of a design, that is then sent to a factory to be made into a prototype.

Bespoke Tailoring

Out of the guilds formed during the Middle Ages came a group of elite, mostly male, tailors who had to work within the many restrictions placed on them by those guilds based on their skills. Some guilds became extremely powerful. Of particular note was the French tailors' guild, the Maîtres Tailleurs d'Habits. By 1740, however, made-to-measure or bespoke tailoring had become popular in London as expert tailors began to set up shop in and around Savile Row, and on Cork Street, St. James Street, and Jermyn Street, to attract the custom of English gentlemen. Beau Brummel, the epitome of the well-dressed man, patronized these shops and helped to make English tailoring famous.

Savile Row is known mostly as the center of men's bespoke tailoring, but women are also catered for. Over a period of several weeks, involving at least 50 hours of hand tailoring, a series of fittings is performed, each taking the garment through successive stages of production, allowing the client to witness the true bespoke experience of having his or her clothes built around them. In the late 1960s the Beatles popularized the Row again, when suits (apart from George Harrison's) were made for their *Abbey Road* album cover by Tommy Nutter of Nutters of Savile Row. Nutter's other celebrity clients including Bianca and Mick Jagger, and Elton John, while fellow bespoke tailor, Anthony Sinclair, was famous for creating the Conduit Cut for Sean Connery for his first James Bond film.

The 1990s and 2000s experienced a "New Bespoke Movement." New designers such as Alexander McQueen (who had worked as an apprentice at Anderson & Sheppard and Gieves & Hawkes, both in Savile Row) and Ozwald Boateng (who started his career with help from Tommy Nutter) incorporated tailoring techniques into their women's ready-to-wear collections.

The Seamstress as Designer

While the main role of the designer is to design, many designers past and present have realized that to excel at their craft they must also be "hands on." Jeanne Paquin started out as a seamstress at the French firm Maison Rouff. In 1891, together with her businessman husband, Isidore René Jacob, she opened the House of Paquin. The couple then proceeded to build one of the largest international haute couture houses of their time.

Designer Madeleine Vionnet started her career as a dressmaker's apprentice at age 12 for Madame Bourgueil, which prepared her for creating masterpieces that are still recognized as sewing marvels today. Italian designer Nina Ricci likewise began her career as a dressmaker's apprentice at a young age, before joining Maison Raffin at the age of 25. She eventually opened her own couture house in 1932, when she was 49.

Cristóbal Balenciaga was a man devoted to his craft. He would personally rework a completed and approved design until its construction seams became invisible, which was why he became known as "the Master." Apprenticeships at the house of Balenciaga attracted several who would go on to become famous designers in their own right, including André Courrèges, Hubert de Givenchy, Oscar de la Renta, and Emanuel Ungaro—all designers whose respect for garment construction is evident in the execution of their designs.

Many designers were inspired by their seamstress mothers. The mother of Spanish-born designer Paco Rabanne, for example, worked as a seamstress at the House of Balenciaga; Gianni and Donatella Versace's mother, Francesca, was a dressmaker with her own shop; and Alberta Ferretti's mother was a successful dressmaker with an *atelier* and as many as 18 seamstresses.

Coco Chanel

Coco Chanel was taught to sew by nuns when she was placed in an orphanage at an early age. Although she started out as a millinery designer, Chanel would become one of the most important designers of all time, in large part due to her attention to garment construction detail. Possibly no other garment in the history of fashion has received more attention than the iconic "Chanel jacket," which was made using a specially commissioned loose-weave tweed from the Linton Weaving Mill in Scotland. Today, the fabric is produced by the House of Lesage.

The Chanel jacket is notable for several tailoring innovations: front and back princess panels for a better fit; extra-wide seam allowances in both the garment shell and lining for easy alteration; quilting the silk lining directly to the shell fabric (no underlining), which helps maintain the jacket's shape while preventing the fabric from becoming loose or distorted; and pieces that are cut straight and then shaped using heat and moisture, so that seams can be matched both horizontally and vertically on plaids and other patterned fabrics. Chanel jacket sleeves are also engineering marvels, starting with a three-piece sleeve pattern that results in a closer-fitting sleeve with a slight natural curve. This allows the sleeve button vent to be in a forward position instead of farther back, as they are on a man's jacket sleeve. (The jacket sleeves were originally designed as three-quarter length so that the wearer's wrist jewelry would be visible.) The jacket also contains an actual chain, hand-stitched along the hem to counterbalance the jacket's heavy buttons and to help weight the jacket so that it hangs smoothly on the body. Other details include hand-stitched patch pockets, hand-worked buttonholes on the face, and faux bound buttonholes on the reverse for a cleaner look. Chanel jackets include expensive buttons and embellishments, such as braided, fringed, and ribbon trims that are sewn by hand around the edges of the jacket, sleeves, and pockets.

In 1997, a subsidiary company called Paraffection (loosely, "for the love of") was established by Karl Lagerfeld at Chanel, with the aim of safeguarding the artisanal skills offered by a number of independent ateliers. These specialist workshops were long-established suppliers to Chanel, as well as to many other couture houses, but were in danger of closing. Over the following years, Chanel acquired various ateliers in turn, including Lesage (specialist embroidery), Desrues (costume jewelry and buttons), Guillet (fabric flowers), Maison Michel (millinery), Lemarié (feathers and flowers), Robert Goossens (gold- and silversmithing), and Massaro (shoemaking). Annual Métiers d'Art collections are specifically designed to showcase the work of these master craftsmen.

Learning How to Sew

The first thing you will need when learning how to sew is familiarity with the tools that you will be using. The most fundamental of these are hand-sewing needles and pins. Choosing the correct needles and pins for a particular project will mean the difference between producing a professional-looking garment or one that is damaged—or even unwearable. You will also need to know how to use a thimble and a pincushion. Not all threads are alike, either. Choosing the wrong thread can cause puckered seams, or create problems when laundering or dry-cleaning a garment.

Pressing your work as you sew is one of the golden rules of garment construction. Knowing the tools and techniques for doing this will result in clothes that look professional rather than homemade.

To truly understand a garment's design and functionality, you will need a good working knowledge of the components that make up a garment, such as where and when to use interfacings, underlinings, interlinings, and linings.

You will also need to master the art of selecting and applying fastenings to your garments, whether you opt for buttons and buttonholes, or zippers, and how best to use your machine to achieve the desired effect in each case.

Your garments will benefit enormously if you have the skills to produce a variety of seam and hem finishes, so that you can always choose the one best suited to your design and the weight of your fabric.

Naomi Campbell modeling a Chanel couture jacket, Fall/Winter 2002.

This book will take you through a series of lessons designed to build up a working knowledge of all of the elements involved in constructing a garment from start to finish. You will learn both hand-sewing and machine-sewing techniques, and build up a comprehensive repertoire of skills that you can then employ on a wide variety of garments, and in many types of fabric.

The Basics

If you are new to sewing, the first thing you will need to do is research and buy a sewing machine. There are many different models to choose from and we advise that you try out a few machines before making a purchase. Machine prices are based on several factors, including whether they have features such as buttonhole and embroidery capabilities, and whether they are computerized or not. Computerized machines have more features, although beginners may find mechanical sewing machines less daunting and easier to use. Focus on choosing the machine that best fits your pocketbook and your sewing aspirations.

You will then need to arm yourself with a number of other smaller tools, so this book begins with a summary of the basics. Our rundown on needles, pins, thimbles, and pincushions is something that you will refer back to repeatedly throughout your sewing career. It contains details of the types of needles and pins available for all sorts of design projects, including hand-sewing needles, sewing-machine needles, and the specific needles used for silk, knits, and everything in between. You will also learn the anatomy of needles and pins, and ways to make threading needles easier. Reading a package of domestic or industrial sewing-machine needles can be somewhat confusing; we will clarify the options so that you will always be able to select the best one for your project. To make hand sewing less painful, we will teach you all about thimbles—the types available, and why and when to use them. And the workroom of no sewer, draper, or pattern maker is complete without several types of pincushion, so we will cover what you need to know here, too.

Just as important as choosing the right needle for your project is picking the correct thread. Our Thread lesson will explore what threads are made from, and the difference between a spun, core-spun, multifilament, and monofilament thread. You will also learn what textured threads are used for, and when to use elastic thread. Although most beginners never think about thread weight, using a thread that is too heavy for your fabric can cause a lot of problems for your seams. The reverse is also true: using a lightweight thread for a heavyweight fabric will cause seams to split. Your choice will need to take certain elements into account, but we will provide you with a thread size chart to make this process easy. Other important topics covered in this lesson are thread finishes, how a spool of thread should be placed on the sewing-machine spindle, and guidelines for selecting the correct color thread for your project.

Hand-stitching techniques that you will learn include basting (tacking), which is a technique used instead of tracing paper and a tracing wheel to transfer seam lines and other guidelines onto expensive or delicate fabrics. It is also used when temporarily sewing a garment together for a fitting. You will also learn various seam and hemming stitches, including overcast stitch, slip stitch, catch stitch,

double overcast, and blind stitch. A thread bar is another hand stitch that you will often use when creating a loop for buttons, hooks, and lacings, while a French tack, or loop, is perfect for holding a belt or a lining in place. To add a decorative touch to a garment, we will also teach you how to sew a pick stitch and blanket stitch. All of these stitches will then be employed in the lessons that follow later in the book.

Pressing Tools & Techniques

One of the biggest mistakes that beginners make is forgetting to press their work throughout the construction process. The importance of this step cannot be underestimated, so in this chapter we will demonstrate how to press a variety of fabrics, ranging from light- to heavyweight options, napped fabrics, and even leather, which must be dealt with carefully so as to avoid damaging and drying out the skin. You will also learn the correct way to press curved seams, sleeves, and other tailored elements, and discover the tools that you will need to produce garments that look as professional as possible.

Interfacings, Underlinings, Interlinings, & Linings

From a garment's outward appearance, one would never know that sometimes one or more other layers of material exist inside it—namely interfacing, underlining, interlining, and lining. These materials play an important role in a garment's look and durability. Interfacings come in woven and nonwoven options and are either sewn or ironed in place to provide shape, structure, and stability to key areas of a garment. From the lightest interfacings through to heavy hair canvas and buckram, this lesson will give you the knowledge to make the best interfacing choice for each of your projects.

Another of these hidden layers is the underlining layer—a layer of material that is used on the underside of a garment's outer shell fabric. As with interfacing, there are a number of different options available, so you will learn how to choose an underlining based on fabric weight, and how to apply it correctly.

Interlining is attached to a lining for added warmth, and we will discuss the various choices available, from loft products sold by the yard to down fillings, feather fillings, and down/feather blends that are quilted or infused into channels on a garment.

Lastly, you will learn the role that lining plays in the construction of a garment, and how to work with the numerous options available.

Seam Finishes

Our chapter on seam finishes is divided into two basic categories: finishes suitable for lightweight fabrics (such as organza, voile, chiffon, and georgette), and those suited to medium-weight fabrics (cotton, linen, wool, or blends).

Lightweight Fabrics

For lightweight woven fabrics you will learn how to sew four different finishes: a single edge-stitch seam, a double-stitched seam, a French seam, and a mock French seam. Each of these seam choices has its own advantages. For full sheer skirts and dresses, for example, where there is no stress on the seam, a single edge-stitch seam is a great choice, whereas a double-stitched seam is a better option for seams that will be subject to moderate stress. A French seam is particularly popular on sheer fabrics, although the clean finish it offers can work well on any lightweight fabric seam. The mock French seam mimics the French seam, but with a fewer steps.

Medium-weight Fabrics

We then move on to a number of seam finishes suitable for medium-weight woven fabrics, beginning with the classic flat-felled seam found on jeans. We also demonstrate how to achieve a tailored look with a Hong Kong seam, which, while very labor intensive, is great for unlined jackets or when you are looking to add extra value to your garment. Another popular seam when working with fabrics that do not fray is a pinked and open seam. Perhaps the most popular seam finish of all, the overlocked and open seam is created using an overlocker (or serger). In addition to these basic seam finishes you will also learn several decorative finishes: a double-faced seam, used on double-faced wool garment edges and seams; a slot seam, which provides an effective design element; and a lapped seam, which is often used on non-fraying fabrics as well as on leather, suede, vinyl, and faux leather.

Hem Finishes

Choosing the correct hem finish for your project plays a key role in determining the look of your garment. The wrong hem finish can cheapen the appearance of a garment and may cause the hem to pucker. As when choosing the right seam finish for a garment, you must learn to assess the requirements of your fabric in order to select the most appropriate hem.

Lightweight Fabrics

When working with lightweight woven fabrics, there are several finishes that can work, depending upon the design of the garment. For example, in couture, a sheer hem is sewn using a hand-rolled hem finish. The most economical hem choice, however, is either a baby hem created with a sewing machine hemming foot or, in the absence of a machine hemming foot, a tailored edge (baby hem) finish. Other hem finishes can add an interesting decorative touch, and in this chapter we explore three of these—adding a horsehair trim to the hem to provide structure; adding a ribbon for a neat, clean hem that can be created on the inside or outside of the garment; and a wide self hem that produces a simple design detail by doubling up the fabric at the hem.

Medium-weight Fabrics

When it comes to medium-weight woven fabrics, most ready-to-wear clothing has a hem edge finished with hem tape or an overlocked hem edge, so we demonstrate both of these techniques. Then, for a more luxurious hand-finished look, we show you how to create a Hong Kong hem, which involves binding the hem edge with either lining or a lightweight organza. A less tedious option is a pinked and stitched hem, although this finish is not a viable option for fabric that has a tendency to fray.

Buttons & Buttonholes

It is very easy to select buttons as an afterthought, but taking the time to consider the size, shape, and material of your buttons can make the difference between a mediocre result and an impressive one; signature buttons or buttonholes can even become your hallmark as a designer. The placement of your buttonholes alone can be what makes your design stand apart from the rest. If you have any doubts about the importance of buttons and buttonholes, do a contrast test. Place buttons in a color that matches your fabric on your garment, then remove them and replace them with a set in a contrasting color—you will see the impact instantly. The same goes for using contrast thread when creating your buttonholes.

You will therefore learn all about buttons—shapes, sizes, and composition. You will also be introduced to the rules of button placement, which includes whether a button should be planned to sit horizontally or vertically, and the differences between men's and women's garments. As for buttonholes, you will learn what size your buttonhole should be, the various shapes to choose from, and what types of thread you can use to make them.

Hand-sewn Buttons

Although it may appear to be the easiest sewing task of all, learning the correct way to sew a button is a lesson that you should not skip. We will show you how to sew both a four-hole button (with different stitch configurations) and a shank button.

Machine-made Buttonholes

The final lesson of this chapter will demonstrate how to produce two standard types of buttonhole: a straight buttonhole and a keyhole variation. You will learn how to use the buttonhole foot attachment that comes with your machine, following a step-by-step approach that will guarantee neat results every time.

Knits

Knits behave very differently to woven fabrics, so you will need to develop a good understanding of their inherent properties so that you can accommodate these when sewing. However, working with knits is easy, once you know how.

Each knit type has its own structure, so at the start of this chapter you will learn the difference between a weft and a warp knit, and the types of knits in each category. You will learn about jerseys, single knits and double knits, interlocks, and ribs, and about the different types of warp knits such as tricot and raschel. Knits are offered in a multitude of fibers such as cotton, polyester, wool, and various blends.

You will then move on to our lesson entitled Knit Fabric Principles. In this lesson you will learn about the four key characteristics: stretch, recovery, weight, and shrinkage. Not only will this lesson explain the difference between a one-way, two-way, and four-way stretch knit, but it will also demonstrate each on a dress form (tailor's dummy) so that you can learn about "stretch ratio" and see at first hand how important choosing the right knit fabric is to the design, pattern-making, and sewing processes.

Certain seam and hem finishes are unique to knits, because of the stretch inherent in knit fabrics. We will demonstrate the techniques involved in achieving each of these. You will also learn different neckline finishes so that you will be able to add a professional touch to your knit garments.

Binding & Spaghetti Straps

You have several choices when it comes to finishing necklines, armholes, sleeve openings, and waistbands—or, in fact, any raw edge on a garment. In this chapter we will demonstrate several ways to sew a bias binding to a raw edge, using an edgestitch, a crack stitch, and a slip stitch, all of which will provide a neat, clean edge. You will also be able to compare the process of finishing the binding on your sewing machine with finishing it by hand; the latter being slower but allowing you greater control. In addition to these bindings, you will also learn how to sew a French piping, which is often used when finishing edges on sheer and very lightweight fabrics. While the Spaghetti Straps lesson demonstrates the process of creating a thin bias strip and turning it inside out to form a strap for a dress, this technique has other uses, too—try using it to create a belt, a trim, or even a looped button closure.

Pockets

While tailoring techniques are usually taught at the intermediate level, the Single- and Double-Welt Pocket lessons in our next chapter are so easy that a beginner can take on the challenge with great results. These pockets can be positioned vertically, horizontally, and, with practice, on the bias of a garment. The welts can be made from self fabric, a contrast fabric, or a contrast color. Single- and double-welt pockets can be used on jackets, dresses, coats, and pants (trousers). And, once you master these lessons, you will most likely find other types of garments to which to add them, to show off your new skills.

Setting Zippers

Many beginners avoid having to sew a zipper into their garments. Our chapter on Zipper lessons will definitely change that. While we do recommend that you practice and baste your zippers prior to sewing them until you get the hang of it, the step-by-step nature of these lessons will take a lot of the worry out of the process. It is recommended that you reinforce the zipper area with a strip of either press-on or sew-in interfacing to stabilize the garment opening before you begin.

We will demonstrate how to set the most common zippers: the centered zipper, the lapped zipper, and the invisible zipper. When setting a lapped zipper into a garment that has a neck facing, professional sewing-machine operators use a particular method, which we share with you here. We will also teach you how to insert an exposed separating zipper—often used on outerwear, or for visual impact—and a fly front zipper, for use on pants. Our final zipper lesson is an embellished, hand-stitched zipper. We will show you how to use a prick stitch to attach your zipper while adding a row of decorative beads down the zipper opening at the same time. This method is perfect for evening dresses that require an extra decorative touch, or when working with delicate fabrics that would be damaged by the zipper foot of a machine.

Sewing Tools

The tools that you will need for sewing begin with an assortment of hand-sewing needles, threads, a thimble, beeswax (or a thread conditioner such as Thread Heaven), and a pincushion. You will also need several types of scissors: fabric shears, embroidery scissors, and pinking shears, as well as clippers and a seam ripper for removing unwanted stitches.

As mentioned previously, a sewing machine will be used to sew many of the projects in this book. Although we use different models in the lessons, choose one according to your budget and the functions that you might need. In addition to the machine's regular presser foot, you will need right- and left-side zipper feet, as well as an invisible zipper foot. And a sewing machine gauge can help with stitching margins as you sew.

For making thin spaghetti straps you will need a loop turner. In addition to dressmaker's pins you will also need silk pins for working with sheer and fine fabrics. Pressing your projects during the construction process is critical, so you will need an iron and an ironing board, plus an assortment of other tools, such as a sleeve board, pressing cloth, seam roll, pressing ham, pressing mitt, and, for napped fabrics, a velvet board. For marking your fabric you will need tailor's chalk, a 2HB lead pencil, a white pencil, and a variety of rulers. Tiger Tape and ¼" (6mm) style tape will be needed for hand sewing. And finally, to protect your table surface, you will need a cutting mat. The equipment summarized in the checklist below should cover most of your needs.

Checklist of Sewing Tools

- [ ] Cutting mat
- [ ] Sewing machine
- [ ] Sewing machine feet: right-side zipper foot, left-side zipper foot, invisible zipper foot
- [ ] Hand-sewing needles: sharps, sizes 8, 9, 10 & 12
- [ ] Hand-sewing needles: quilting/betweens, size 10
- [ ] Embroidery needle, size 1
- [ ] Beading needles, sizes 10 & 12
- [ ] Beeswax or Thread Heaven
- [ ] Dressmaker's pins
- [ ] Silk pins
- [ ] Seam ripper
- [ ] Loop turner
- [ ] Sewing gauge
- [ ] 12" (30.5cm) clear plastic ruler

- [ ] 18" (46cm) clear plastic ruler
- [ ] 1 x 6" (2.5 x 15cm) clear plastic ruler
- [ ] Embroidery scissors (sharp point)
- [ ] 9" (23cm) fabric shears
- [ ] Pinking shears
- [ ] Clippers
- [ ] Tailor's chalk
- [ ] White pencil
- [ ] 2HB pencil
- [ ] Needle threader
- [ ] Pointer
- [ ] Open-top thimble
- [ ] Regular thimble
- [ ] Pearl cotton thread
- [ ] 6-strand cotton embroidery floss (thread)

- [ ] Cotton thread
- [ ] Silk thread
- [ ] Buttonhole twist thread
- [ ] Tiger Tape
- [ ] Scotch tape
- [ ] Adhesive ¼" (6mm) style tape
- [ ] Pressing cloth
- [ ] Iron & ironing board
- [ ] Sleeve board
- [ ] Seam roll
- [ ] Pressing (tailor's) ham
- [ ] Pressing mitt
- [ ] Velvet (needle) board
- [ ] Clapper

1 Hand Sewing

As any industry professional will tell you, using the correct tools will make all of your projects the best that they can be. This first chapter contains all you need to know about hand and machine **needles, pins, thimbles, and pincushions**. It is a handy reference to use while working through the sewing lessons that follow. You will discover how sewing **threads** are made, how they are sized and packaged, and which type, and how much, to buy for a project.

The key **hand stitches** begin with a basting (tacking) stitch, which you will need for almost every project. Techniques include attaching fabrics of different textures to avoid slippage, transferring marks and guidelines to fabric with thread tracing or tailor's tacks, and using a pad and fell stitch to secure a canvas interfacing.

Other featured stitches are used variously for joining seams, securing appliqués, finishing hems, and even creating closures. We include two decorative hand stitches—the blanket and the pick stitch—that allow you to finish the edges of collars and sleeves with a flourish.

Decorative pincushion and flat-head pins, thimble, and thread.

Introduction to Needles, Pins, Thimbles, & Pincushions

Learning objectives

- ☐ Understand the anatomy of a hand-sewing needle; gain an overview of different hand-sewing needles and what they are used for

- ☐ Choose and fit a thimble and discover other sewing aids

- ☐ Survey the main types of pincushion

- ☐ Know the different pins, their sizes and uses, and when to use each type

- ☐ Explore sewing-machine needles—anatomy, needle size and class charts, and when to use each type

Needle Anatomy and Sizes

All hand-sewing needles share the same basic anatomy. At the top is the eye, which is the opening through which the thread passes. The shaft runs from the eye down to the point, or tip. The point, in turn, is the part of the needle that penetrates your fabric, and the diameter of the needle describes its width, or thickness.

Hand-sewing needles come in many different lengths and thicknesses. They are chosen based on the thickness of the fabric or material of a particular project. For most needles, the rule is: the higher the number, the shorter the shaft and the smaller the needle's diameter. For example, size 10 sharps will be shorter and finer than size 5 sharps. This sizing convention dates back to the beginning of the nineteenth century. The exception to this rule are beading needles, where the number given indicates only the width of the needle's eye and not the needle's length, since beading needles come in varying lengths.

The size of a needle's eye, whether it is small, round, oval, medium, or large, will determine the thickness of thread that can pass through it. A suitable eye opening, therefore, depends on the project. For example, the eye of an embroidery needle needs to be larger than the eye of a beading needle, while sharps and betweens (or quilting needles) have round eyes. Some needles are available with 18-carat gold or gold-plated eyes, which help the needle maneuver quickly through the fabric, resulting in less stress on your fingers.

Hand-sewing needles are also available with various types of tip. Depending on your project, you may choose one that is very sharp (sharps are so-named for this feature), or perhaps a beading needle with a slightly rounded tip, which is designed to avoid splitting your thread as you pass more than once through a bead. A ballpoint needle is very rounded at the tip and is used for stretch wovens and knits, where it passes between the threads of the fabric rather than piercing them and creating a hole. And a tapestry needle has a blunt tip, allowing the needle to pass through the material without damaging the needle. It is always very important to avoid using a needle with a damaged tip. If you do, you will ruin your work.

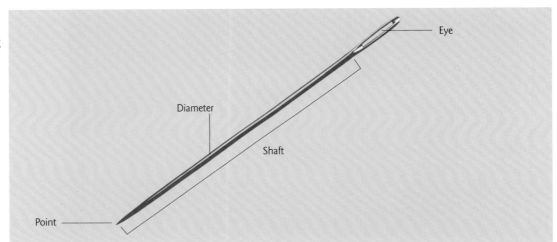

Self-threading Needles

Many people have difficulty threading a needle, especially when the eye is very small, which is why self-threading needles can be helpful. These are needles that can be threaded from either the top or the side. Those that thread from the top are known as calyx-eye needles. Those that thread from the side are called spiral-eye needles. Self-threading needles are not recommended, however, when working with fine fabrics.

Instead of a self-threading needle you can also use a needle threader to help thread a needle.

Tip
Some sewing machines come with built-in needle threaders, but if yours lacks this feature, needle threaders specifically designed for use with sewing machines are also available.

Needle Threaders

Needle threaders are available in various models. Just slip the needle threader wire into the needle's eye. Then feed the thread through the wire opening of the needle threader before pulling the threader back out of the eye with a tug.

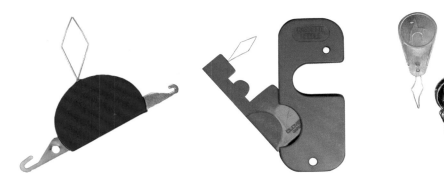

Sharps

Sharps are the most popular hand-sewing needles for general purposes. They have a round eye and, as mentioned, a sharp point. They are available in sizes 1 to 12. Sizes 2, 3, and 4 are suitable for medium to heavy fabrics, while sizes 5 to 10 are used for light to medium fabrics, with sizes 8 and 9 being good all-purpose needles within this weight category. Sizes 11 and 12 are best for fine fabrics and for creating small, delicate stitches.

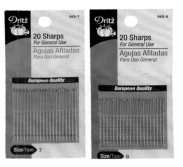

Sharps Size Chart

This chart lists the various sizes of sharps, along with their length and diameter.

Needle Size	Needle Length	Needle Diameter
1	48.5mm	1.02mm
2 & 3	44mm	0.86mm
4 & 5	40mm	0.76mm
6 & 7	37mm	0.69mm
8 & 9	34mm	0.61mm
10	32.5mm	0.53mm
11	31mm	0.46mm
12	29.5mm	0.41mm

Betweens/Quilting Needles

Betweens, or quilting needles, are short needles with a round eye. They are easy to handle, due to their size, and are mostly used in quilting and detailed work. Tailored garments, especially where pad stitching is involved, are one example of a project that will require betweens. They are available in sizes 1 to 12, and are also available gold and platinum plated for reduced friction.

Betweens/Quilting Needles Size Chart

This chart lists the various sizes of betweens, along with their length and diameter.

Needle Size	Needle Length	Needle Diameter
1	41mm	1.02mm
2 & 3	39mm	0.86mm
4 & 5	35mm	0.76mm
6 & 7	31.5mm	0.69mm
8 & 9	28.5mm	0.61mm
10	25.5mm	0.53mm
11	22.5mm	0.53mm
12	22.5 mm	0.41mm

Beading Needles

Beading needles are used for beading, so are fine enough to be able to pass easily through bead and sequin holes. They are longer in length than sharps so that multiple beads can fit on the needle shaft. Beading needles are sometimes made from stainless steel for durability and strength. In addition to being used for beading, these needles are also used for thread-basting fine fabrics. Their tips are slightly rounded to avoid splitting the fabric yarn and the threads while beading.

Although beading needles are sized from 10 to 15, these numbers—unlike with other hand-sewing needles—do not indicate the length of the needle; they only refer to the diameter of the needle's eye. A beading needle in a single size is offered as sharp, short, long, or extra long.

The average beading needle is a size 10, which fits a size 11 seed bead. (Seed bead sizes are determined by how many beads can sit end to end in 1 inch/2.5cm.) However, short beading needles are also available. Always use a needle at least one size smaller than the size of the bead that you are working with. And consider how many times the thread will need to pass through the bead—the thread will take up space in the hole, so you need to plan accordingly.

For delicate work, choose a ballpoint beading needle. Other types of beading needles include curved needles; needles with large eyes (called "big eyes") or collapsible eyes; and needles with twisted wire shafts. English beading needles are more flexible; they tend to be a bit longer and curve with use. Japanese beading needles are stiffer and may break, depending upon the project.

Left to right: Ballpoint beading needles; Big-eye beading needles; Collapsible-eye needle; Twisted wire beading needle; Flexible twisted wire beading needles; Curved beading needles.

Beading Needles Size Chart

This chart lists size, diameter, and length, with sharp, short, long, and extra-long variants.

Needle Size	Needle Length	Type	Needle Diameter
10	55mm		0.44mm
10	32mm	Sharp	0.44mm
10	37mm	Short	0.53mm
10	51mm	Long	0.53mm
10	116mm	Extra long	0.44mm
11	31mm	Sharp	0.43mm
11	53mm		0.38mm
12	29mm	Sharp	0.33mm
12	59mm	Long	0.38mm
12	76mm	Extra long	0.38mm
12	51mm		0.33mm
13	49mm		0.03mm
15	45mm		0.25mm

Embroidery & Crewel Needles

Embroidery needles are similar to sharps in that they have sharp points. However, embroidery needles have a larger, oval eye to allow thicker threads (such as six-strand embroidery floss) to pass through them. Crewel needles have slightly longer eyes. They can be used for general-purpose sewing, but because of the larger eye they are most often used when a thicker, stronger thread is needed—when basting, smocking, quilting, decorative topstitching in appliqué, or cross-stitching, and for crewel work using worsted wool, ribbon, and linen twill. Embroidery and crewel needles are available in sizes 1 to 10.

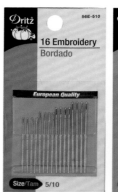

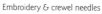

Embroidery & crewel needles

Ballpoint Needles

Ballpoint needles are used for sewing stretch and knit fabrics. The rounded point of the needle will not break the fibers or stretch them out of shape, but instead will pass between them and therefore retain the integrity of the fabric. They are available in sizes 5 to 10.

Glovers/Leather Needles

Glovers have triangular points that make it easier for the needle to penetrate leather and leatherlike materials. They are available in sizes 1 to 12. The length and diameter specifications for glovers are the same as for sharps.

Milliners/Straw Needles

Milliners are the longest of the hand-sewing needles, and have a small, round eye. They are used for gathering, smocking, pleating, basting, and millinery work. They are also available with 18-carat gold eyes, and gold or plantinum plated, which helps them maneuver quickly through fabric, creating less stress on your hands. They are available in sizes 3 to 11.

Needlelike Tools

A bodkin is a long, thick, needlelike tool with a large, elongated eye, sometimes available with a ballpoint end that prevents it from piercing the fabric. Bodkins can be flat, round, or textured for working with slippery fabrics, and are generally used for threading elastic, ribbon, or tape through casings and lace openings. A plastic elastic threader is another tool that can be used to pull elastic through a casing.

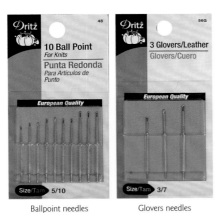

Ballpoint needles   Glovers needles

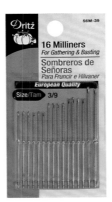

Milliners needles

Bodkins

Elastic threader

Tapestry Needles

Tapestry needles have a large eye and a blunt tip. They are used for needlepoint on embroidery canvas or on any type of even-weave or other loosely woven fabric. The blunt tip allows the needle to pass through the fabric without damaging it. Sizes range from 13, being the heaviest, up to 28, the finest. They also are available gold or platinum plated. Double-ended tapestry needles, with the eye in the middle, are also available and convenient when working with fabric mounted in a frame.

Tapestry needles   Tapestry petite needles   Cross-stitch needles

Tapestry Needles Size Chart

This chart lists the various sizes of tapestry needles, along with their length and diameter.

Needle Size	Needle Length	Needle Diameter
13	69mm	2.34mm
14	58mm	2.03mm
16	52.5mm	1.63mm
18	48.5mm	1.27mm
20	44mm	1.09mm
22	40.5mm	0.94mm
24	37mm	0.76mm
26	34mm	0.61mm
28	32.5mm	0.53mm

Chenille Needles

Chenille needles are similar to tapestry needles in that they have elongated eyes, and the same length and diameter. Unlike tapestry needles, however, chenille needles have very sharp points so that they can penetrate close-weave fabrics. They are used in crewel work and ribbon embroidery, and come in sizes 13 to 26.

Appliqué Needles

Appliqué needles are similar to sharps in that they have a round eye, the same diameter, and a sharp point. Since these needles are primarily used for appliqué and patchwork, they are available only in sizes 9, 10, and 12, and have a gold-plated eye for additional sewing ease.

Darning Needles: Short & Long

Darning needles are available in different types: short darners (also known as cotton darners), long darners, and yarn darners. Short darners have long eyes and pointed tips. They are used for mending and are available in sizes 1 to 9. Long darners, also with pointed tips, are sized 1 to 9 and have the same diameter as short darners. However, they differ in that they have extra-long eyes and are longer in length. In addition to mending, they are used for basting layered fabrics together.

Yarn Darners

The yarn darner is the thickest darning needle and has a very large eye so that yarn can easily pass through it. However, this type of darner has a blunt tip. Yarn darners are used for mending and for joining knit and crochet pieces together. They are available in sizes 14 to 18. Plastic and latch-hook eye versions are also available.

Darning Needles Size Charts

These charts list the sizes, thicknesses, and lengths of the various darning needles available.

Short/Cotton Darning Needles

Needle Size	Needle Length	Needle Diameter
1	57.5mm	1.02mm
3	54mm	0.86mm
5	51mm	0.76mm
7	48mm	0.69mm
9	45mm	0.61mm

Long Darning Needles

Needle Size	Needle Length	Needle Diameter
1	75mm	1.02mm
3	70mm	0.86mm
5	64mm	0.76mm
7	58mm	0.69mm
9	52mm	0.61mm

Yarn Darning Needles

Needle Size	Needle Length	Needle Diameter
14	75mm	2.03mm
15	69mm	1.83mm
16	66mm	1.63mm
17	63mm	1.42mm
18	60mm	1.27mm

Upholstery Needles

Upholstery needles are long, heavy needles with pointed tips, and are available straight or curved. They are used for sewing heavy fabrics, upholstery work, tufting, and for tying quilts. Curved needles are used for difficult situations where a straight needle is not practical. Straight upholstery needles are sized 3" (75mm) to 24" (610mm) long, while curved upholstery needles range from 1½" (38mm) to 6" (150mm) long. These needles are available in light and heavy gauge.

Sailmaker Needles

Sailmaker needles are similar to leather needles, but the triangular point extends farther up the shaft. These needles are used for sewing thick canvas or heavy leather.

Doll Needles

Perhaps the longest needle of all is the doll needle, which measures 3" (75mm) long, has a long eye, and is used for doll-making, soft sculpture, and for sewing upholstery.

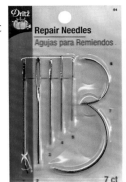

Curved upholstery needles · Doll needles

History of Thimbles

Prehistoric man, when creating body coverings, most likely fashioned some kind of thumb guard so as to be able to push bone needles through animal skins. The earliest known metal thimble dates back to China's Han Dynasty (between 206 BCE and 202 CE), while bronze thimbles were possibly used by the Romans in around the first century CE.

Thimble Types

Today, several different thimble types are available, depending upon the project that you are working on. The most popular models with dressmakers are dome-top thimbles, while flat-top thimbles are used by quilters, and open-top and band thimbles are preferred by tailors. Thimbles consist of nickel-plated steel with dimpled surfaces that "grab" the end of a needle, providing the leverage for it to be pushed easily through the fabric. Some thimbles are available in a combination of nickel plating and brass.

Rubber Thimbles

While metal thimbles are the most common, many sewers prefer the softness and flexibility of a rubber thimble. These may feature a recessed top, a domed top, or even come with open areas for better breathability. A variation that combines structure with flexibility is the Protect and Grip thimble, which has a rubber body and a metal top. Adjustable rubber thimbles are also available, which are molded to the wearer's finger and are designed to prevent broken nails.

Leather Thimbles

Many people find leather thimbles more comfortable to use than a metal thimble because they are malleable. There are several types available, including one with a knit insert for better flexibility. Some are fitted with a metal tip. Also available are small leather thimble bands, and structured leather thimbles. Leather palm-type thimbles are a useful option when sewing very heavy materials.

Other Types of Thimbles

Metal thimbles are also available in other forms, including a fingertip model and an adjustable ring variation.

Fingertip thimble

Adjustable ring thimble

Keepsake Thimbles

People have collected thimbles as keepsakes since the sixteenth century, and today, collectors are known as "digitabulists." Precious-metal thimbles are made from silver and silver plate, gold, brass, and pewter, while other keepsake thimbles can be embedded with precious stones. More delicate thimbles are made of porcelain, ceramic, cloisonné, horn, and even painted papier-mâché.

Silver thimble Gold thimble Brass thimble Pewter thimble Porcelain thimble

Ceramic thimble Cloisonné thimble Horn thimble Papier-mâché painted thimbles

Thimble Sizes

Although there are no global standard sizes for thimbles, thimble gauges like this one provide a guide, with English sizes running from a size 4 up to a size 13, alongside metric equivalents, running from 13mm up to 20mm.

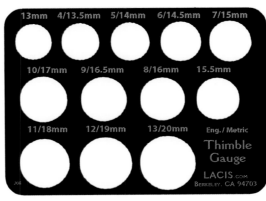

13mm	4/13.5mm	5/14mm	6/14.5mm	7/15mm
10/17mm	9/16.5mm	8/16mm	15.5mm
11/18mm	12/19mm	13/20mm	Eng./Metric

Thimble Gauge

LACIS.com
BERKELEY, CA 94703

Thimble gauge

How to Fit a Thimble

To know that your closed-top thimble fits properly, the joint of your middle finger must pass through the thimble opening and lightly touch the top of the thimble. For an open-top thimble, the thimble should not be too tight or too loose. A closed-top thimble (most often used in dressmaking) goes on the middle finger of the dominant hand and the top of the thimble is used to push the needle through the fabric. Open-top thimbles (used by tailors) enable the wearer to manipulate fabric more easily as they curl their finger and use the side of the thimble to push the needle through.

Hand-sewing Aids

Although they cannot push a needle through fabric like a thimble, latex finger covers known as Quilter's Tips can be used on the pointer finger and thumb to help grip a needle and pull it through the fabric, or to help guide fabrics through a sewing machine. If you cut or prick your finger, these will prevent blood staining the fabric. Thimble-It® is a product designed to stick to your fingers while you sew, to help push the needle through the fabric. Another product designed with quilters in mind are quilter's gloves.

Quilter's Tips

Thimble-It®

Quilter's gloves

Tomato & Strawberry Pincushions

Pincushions provide easy access to pins during the sewing, draping, fitting, and pattern-making processes. The pincushion was already in use by the Middle Ages, and it was during the Victorian era that the now ubiquitous tomato pincushion with a strawberry attached became popular.

The tomato part of the pincushion was originally filled with sand, wool roving, or sawdust. However, today it is usually filled with ground walnut shells or sawdust. The small strawberry, and sometimes the tomato, is filled with emery sand, or emery powder. When you stick your needle or pin into the strawberry portion of the pincushion, it cleans and sharpens your needle, making your work quicker and easier. Emery sand and walnut shells are available online, if you choose to create your own pincushion.

Decorative Pincushions

Other, more decorative types of pincushions are also available, such as the Chinese motif and multicolored pincushions shown here.

Magnetic Pin Holder & Wand

Another convenient way to access your pins is to use a magnetic pin holder, or cup. For gathering up pins that have fallen, a magnetic pin wand is ideal.

Wrist Pincushions

Pincushions that can be worn on your wrist are very convenient, especially when draping. Two popular models are the wristband pincushion with a magnetic strap, and the magnetic wrist pin magnet.

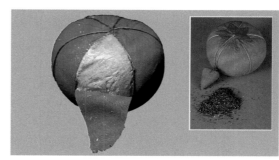

Fillings of sawdust and emery sand (inset)

Tomato/strawberry pincushions come in various sizes, from small to extra large, and in different colors

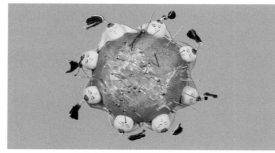

Decorative pincushion

Decorative pincushion

Magnetic pin holder

Wrist pincushion

Magnetic pin holder

Wrist pin magnet

Straight Pins

Straight pins are a key tool in the design process. Whether they are used in draping, pattern making, or sewing, choosing the appropriate pin is always important. The most popular straight pins are made of nickel-plated steel. Nickel plating helps prevent steel pins from rusting and provides improved resistance to wear. Metal pins are able to stick to a magnet, which is useful when gathering pins after a spill.

The anatomy of a straight pin consists of a head, shaft, and tip. The head and tip will vary from one pin to another, as will the length and thickness of the shaft, so these are the things to consider when choosing the right pin for your project.

Pin Quality

Not all pins are manufactured in the same way. Japanese Tulip Hiroshima nickel-plated pins and needles, for example, undergo a polishing process that produces a superior result. English Dorcas pins and needles are made from hardened and tempered nickel-plated steel. Options like these are much more expensive than regular pins and needles.

Pinheads

The typical straight pin has a blunt nub called a "flat head," made of the same metal as the pin shaft. Flat-head pins are popular because they can be pressed with a hot iron.

Straight pins with round plastic heads—also known as craft pins—are easy to handle due to their large heads. The round heads can be made of plastic, pearlized plastic, glass, or metal, and are available in a variety of lengths and thicknesses.

Nickel-plated pins

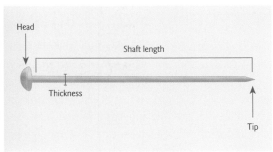

Anatomy of a straight pin

Tulip Hiroshima pins

Dorcas pins

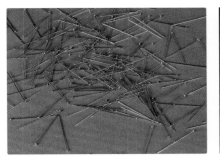

Flat-head pins

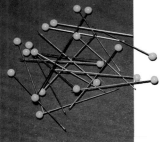

Round-head pins

Pearlized craft pins

Glass-head craft pins

Straight Pin Size Chart

This chart lists various pin categories, their numeric sizes, diameters, lengths, and uses. The shortest pin is a size 8 Lill, which is ½" (13mm) long. Sizes then range up through the most commonly used dressmaker's pin—a size 17, which is 1¹⁄₁₆" (27mm) long—to a size 32 bank pin, at 2" (51mm) long. You will notice that the rule applied to needle size—the higher the number, the finer and shorter the needle—does not apply to pins.

Choosing the Correct Pins

Selecting the correct pin for a sewing project is just as important as selecting the fabric and thread. Choose your pins based on the type of project and the fabric type and weight, using the Straight Pin Size Chart as your guide. Remember that ballpoint pins should be used with knits. The diameter of a pin is also important as you do not want pins to leave permanent holes in your fabric. Pin diameters range from patchwork pins measuring 0.4mm to bank pins measuring 1.16mm. Be sure that the pin will not leave a rust mark, or melt when hit with a hot iron.

Hand Sewing

Pin	Pin Type	Metal Type	Size	Diameter	Length	Uses
	Lill	Nickle-plated & gold-plated steel	8	0.021" (0.5mm)	½" (13mm)	Sequins / Beading / Craft work
	Pleating (extra fine)	Nickel-plated steel	12	0.021" (0.5mm)	¾" (19mm)	Pleating / Quilting / Appliqué
	Bead (extra-large head)	Nickel-plated steel	14	0.030" (0.8mm)	⅞" (22mm)	Beading / Quilting
	Patchwork	Steel (often with glass heads)	30	0.020" (0.4mm)	1½" (38mm)	Sheers / Delicate fabrics / Quilting
	Satin (extra fine)	Stainless steel	17	0.021" (0.5mm)	1¹⁄₁₆" (27mm)	Sheers / Silks / Delicate fabrics
	Satin (extra fine)	Nickel-plated steel	21	0.021" (0.5mm)	1⁵⁄₁₆" (33mm)	Sheers / Silks / Delicate fabrics
	Satin (fine)	Nickel-plated steel	17	0.0255" (0.7mm)	1¹⁄₁₆" (27mm)	Lightweight and delicate fabrics
	Silk (fine)	Nickel-plated steel	17	0.0255" (0.7mm)	1¹⁄₁₆" (27mm)	Sheers / Silks / Delicate fabrics
	Silk	Nickel-plated steel	20	0.030" (0.8mm)	1¼" (31mm)	Silks / Delicate fabrics
	Dressmaker (medium)	Nickel-plated steel	17	0.0285" (0.7mm)	1¹⁄₁₆" (27mm)	Medium-weight fabrics
	Dressmaker (medium)	Brass	17	0.0285" (0.7mm)	1¹⁄₁₆" (27mm)	Medium-weight fabrics
	Dressmaker (medium)	Nickel-plated steel	20	0.030" (0.8mm)	1¼" (31mm)	Light- to medium-weight fabrics
	Dressmaker (medium)	Nickel-plated steel	24	0.036" (0.9mm)	1½" (38mm)	Heavyweight fabrics
	Bank (heavy)	Nickel-plated steel	17	0.036" (0.9mm)	1¹⁄₁₆" (27mm)	Heavyweight fabrics
	Bank (heavy)	Nickel-plated steel	20	0.036" (0.9mm)	1¼" (31mm)	Heavyweight fabrics
	Bank (heavy)	Nickel-plated steel	24	0.045" (1.16mm)	1½" (38mm)	Heavyweight fabrics
	Bank (heavy)	Nickel-plated steel	28	0.045" (1.16mm)	1¾" (44mm)	Heavyweight fabrics
	Bank (heavy)	Nickel-plated steel	32	0.045" (1.16mm)	2" (51mm)	Heavyweight fabrics

Specialty Pinheads

Another type of craft pin is the decorative flat-head pin. These pins are a good choice when working with open-weave fabrics, because the large, flat head prevents them from getting lost in the work.

T-pins range in length from 1" to 2" (25 to 50mm) and are somewhat thicker than dressmaker's pins. They are used for quilting and craft projects, and the 2" (50mm) length is used to pin together multiple layers of heavyweight fabrics.

Open-eye pins are used in jewelry making and are too soft for use in garment making.

Fork blocking pins are U-shaped pins used when blocking knits and for craft projects.

Decorative flat-head pins

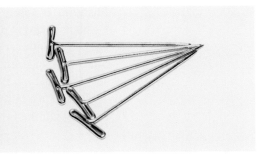

T-pins

Open-eye pins

Fork blocking pins

Draping Pins

When draping in muslin (calico), the best choice is size 17 dressmaker's pins.

When draping in your actual fabric, whether it be a sheer or a silk or silk-like material, you can use size 17 silk pins, size 17 extra-fine satin pins, ultra-fine glass-head pins, size 20 super-fine sharp pins, or the finest pin—the patchwork pin—which is only 0.4mm in diameter.

When draping in your actual knit fabric, use size 17 ballpoint pins.

Dressmaker's pins

Silk pins

Extra-fine satin pins

Super-fine sharp pins

Patchwork pins

Ballpoint pins

Pushpins & Safety Pins

Pushpins (drawing pins), used in pattern making, are ½" (12.7mm) and ¾" (19mm) in length. Safety pins, in sizes ¾" (19mm), 1" (25mm), 1½" (38mm), and 2" (50mm), are used in sewing. The length of a pushpin and the choice and size of a safety pin depends upon your individual project.

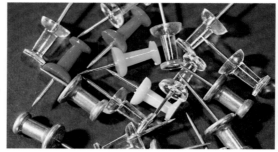

Pushpins

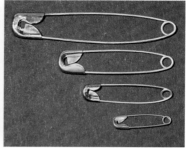

Safety pins

Sewing-machine Needle Anatomy

A domestic or home-sewing lockstitch machine needle is made up of several parts. The shank is the top of the needle, which is inserted into the machine. The shaft is the body of the needle below the shank, and the groove is the slit that runs down one side of the needle to its eye. The scarf is an indentation above the eye, on the opposite side of the needle to the groove. A long scarf helps eliminate skipped stitches by allowing the bobbin hook to loop the thread more easily. The eye is the hole through which the thread passes, and the point is the needle tip below the eye. The point of the needle is shaped to provide the most suitable penetration of the material being sewn, according to its nature and the desired stitch effect.

Domestic-needle shanks are flat on one side, while industrial-needle shanks are fully round and slightly longer than domestic needles.

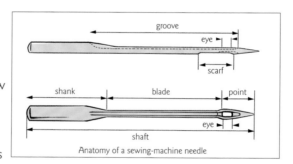

Anatomy of a sewing-machine needle

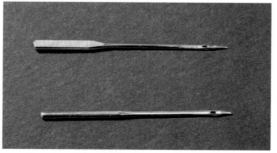

Domestic machine needle (above) and industrial version (below)

Machine Needle Sizes

Selecting the correct machine needle for your project and fabric weight is just as important as selecting the fabric, thread, lining, and interfacing. The European metric needle-sizing system, also known as NM, is numbered from 55 to 250, while the American sizing system is numbered from 6 to 27. The most popular sizes are European from 60 to 110, and American from 8 to 18. Needle packages, both domestic and industrial, list both European metric and American needle sizes on their packaging.

For both systems, the rule is: the lower the needle number, the finer the needle, and therefore the lighter the fabric weight. And the higher the needle number, the larger the needle and the heavier the fabric weight.

Many times, the thread you will be using for your project will also determine the needle size you choose. For example, when using a fine, delicate thread, be sure to use a smaller needle size.

Domestic and industrial needle packages list both European metric and American needle sizing

Machine Needle Size Chart

This chart provides suggested needle sizes based on various fabric weights.

European Metric (NM) Needle Size	American Needle Size	Metric Needle Diameter	American Needle Diameter	Fabric Weight
55	6	0.5mm	0.0215"	Sheer and lightweight
60	7	0.6mm	0.023"	Sheer and lightweight
60	8	0.6mm	0.0245"	Lightweight
65	9	0.7mm	0.026"	Lightweight
70	10	0.7mm	0.028"	Lightweight
75	11	0.8mm	0.030"	Medium-weight
80	12	0.8mm	0.032"	Medium-weight
85	13	0.9mm	0.034"	Medium-weight
90	14	0.9mm	0.036"	Medium-weight
95	15	1.0mm	0.038"	Medium-weight
100	16	1.0mm	0.040"	Heavyweight
105	17	1.1mm	0.042"	Heavyweight
110	18	1.1mm	0.044"	Heavyweight and leather
120	19	1.2mm	0.046"	Heavyweight and leather
125	20	1.2mm	0.048"	Very heavyweight
130	21	1.3mm	0.051"	Very heavyweight
140	22	1.4mm	0.057"	Very heavyweight
160	23	1.7mm	0.065"	Very heavyweight
180	24	1.8mm	0.072"	Very heavyweight
200	25	2.1mm	0.081"	Extremely thick layers
230	26	2.3mm	0.091"	Extremely thick layers
250	27	2.5mm	0.100"	Extremely thick layers

Needle Classes

Whether you are using a home sewing machine or an industrial machine, regardless of manufacturer, you will need to know what needle class, or system, your machine uses. A needle class defines the dimensions of a needle to suit the machine type. Using the wrong needle will damage your machine, and therefore you should always consult your machine's manual when choosing machine needles.

Domestic versus Industrial Needle Classes

In addition to the physical differences between domestic and industrial needles, each has their own identifying class, or system, and those codes may vary by needle manufacturer. For example, a size 75/11 "Universal" type lockstitch needle is listed as 130/705H on a package of Schmetz domestic needles, while the same size of needle for an industrial lockstitch sewing machine is listed as DBx1 on a package of industrial needles by Organ Needles (see both, below left). When selecting needles for your machine and your project, therefore, always check the needle manufacturer's

own classification system for domestic and industrial needles.

The domestic needle-maker's cataloging system will be listed on the needle package—for example, 15x1H, 130/705H, 2020, H-E, HAx1, and so on. It is very important that 15x1 needles are not used in machines designed for 206x13's; this may result in serious damage to the bobbin case. Again, check your machine's operating manual for the needle system.

Schmetz domestic universal 130/705H needles for home sewing

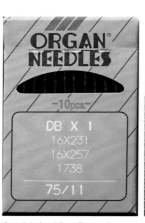

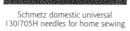

Organ's industrial needles are also sized 75/11; note how the annotations differ from the Schmetz domestic package

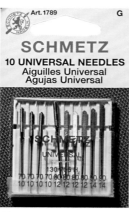

Schmetz assorted domestic universal 130-705-H needles

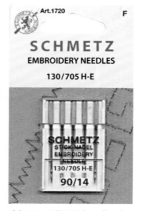

Schmetz 130/705-H-E needles; the letter E stands for embroidery

Industrial Sewing Machine Needle System Chart

Industrial Machine Type	Needle System
Single-needle machines	16 x 257
Single-needle machines	16 x 231
Single-needle and heavy zigzag machines	135 x 5
Zigzag and double-needle machines	135 x 7
Walking-needle sewing machines	135 x 17
Overlock sewing machines	B-27
Blindstitch sewing machines	251
Button-sewing machines	175 x 7
Buttonhole-sewing machines	750
Coverstitch machines	128G
Multi-needle sewing machines	113GS

Machine Needle Dos & Don'ts

- Always ensure that the needle belongs to the correct needle system for the sewing machine
- Make sure the needle size / eye fits the thread size being used
- Always start a new sewing project with a new needle
- Make sure the needle is pushed all the way into the needle holder
- Ensure that the angle of the needle is correct
- After inserting a needle in the machine, turn the machine hand wheel manually to make sure that the needle is not making contact with any parts
- To avoid skipped stitches, use a ballpoint needle for knit and stretch fabrics
- Replace the needle if it becomes bent, or if the tip becomes damaged while sewing

Schmetz Color Coding

Schmetz domestic sewing-machine needles use a color coding system for easy identification.

The top color band indicates the needle type, and the lower color band indicates the needle size. Though it is very hard to read, the size of the needle is also engraved on the shank of the needle. However, some Schmetz domestic machine needles, such as their Universal, Hemstitch, Double Eye, and Quick Threading needles, use only one color band to identify needle size.

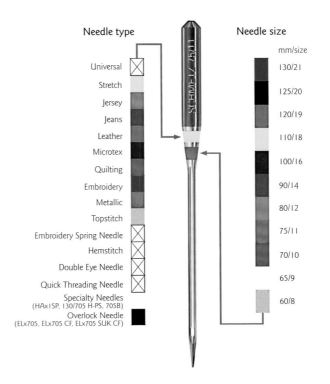

Needle type

- Universal
- Stretch
- Jersey
- Jeans
- Leather
- Microtex
- Quilting
- Embroidery
- Metallic
- Topstitch
- Embroidery Spring Needle
- Hemstitch
- Double Eye Needle
- Quick Threading Needle
- Specialty Needles (HAx1SP, 130/705 H-PS, 705B)
- Overlock Needle (ELx705, ELx705 CF, ELx705 SUK CF)

Needle size

mm/size
- 130/21
- 125/20
- 120/19
- 110/18
- 100/16
- 90/14
- 80/12
- 75/11
- 70/10
- 65/9
- 60/8

Machine Needle Points

Needle points, or tips, are shaped to provide the best penetration of the material being sewn. The point shape, in combination with the point, determines its performance. Points fall into two broad categories—round and sharp. Rounded points are used for sewing wovens, with ballpoint needles used specifically for knits. Sharp, cutting points, either spear- or wedge-shaped, are used for nonwovens such as leather and faux leather.

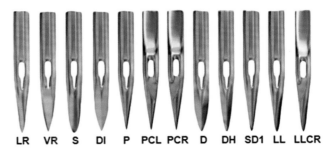

R SPI SES SUK SKF SKL   LR VR S DI P PCL PCR D DH SD1 LL LLCR

Needle points from round (left) to sharp (right)

Reading a Domestic Sewing-machine Needle Package
The example shown here is a pack of Schmetz needles, which lists the needle type (in this case, an embroidery needle), its size (Metric/American = 90/14), and the needle system to which it belongs (here, 130/705 H-E).

1 Needle type
2 Needle system
3 Needle size

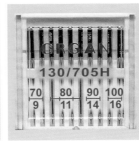

Mixed-size Packages
Many needle manufacturers sell packages of needles in assorted sizes, as with this set of domestic Universal needles by Organ. The class number provided is 130/705H, and the package contains at least two needles in each of the following sizes—70/9, 80/11, 90/14, and 100/16.

Types of Sewing-machine Needles

Within the rounded and sharp needle-point categories, there is a multitude of needle tips and sizes to choose from. Universal needles, for example—the most commonly used—are available in many different sizes. This chart will help you decide which needle type is best for your project, based on your fabric type and weight.

Needle Type	Needle Sizes	Description/Applications
Universal	60/8, 65/9, 70/10, 75/11, 80/12, 90/14, 100/16, 110/18, 120/19	General all-purpose needle with slightly rounded point used for wovens and some knits.
Quick Threading	75/11, 80/12, 90/14, 100/16, 110/18	Universal needle with a slip-in threading slot to make threading easier. Used on wovens and knits.
Double Eye	80/12	A Universal needle with two eyes, used on wovens and knits. Used with two threads for topstitching, shading and texturing effects, and for embroidery.
Stretch	75/11, 90/14	The medium ballpoint, special eye, and scarf are specially designed to prevent skipped stitches. For use on elastic materials and highly elastic knitwear.
Jersey	70/10, 80/12, 90/14, 100/16	Medium ballpoint for use on knits and stretch fabrics. Will not break or damage knit fibers.
Jeans	70/10, 80/12, 90/14, 100/16, 110/18 *Twin 4.0mm/100	Modified medium ballpoint with reinforced blade. For use on denim, canvas, upholstery fabrics, and fabrics of similar weight.
Hemstitch/Wing	100/16, 120/19	Consists of a wing on each side of the needle, which opens the fabric fibers, creating a decorative stitch. Used on zigzag machines together with the correct throat plate and presser foot. Excellent for light- or medium-weight loosely woven fabrics and decorative cutwork and heirloom sewing.
Double Hemstitch	2.5mm/100	A combination Wing and Universal needle with a 2.5mm separation on a combined shank. Used for decorative stitching in dual rows on light- or medium-weight loosely woven fabrics and decorative cutwork.
Leather	70/10, 80/12, 90/14, 100/16, 110/18	Wedge-shaped point with a tri-point knife edge to penetrate leather, faux leather, and vinyl without ripping it.
Industrial Machine Leather	55/7, 60/8, 65/9, 70/10, 75/11, 80/12, 90/14, 100/16, 110/18, 120/19, 125/20, 130/21, 140/22, 160/23, 180/24, 200/25	Wedge-shaped point with a tri-point knife edge to penetrate leather, faux leather, and very heavy nonwoven synthetics.
Metallic	80/12, 90/14 *Twin-2.5mm/80, 3.0mm/90	Used for metallic threads, it has a long elongated eye, a fine shaft, sharp point, and a deep scarf in front side of the needle. This needle helps eliminate skipped stitches and fraying of thread.
Microtex	60/8, 70/10, 80/12, 90/14, 100/16, 100/18	Fine needle with slim, very sharp point for silk and microfibers.
Quilting	75/11, 90/14	Tapered needle wth sharp point to make sewing of multiple seams and layers easier. The acute point also helps prevent "bearding" or migration of the batting (wadding) through the fabric.
Embroidery	75/11, 90/14, *Twin 3.0mm/75, 3.0mm/75	Light ballpoint, larger eye, and deeper scarf in front side of the needle to prevent skipped stitches; guards against excess friction to protect fragile threads as they are pulled through the fabric.
Embroidery Gold Needles (Titanium)	75/11, 90/14	Titanium needles have a nitride coating, a slightly rounded point, and an enlarged eye. The coating resists adhesive residue on fabrics. These needles are perfect for coarse and densely woven fabrics, as well as fabrics with fragile specialty threads.
Embroidery Spring	70/10, 75/11, 80/12, 90/14, 100/16	Needle with a spring around the needle used for free motion and embroidery on lightweight fabrics. The spring's function is to keep pressure on the fabric to keep it from stretching while embroidering.
Twin	1.6/70, 2.0/80, 2.5/75, 3.0/90, 6.0/100, 8.0/100	Two needles on a crossbar that can only be used on a zigzag machine that zigzags 6.5mm. Perfect for sewing pin tucks, decorative seams, hems, and heirloom sewing.
Stretch Twin	2.5mm/75, 4.0mm/75	Two stretch needles mounted to one shank, creating two rows of stitches simultaneously.
Topstitch	80/12, 90/14, 100/16	Extra-long eye to accommodate heavy or multiple strands of thread for topstitching. The needle's deep scarf prevents the thread from fraying while stitching.
Triple	2.5/80, 3.0/80, 4.0/100	Three needles on a crossbar so that you can stitch three rows at once. May be used for machine embroidery and heirloom sewing.
5 HLx5 High Speed	75/11, 90/14, 100/16	Chrome-plated, short, flat-shank needle designed specifically for high-speed professional quilting machines (e.g. Janome 1600P series). Can be used on jersey, denim, fake fur.
Home Serger Needles	65/9, 70/10, 75/11, 80/12, 90/14, 100/16, 110/18, 125/20	For use on home sergers (overlockers) only, and not on domestic or industrial lockstitch machines or embroidery machines. Sizes 65/9 & 70/10 for fine wovens and knits. Sizes 75/11–90/14 for medium-weight wovens and knits. Sizes 100/16–25/20 for heavyweights and elastic materials.
Industrial Overlock Straight	55/7, 60/8, 65/9, 70/10, 75/11, 80/12, 85/13, 90/14, 100/16, 110/18, 120/19, 125/20, 130/21, 140/22, 160/23, 180/24	Straight overlock needles in various shank lengths and shapes. Used to finish edges and for seaming. Sizes 65/9–70/10 for fine wovens and knits. Sizes 75/11–100/16 for medium-weight wovens and knits. Sizes 110/18–180/24 for heavyweights and elastic materials.
Industrial Overlock Curved	55/7, 60/8, 65/9, 70/10, 75/11, 80/12, 85/13, 90/14, 100/16, 110/18, 120/19, 125/20, 130/21, 140/22	Curved overlock needles in various shank lengths and shapes. Used to finish edges and for seaming. Sizes 65/9–70/10 for fine wovens and knits. Sizes 75/11–100/16 for medium-weight wovens and knits. Sizes 110/18–140/22 for heavyweights and elastic materials.
Industrial Blindstitch	60/8, 65/9, 70/10, 75/11, 80/12, 85/13, 90/14, 100/16, 110/18, 120/19, 125/20, 130/21, 140/22	Curved blind-stitch needle. The lower the number, the lighter the fabric weight; the higher the number, the heavier the fabric weight.

*Twin & Triple needle sizing includes the mm distance between the 2 or 3 needles, and the NM needle size—for example, twin Embroidery Needle 3.0mm/75.

Introduction to Threads

Learning objectives

- [ ] Find out all about sewing threads—what they are made from, and how they are manufactured
- [ ] Understand thread weights and sizes, the different systems and what they mean
- [ ] Choose the right thread, using sizing charts and general guidelines on material and color
- [ ] Know how to estimate the quantity of thread needed, using the type of stitch, seam, stitches per inch, and fabric weight

Gütermann thread assortment holder.

Module 1:

What is a Sewing Thread?

The Definition of a Sewing Thread

"A sewing thread is a flexible, small-diameter yarn or strand, usually treated with a surface coating, a lubricant, or both, intended to be used to stitch one or more pieces of material or an object to a material," as defined by ASTM International. (ASTM Standard D123-13)

Sewing Thread versus Yarn

Again, according to ASTM International: "Yarn is defined as a generic term for a continuous strand of textile fibers, filaments, or material in a form suitable for knitting, weaving or otherwise intertwining to form a textile fabric."

A sewing thread is designed to pass rapidly through a sewing machine to form a stitch used to hold a garment together, whereas a yarn is used to make fabric. However, the terms yarn and thread are sometimes used interchangeably.

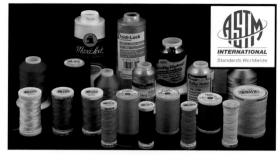

Module 2:

Natural & Synthetic Fibers

Sewing threads are derived from three main sources: natural fibers, such as plants and animals; plant sources that require processing, known as regenerated fibers; and fibers that are manufactured from chemicals.

Plant sources of natural fiber include cotton and flax. (Flax is the fiber used to make linen cloth.) Animal sources include the cocoon produced by the silkworm. Before the development of cotton in the late nineteenth century, silk and linen threads were the most commonly used. Today, the most common fiber used for thread is cotton.

One example of a regenerated fiber is rayon—also known as "artificial silk"—which is produced from wood pulp that has undergone extensive processing, or regeneration. Although rayon fibers make beautiful thread, they are mostly used for hand and machine embroidery.

The third fiber type is manufactured from chemicals. Nylon and polyester are two examples.

Cotton

Flax

Silkworm

How are viscose and rayon made?

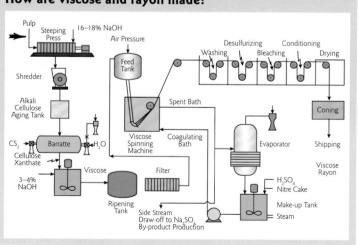

Module 3:
Staple Fibers & Filaments

A length of yarn consists of either many short fibers ("staple fibers") twisted together, or of one continuous length of fiber ("filament").

Staple fibers are measured in inches and vary from fractions of an inch to about 36" (91cm) long. Staple fibers come from natural sources, such cotton and linen. Think of the jar of cotton balls hidden at the back of the medicine cabinet. Cotton fibers range in length from ½" (1.3cm) to 2½" (6.3cm).

Flax, the plant fiber used to make linen fabric, is also produced as a staple yarn, and its staple fibers range in length from 2" (5cm) to 36" (91cm).

Synthetic fibers, such as rayon, nylon, and polyester, are produced as filament—in one continuous length. Although manufactured fibers are produced in long lengths, they may also be cut into staple fibers and then spun into yarns.

Although silk is a natural fiber (from the silkworm), it is actually a filament. A continuous strand from one silkworm cocoon may measure a mile long.

Cotton balls

Linen fibers

Silkworm cocoons

Module 4:
How Threads Are Made

Sewing threads may be made by hand or by machine.

To spin yarn by hand using a spinning wheel, as shown here, the operator turns the wheel with a foot pedal while holding the loose fibers with one hand. As the loose fibers are fed into the device with the other hand, the motion of the wheel twists them together to form a yarn around a spool.

The twist applied to a yarn to hold the fibers together can be directed to the left or the right. A left-hand twist is known as an "S" twist, while a right-hand twist is called a "Z" twist. Most sewing machines use thread with a "Z" twist.

Spinning thread by hand

A mill worker examines cotton yarn

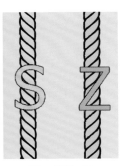

"S" and "Z" twists

44

Thread Types
The most common sewing thread types are: 1. spun, 2. core-spun, 3. monofilament, 4. multifilament, and 5. textured. Variations include elastic thread and heavy-duty thread.

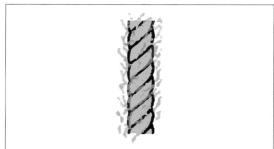

Spun Thread
Most threads start with staple fibers, which are twisted together to make a single yarn or spun yarn. The "fuzzy" surface of the yarn is from the short fibers. When a single yarn is untwisted, it comes apart into fibers. The process of twisting staple fibers together creates a strong and flexible thread.

Two single yarns can then be twisted together to produce a ply yarn, or plied yarn. When a ply yarn is untwisted, it comes apart into two single yarns. Ply yarns are commonly used for basic seam construction.

Core-spun Thread
A core-spun thread has a core of a polyester filament covered with cotton or polyester staple fibers. It is the most costly thread, and is good for fabrics that have a finish or a tendency to pucker.

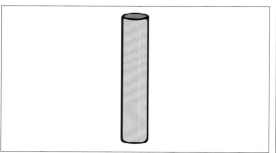

Monofilament Thread
A monofilament thread is a single strand of filament fiber. These threads are finer and stronger than spun thread, and less costly. They are commonly used in industrial hemming machines used to stitch the chainstitch often seen in ready-to-wear clothing.

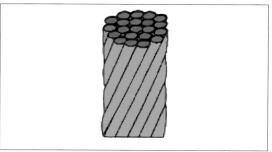

Multifilament Thread
A multifilament thread consists of several strands of filaments. Since multifilament threads are made from continuous manufactured fibers, they require only a slight twist to hold them together.

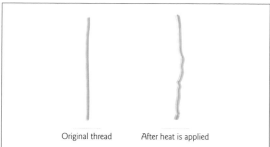

Original thread   After heat is applied

Textured Thread
Applying heat to a manufactured fiber creates a textured thread. The heat increases the bulk of the thread and creates a softer finish. Such threads are used in the loopers of overlock machines (sergers) to finish the raw edges of seams and make rolled hems.

Elastic Thread
Another type of thread is elastic thread. This has an elastic core and is used to create gathers, shirring, crimping, and smocking (when used in the bobbin of a sewing machine).

Heavy-duty Thread
When running a shirring or gathering stitch, a heavy-duty (core-spun) thread is used in the bobbin of the sewing machine. It can also used to hand sew gathers—for example, on a sleeve cap or along the waistline of a gathered skirt.

Over time, several different methods have developed for measuring the weight, or linear density, of a fiber. These include, for example:
• Number English (Ne), or cotton count
• The denier system, originated in France
• The tex system, developed to provide a single global system

Although not all manufacturers use the same system, all thread-sizing systems fall into one of two categories:
• "fixed weight" (indirect) systems
• "fixed length" (direct) systems
The thread weights for both of these systems are based on the spun greige (pronounced "gray") yarn. Greige yarn is unprocessed yarn that has not yet been finished by bleaching or dyeing.

Greige thread spool

Fixed-weight Systems

Cotton count, thread weight, metric count, and metric ticket are all fixed-weight systems. The abbreviations for the system used for a particular thread are usually marked in parentheses on the spool's label.

Cotton count (Ne, NeC, NeB, C Ne)
Thread weight (Wt.)
Metric count (Nm)
Metric ticket (No., No./Tkt., Tkt.)

Fixed-weight systems refer to the length of thread required to weigh a specific amount:
• The weight of the thread is constant, measured in units of pounds and ounces, or metric grams.
• The numbers used for this system therefore refer to the length, which will vary from one thread to another.

Since fixed-weight systems use an indirect numbering relationship:
• The higher the number, the finer the thread.
• The smaller the number, the heavier the thread.
So, a thread size of 120 is finer than a thread size of 30.

We will now look at the individual systems within this category.

The cotton count system uses the fixed weight of one pound; the length in yards is the variable used to determine the size of the thread. The cotton count system uses the length of a hank as a unit of measurement (one hank being equal to 840 yards).

The numbering for this system is expressed in a two-part format—for example, 40/1, 50/2, or 45/3. The first number refers to the number of 840-yard hanks in 1 pound, while the second number refers to the number of plies.

A cotton count of Ne 40/1 translates into a quantity of 40 hanks (each measuring 840 yards), or 33,600 yards (40 x 840) of a single thread. When comparing cotton count threads, the number of plies must always be taken into account. A cotton count thread that is described as a 50/2 thread is two plies of a size 25 thread (50 divided by 2 = 25).

Now compare a 50/2 thread to a 45/3. Which thread is heavier? 45 divided by 3 equals 15. Since the cotton count has an inverse relationship, the Ne 45/3 is equivalent to 15, which is heavier than the Ne 50/2 (equivalent to 25).

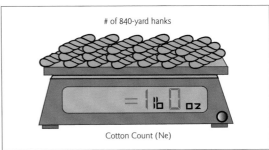

# of 840-yard hanks

Cotton Count (Ne)

Cotton count system

Thread weight (Wt.) is a variation of the cotton count system and refers to the number of meters needed to weigh 1 gram. A thread described as 50 Wt means that 50 meters of that thread weigh 1 gram.

The metric count (Nm) system is the number of 1-meter hanks of a single thread that weigh 1 gram.

The metric ticket (No., No./Tkt., Tkt.) is a variation of the metric count system. It is based on the number of meters of thread needed to weigh 3 grams.

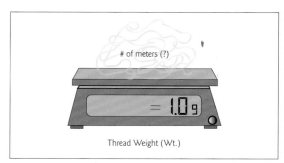

# of meters (?)

= 1.0 g

Thread Weight (Wt.)

Thread weight system

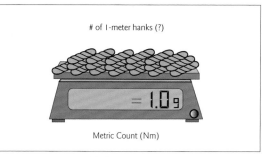

# of 1-meter hanks (?)

= 1.0 g

Metric Count (Nm)

Metric count system

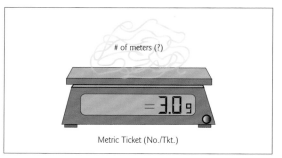

# of meters (?)

= 3.0 g

Metric Ticket (No./Tkt.)

Metric ticket system

Fixed-length Systems

Both the denier and tex systems are fixed-length systems. As with the systems discussed above, the abbreviations for these systems will usually appear in parentheses on a spool of thread.
Denier (Td, d)
Tex (TEX, T)

Fixed-length systems refer to the weight of a given length of thread. Since the numbers used have a direct relationship with the thread:
• The smaller the number, the finer the thread.
• The larger the number, the heavier the thread.

A thread size of 30, therefore, is finer than a thread size of 120. Direct systems are easier to follow than indirect systems.

The denier system is commonly used for filament fibers and measures the weight in grams of 9,000 meters of thread. (One denier as a unit of measurement is based on a strand of silk—9,000 meters of silk weigh 1 gram.)

Imagine 9,000 meters of a lightweight polyester thread. This will weigh less than 9,000 meters of a heavyweight thread.

The tex system is commonly used for filament fibers and measures the weight in grams of 1,000 meters of thread.

A common tex size for an all-purpose thread is 30. This means that 1,000 meters of that thread weigh 30 grams, which is expressed as T-30, or Tex 30. Topstitching thread, which is heavier than all-purpose, would have a tex size of 60 or more.

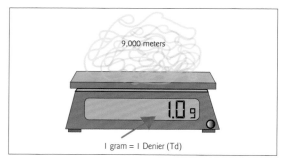

9,000 meters

1.0 g

1 gram = 1 Denier (Td)

Denier thread

1,000 meters

30.0 g

30 grams = Tex 30

Tex thread

Thread Sizing

To convert a thread size to another system for comparison, use the table below.

	Fixed Weight: Indirect System				Fixed Length: Direct System	
	Cotton Count	Thread Weight	Metric Count	Metric Ticket	Tex	Denier
Weight	Ne, NeC, NeB, C Ne	Wt.	Nm	No., No./Tkt, Tkt., or Ticket	TEX or T	Td, d
Definition	The number of 840-yard hanks in 1 pound. A two-part format. The thread size of 50/2 translates into a quantity of 50 840-yard hanks in 1 pound, made with two plies of size 50 yarn.	Thread weight (Wt.) is a variation of the cotton count system. It is the **number of meters of thread that weigh 1 gram.** For a 2-ply thread, the first number of the cotton count system without listing the number of plies. The thread size of 50/2 in the cotton count system is equivalent to a 50 Wt. thread.	Metric count (Nm) is the **number of 1-meter hanks of a single thread that weigh 1 gram.** The thread size of Nm 80/2 refers to two yarns, each of 80m, weighing 2g.	The metric ticket (No., No./Tkt, Tkt.) is a variation of the metric count (Nm) system and refers to **the number of meters of thread that weigh 3 grams.**	The tex unit of measurement, commonly used for continuous filament fibers, is based on a fixed length of 1,000 meters weighing 1 gram. A length of 1,000 meters is weighed and the size of the thread is determined by the weight in grams. **Weight in grams of 1,000 meters**	The denier unit of measurement, commonly used for continuous filament fibers, is based on a fixed length of 9,000 meters weighing 1 gram. **Weight in grams of 9,000 meters**
Formula	# of hanks (?) = 1 pound 1 hank = 840 yards	# of meters (?) = 1 gram	# of 1 meter hanks (?) = 1 gram	# of meters (?) = 3 grams	# of grams (?) = 1,000 meters	# of grams (?) = 9,000 meters

Key to understanding thread count, too, is the expression.
For comparison, an all-purpose thread with a Tex size of 30 is equivalent to these
values, shown in the table below:
- Cotton count of 50 or 50/2
- Thread weight of 50
- Metric count of 33
- Metric ticket of 100
- Denier of 270

	Fixed Weight: Indirect System				Fixed Length: Direct System	
	Cotton Count	Thread Weight	Metric Count	Metric Ticket	Tex	Denier
Symbol	Ne, NeC, NeB, C Ne	Wt.	Nm	No., No./Tkt, Tkt., or Ticket	TEX or T	Td, d
Expression	C Ne 50 or 50/2	50 Wt.	Nm 33.33	No. Tkt. 100	T-30	d 270

Module 7:

Thread Packaging

Sewing threads are "put up" (the industry phrase for packaging) in different types of packages and lengths, according to the type of thread, the machine, and the sewing requirements.

The four most common put-ups available to consumers are:
• Spool
• Cop
• Cone
• Vicone

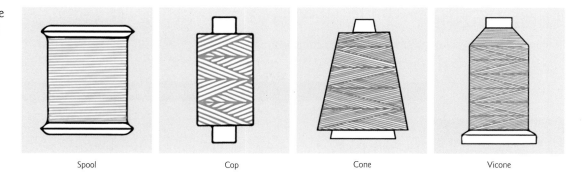

| Spool | Cop | Cone | Vicone |

Module 8:

Winding Thread onto the Spool

The way that a thread is wound onto its put-up will influence how it reels off when used.

Spools of thread are stack wound, with one row of thread parallel to the next. A stack-wound spool is best on a sewing machine's vertical spindle, allowing the thread to reel off the side. If a stack-wound spool is placed in a horizontal spindle, the thread may catch in a small notch on the top of the spool.

A cop thread is cross wound, forming an "X" pattern. It is used on the vertical spindle, allowing the thread to reel off the top, or on a horizontal spindle with a spool cap.

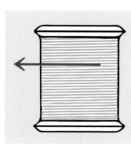

Stack-wound thread

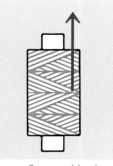

Cross-wound thread

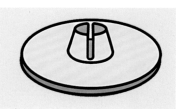

Spool cap

Module 9:

Thread Finishes

The most common thread finishes are:
1. Soft
2. Mercerized
3. Glazed
4. Bonded
5. Lubricated

A soft-finished thread refers to a natural cotton thread or spun thread with only a small amount of lubrication. This type of thread has a fuzzy surface.

Mercerized cotton threads are treated with sodium hydroxide to enhance their strength, luster, and dyeability. Some thread brands refer to a mercerized finish as a "silk finish."

Glazed threads have a surface coating of wax and starches to reduce abrasion and increase durability, perfect for sewing on buttons.

When threads are bonded, a resin is applied to the thread to form a smooth finish.

A silicon lubricant called Sewer's Aid can be used to reduce friction and heat. It is applied to a spool of thread in a zigzag pattern.

Soft finish

Mercerized or silk finish

Glazed finish

Bonded finish

Sewer's Aid

Sewer's Aid applied to thread

Module 10:

Common Thread Types

The main manufacturers for consumer garment sewing threads are:
- Gütermann
- Amann Mettler
- Coats & Clark

Each produces threads in the following categories:
- Fine sewing thread
- Serging (overlocking) thread
- All-purpose thread
- Topstitching thread
- Specialty threads

Sizing Chart for Consumer Sewing Threads

Compare different thread brands and sizes at your local fabric store using this chart. Not all brands of thread are clearly labeled with their sizes. The colored sections at the top provide an easy reference for each brand.

Key to Brands	Gütermann	Mettler	Coats Dual Duty	Other Brands
		Fixed Weight: Indirect System		Fixed Length: Direct System
	Cotton Count	Thread Weight	Metric Ticket	Tex
	Ne, NeC, NeB, C Ne	Wt.	No., No. Tkt., Ticket	TEX or T
Fine sewing		60 Wt.		T-23
		Mettler Silk Finish Cotton 60wt.	Skala 360 No./Tkt. 360 (Tex-8)	
		Dual Duty XP Fine	Skala 240 No./Tkt. 240 (Tex 12)	
			Mara 120 No./Tkt. 120	
Serger			No./Tkt. 120	T-27
		Seracor Serger Thread 50wt.	Miniking Bulky Nylon	YLI Woolly Nylon
				Maxi-Lock Stretch
				Maxi-Lock Serger
				Coats SureLock
All-purpose	C Ne 50 or 50/2	50 wt.	No./Tkt. 100	T-30
	Natural Cotton C Ne 50	Mettler Silk Finish Cotton 50wt.	Sew-All Polyester No. 100	Dual Duty XP Tex 30
			Mara 100 No./Tkt. 100	
			Gütermann A 302	
			Mettler Metrosene No. 100	
			Dual Duty XP General Purpose	
Topstitching		24wt. or more	No./Tkt.	T-35 or more
		Mettler Extra Strong 24wt.	Jeans Thread No. 75	Silk Buttonhole Tex 75
		Dual Duty XP Heavy 15wt.	Extra Strong M 782 No. 40	Dual Duty Plus Denim Tex 35
			Topstitching No. 30	Dual Duty Plus Jean Tex 60
			Mara 30 Topstitching No. 30	XP Heavy Duty S950 Tex 75
Specialty			No. Tkt.	
	Cotton Basting Ne 42/2		Silk S 303 No. 100	Button and Carpet Tex 104

As a general guideline for basic garment construction, an all-purpose thread that is made of 100 percent polyester or 100 percent mercerized cotton will be suitable for linen, cotton, silk, wool, blends, and manufactured fibers.

For all cotton garments, a mercerized 100 percent spun cotton thread may be suitable.

In most cases, 100 percent silk thread would be too strong for basic garment construction. If a seam is stressed, the silk thread may be much stronger than the fabric, resulting in the fabric tearing rather than the thread breaking. (Repairing a broken thread is much easier than repairing a torn fabric.) However, fine silk thread is perfect for pad-stitching fine wools and woolens.

For a professional look, a fine cotton thread with a tex size of 24 or a thread weight of 60 (60 wt.), sewn with 14 stitches to the inch (1.1mm stitch length), works beautifully for the construction and topstitching of a men's or women's dress shirt.

For seams that are serged, or overlocked, a thread made of 100 percent polyester is suitable.

When stretch is needed—for example, in activewear or swimwear—a textured thread made of nylon or polyester provides seams with stretch and softness.

Traditional topstitching on a pair of jeans is stitched with a heavier thread, such as a tex 60 or a metric ticket (No./Tkt.) size of 30. The largest needle recommended for your sewing machine model may determine the final thread size.

A silk buttonhole thread with a tex size 75 makes beautiful hand-sewn buttonholes.

For pad-stitching tailored garments by hand, a prewaxed and precut nylon thread will allow more efficient stitching.

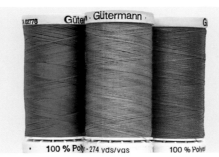

Gütermann 100% polyester thread

100% cotton thread

Seam with broken thread

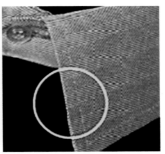

Cotton thread used for topstitching

Serged seam

Topstitching jeans with heavy thread

Silk buttonhole thread

Prewaxed and precut nylon thread

Module 11:

Choosing Thread Colors

Thread color choices may seem endless until you encounter a situation where you cannot find a good match for a particular fabric, but the following tips will help:
- For a dark-colored fabric, select a thread color that is a shade darker
- For a light-colored fabric, select a thread color that is a shade lighter

Keep in mind that color perception varies between individuals so use your best judgment or, better yet, sew a sample with the two best options.

Above, five all-purpose threads are laid out across the fabric. The best color match is number 3. Would the second best be number 2 or 4?

This example also has five all-purpose threads laid out across the fabric. The best color selection is number 4. A second choice would be number 5.

Module 12:

Thread Quantities

Determining the quantity of thread that will be required for a particular project depends on a number of factors.

The Type of Stitch

A stitch is defined by the ASTM as the "repeated unit formed by the sewing thread(s) in the production of seams."

Each stitch is classified by the type of machinery used, and designated a standard number by the International Organization for Standardization (ISO), the body that sets standards for commerce and industry.

For example, the lockstitch is the most common stitch used in sewing and is "formed with two threads; one needle thread and one bobbin thread interlaced with each other" (ASTM-123-13). The ISO classification or stitch class for the lockstitch is #301. The needle view and the bobbin view of the lockstitch is the same on both sides.

In the cross section of the lockstitch, the needle thread and bobbin thread loop into each other, "locking" the stitch.

The second most common stitch used is the overlock stitch, which is formed by one needle thread and two looper threads. The overlock machine is referred to as a serger in home sewing. The ISO class for this stitch is #504.

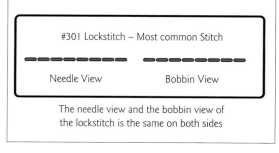

#301 Lockstitch – Most common Stitch

Needle View   Bobbin View

The needle view and the bobbin view of the lockstitch is the same on both sides

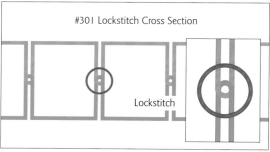

#301 Lockstitch Cross Section

Lockstitch

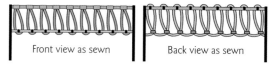

Front view as sewn   Back view as sewn

The Type of Seam

In clothing construction, seams are classified by their type (plain, lapped, bound, or flat) and their position in the finished garment (center-back seam, inseam, or side seam). Seams are finished with a variety of techniques to prevent the raw fabric edges from unraveling, and to neaten the inside of garments. In general, placing one piece of fabric above another and then stitching them together forms the most basic seam type.

In the illustrations on the right, the dotted line is the stitching line and the red line indicates where the fabrics are stitched.

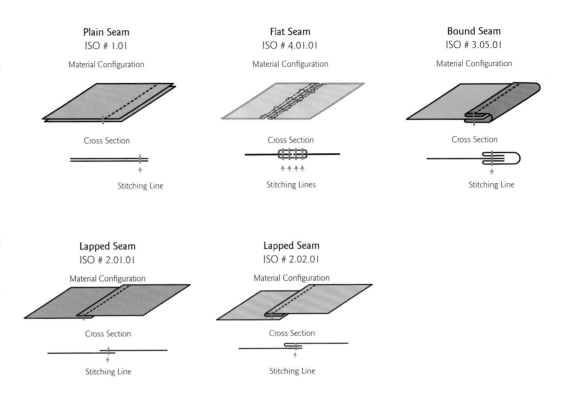

Plain Seam
ISO # 1.01
Material Configuration
Cross Section
Stitching Line

Flat Seam
ISO # 4.01.01
Material Configuration
Cross Section
Stitching Lines

Bound Seam
ISO # 3.05.01
Material Configuration
Cross Section
Stitching Line

Lapped Seam
ISO # 2.01.01
Material Configuration
Cross Section
Stitching Line

Lapped Seam
ISO # 2.02.01
Material Configuration
Cross Section
Stitching Line

The Number of Stitches per Inch

For the basic lockstitch seam, this chart may be used to determine the number of stitches per inch, or spi. For more complicated stitch types, stitch a sample seam on a piece of fabric. Place two marks 1" (2.5cm) apart on the seam, then count the number of stitches.

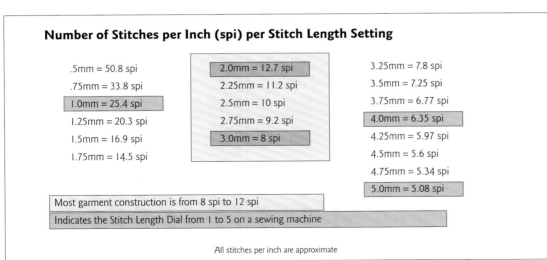

Number of Stitches per Inch (spi) per Stitch Length Setting

.5mm = 50.8 spi	2.0mm = 12.7 spi	3.25mm = 7.8 spi
.75mm = 33.8 spi	2.25mm = 11.2 spi	3.5mm = 7.25 spi
1.0mm = 25.4 spi	2.5mm = 10 spi	3.75mm = 6.77 spi
1.25mm = 20.3 spi	2.75mm = 9.2 spi	4.0mm = 6.35 spi
1.5mm = 16.9 spi	3.0mm = 8 spi	4.25mm = 5.97 spi
1.75mm = 14.5 spi		4.5mm = 5.6 spi
		4.75mm = 5.34 spi
		5.0mm = 5.08 spi

Most garment construction is from 8 spi to 12 spi

Indicates the Stitch Length Dial from 1 to 5 on a sewing machine

All stitches per inch are approximate

Thread Size

A garment such as a pair of jeans would require several different thread sizes.
1. Basic construction: Tex 30 or Metric Ticket (No., No./Tkt., Tkt.) 100
2. Overlocked seams: Tex 27
3. Buttonholes: Tex 60
4. Topstitching: Tex 75

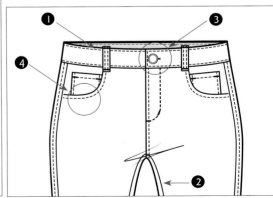

Fabric Weight

The final factor affecting the amount of thread is the relationship between the fabric weight and thread size. A sheer fabric would not withstand sewing with a heavy topstitching thread. Nor would a denim fabric hold together with a fine sewing thread. The fabric weight and thread weight should complement each other.

Use this chart from thread manufacturer American & Efird as a guide:

Fabric Weight/Typical Thread Sizes/Needle Sizes

Fabric Weight	Oz/Sq Yard	Grams/Sq Meter	Thread Tex Size	Needle Size
Fine 18–30 Tex (Top Weight = below 8oz/200g)				
Extra Light	2–4oz	68–136g	Tex 16, 18, 21, 24	60, 65
Light	4–6oz	136–204g	Tex 24, 27, 30	70, 75
Garment types: blouses, casual shirts, lingerie, knitted tops, dresses, sleepwear, swimwear, t-shirts				
Medium 30–60 Tex (Bottom Weight = 8oz/200g or above)				
Medium	6–8oz	204–272g	Tex 30, 35, 40	80, 90, 100
Medium Heavy	8–10oz	272–339g	Tex 40, 45, 50, 60	100, 110
Garment types: athletic wear, coats, jackets, jeans, pants (trousers), rainwear, sweatshirts				
Heavy 60–105 Tex				
Heavy	10–12oz	339–407g	Tex 60, 80, 90, 105	120, 140
Extra Heavy	12–14oz	407–475g	Tex 105, 120, 135+	140, 160
Garment types: denim garments, overcoats, parkas, sweat pants, work wear				

Average Thread Consumption by Garment

The amount of thread may vary from as little as 50 yards (45.7m) on a spool to 6,000 yards (5,486.4m) or more on a vicone.

Product Sewn	Total Yds/Garment	Product Sewn	Total Yds/Garment	Product Sewn	Total Yds/Garment	Product Sewn	Total Yds/Garment
Women's				Men's			
Lined Coat	246	Jeans	250	Slacks	225	Work Shirt	115
Blazer	153	Shorts	151	Jeans	200	Fleece Sweat Shirt	280
Dress	141	Robe	300	Jean Shorts	160	Knit Polo Shirt	130
Skirt	192	Night Gown	135	Work Pants	238	T-shirt	63
Blouse	122	Knit Dress	125	Suit Coat	175	Tank Top	58
Pants	162	Swimsuit	85	Dress Shirt—Long Sleeve	131	Knit Brief	68

A tailor pad stitching a jacket collar and fell stitching a lapel.

Hand Stitches

Learning objectives

☐ Identify the different types of basting (tacking) and what they are used for; use basting and tailor's tacks for marking

☐ Produce fell stitches and pad stitches, and whipstitch seams

☐ Hidden stitches: work slip stitch appliqué, and use catch stitch to hold layers together

☐ Sew a double overcast hem by using blind stitch and double overcast stitch

☐ Bar stitches: work a thread bar, and make a French tack

☐ Edge finishing stitches: learn how to work overcast stitch, blanket stitch, and pick stitch

In this section:

- Hand basting (even and uneven)
- Slip stitch appliqué
- Catch stitch
- Blind stitch with a double overcast stitch

- Thread bar & French tack
- Overcast stitch
- Blanket stitch
- Pick stitch

Hand Basting

Tools and supplies:

- Various fabrics: felt, wool felt, woolen tweed, silk organza, hymo canvas, and cotton fabric
- Size 5 sharps needle
- Size 8 betweens needle
- Cotton thread
- Thimble

This first round of modules will cover the following stitches: even basting, uneven basting, thread tracing, diagonal basting, tailor's tacks, fell stitch, pad stitch, and whipstitch.

These basic hand-basting stitches will form the foundation of many of your sewing projects, and some are also used in the draping process.

Module I:

Even Basting
(Running Stitch)

Step 1
For this lesson, you will need to prepare a piece of felt measuring 9" (23cm) wide by 12" (30.5cm) long. Draw three chalk lines at 2" (5cm) apart. For demonstration purposes, we will be sewing our basting stitches on a single fabric layer.

Step 2A
Thread your size 5 sharps needle with an 18" (46cm) single strand of unknotted cotton thread. Insert your needle into the top of the fabric and pick up two stitches ¼" (6mm) apart on your needle. Then pull the thread through, leaving a 1" (2.5cm) thread tail. Sew a backstitch if you like.

Step 2B
Take the next stitch ½" (1.3cm) away from the last and repeat the steps of picking up two stitches on your needle, each spaced ½" (1.3cm) apart. Do not pull the thread too tightly or the fabric will bunch up. Here we are basting on the chalk line of our sampler. When basting an actual seam, a tip is to baste ⅟₁₆" (2mm) away from the garment's stitching line so that the basting stitch does not get caught in the machine stitch and can be easily removed later. You could also use this stitch to create gathers, though you would want your stitch length to be between ⅛" (3mm) and ¼" (6mm) long.

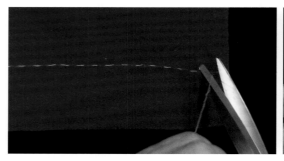

Step 2C
Continue this process until you reach the end of the fabric. An even basting stitch is used most often when two or more fabric seam layers are joined together, as when testing the fit of a garment and/or prior to machine-stitching a garment. Working with a longer needle, such as a size 5 sharps, will allow you to place several stitches onto the needle as you sew, speeding up the process.

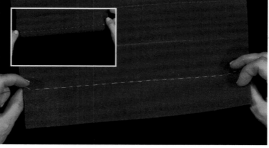

Step 2D
When you have finished basting, turn the piece over to see the stitches on the underside of the piece. When removing basting stitches, always clip the threads every few inches and then pull the stitches out without pulling on the fabric.

Tip
You may choose to use two strands of thread when basting thicker fabric layers, or if you anticipate extra strain on the seam when fitting a garment.

Module 2:

Uneven Basting

Tip

Do not use the uneven basting stitch (even with a double strand of thread in the needle) if there might be stress on the seams during fitting.

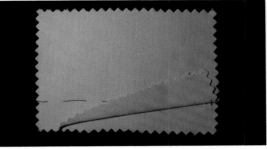

Step 1

Uneven basting is used when you want to baste layers together quickly. However, because this stitch is much longer than the even basting stitch, it is less secure, so should not be used for fitted garments. When basting a hem, make the small stitch side visible on the outside.

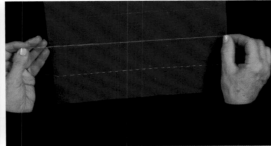

Step 2A

Thread your size 5 sharps needle with an 18" (46cm) single strand of unknotted cotton thread.

Start by taking a ⅜" (1cm)-long stitch on the top of the fabric, followed by a 1" (2.5cm)-long stitch, and then another ⅜" (1cm)-long stitch. Then pull the thread through.

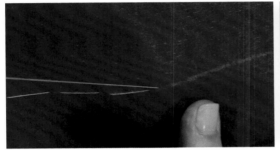

Step 2B

Repeat the stitching process, alternating between the ⅜" (1cm)-long stitch and the 1" (2.5cm)-long stitch. Note that, due to the length of the 1" (2.5cm) stitch, you cannot grab several stitches at a time onto the needle as you did for the even basting stitch.

Step 3

When you reach the end of the seam, sew a backstitch and then trim the end thread.

Step 4

This is how stitches look on the underside of the fabric.

Module 3:

Thread Tracing (Thread Marking/ Guide Basting)

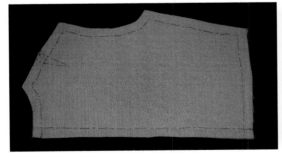

Step 1

A thread-tracing stitch is used in place of tracing paper to mark certain parts of a garment, such as the center front, center back, or the center of a sleeve. It is also used to mark seam allowances, notches, pockets, and buttonholes on fabrics that are either too delicate or too thick to mark with tracing paper or chalk. Smaller-length stitches are used when thread-tracing smaller garment areas such as buttonholes.

Step 2

Thread a size 5 sharps needle with a single unknotted strand of thread. All of the stitching will be done on the wrong side of the fabric.

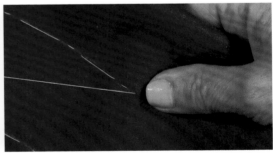

Step 3

Start on the top side of the fabric by making two small stitches ¼" (6mm) apart, followed by a 1" (2.5cm)-long stitch and then two more small stitches. The result is a combination of a ¼" (6mm) stitch, a ¼" (6mm) space, and a 1" (2.5cm) stitch. Repeat until you reach the end. Do not pull too tightly on the thread as you sew, or you will cause bunching.

Step 4
When you reach the end, leave a 1" (2.5cm) thread tail and clip the thread.

Step 5
Turn the fabric to the underside to see the smaller stitches. This is the preferred side, facing out, when basting hems.

Module 4:

Diagonal Basting

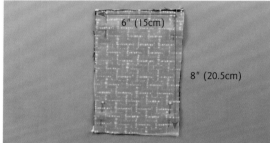

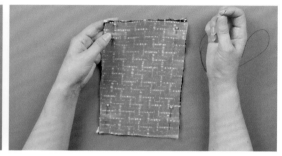

Step 1
For this lesson you will need to prepare a piece of organza and a piece of wool tweed, each measuring 6" (15cm) wide by 8" (20.5cm) long. Pin the two layers together.

Step 2
Diagonal basting is used to hold and control layers during garment construction and while pressing garments.

Step 3
Thread a size 5 sharps needle with a single strand of unknotted cotton thread. Note that the instructor here is using a contrasting red thread. This is just for demonstration purposes. Red thread is not recommended, because it can stain your fabric.

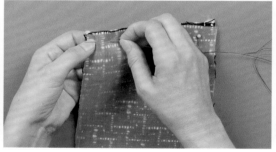

Step 4
Start by removing the pin that is securing the layers in the top left-hand corner.

Step 5
Now make a large stitch, working from right to left, then pull it through.

Step 6
Next, take your needle down and across diagonally, then make another large stitch—once again, work from right to left.

Step 7
Repeat the same process, passing down and across diagonally, and then making a large stitch from right to left.

Step 8
Continue stitching in this way down the length of the fabric.

Step 9
When you get to the end, take your stitch and then another stitch, then trim the end thread.

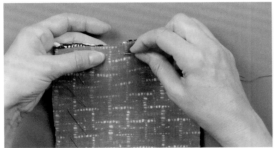

Step 10
You will now start again in the center of the fabric. Knot your thread, then make your first stitch about an inch away from the previous row.

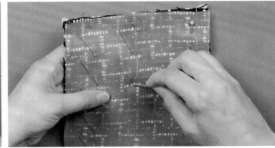

Step 11
Work your way down as before, working each stitch from right to left, and keeping your stitches approximately the same in length. The idea is to hold the fabrics together securely so that, when you come to sew with them, you are using them as one.

Step 12
Continue down the length of the fabric. Make a last stitch, as before, then trim the end thread.

Step 13
Now begin a third row of diagonal stitches. Here, our instructor is using an open-top thimble. This enables her to push the needle with the side of her finger, not the end, as demonstrated.

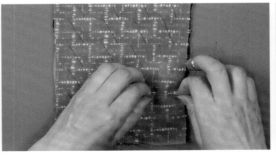

Step 14
Continue stitching down, as for the previous rows. If you were constructing a jacket with an underlining, you would use this stitch on the front, back, and sleeves.

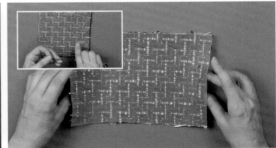

Step 15
As you approach the end, remove the last remaining pin. Create your last stitch, then trim the thread. You have now finished your diagonal basting.

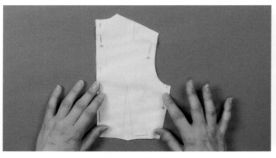

Step 1
You will now learn how to create tailor's tacks—both single and continuous tailor's tacks. Tailor's tacks enable you to transfer markings from your pattern to the fabric. This is a quarter-scale pattern. We have chosen a back view—its two darts will give us the opportunity to demonstrate the two different techniques.

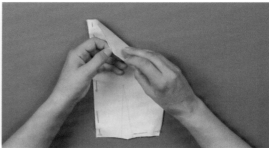

Step 2
You will need to pin your pattern to two layers of fabric and then cut out both layers. The pins hold all three layers together.

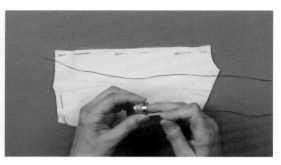

Step 3
Thread your size 5 sharps needle with a double thread, but with no knot at the end. Our instructor here will also be using a thimble.

Step 4
We will start with the single tailor's tack. We are using red thread for demonstration purposes, but otherwise this color is not recommended, since it can stain your fabric.

Step 5
We will start by marking the tiny dart at the top by tailor-tacking the two ends and the point of the dart. Because it is so small, you will only need a single tailor's tack at each point. Working from right to left, take a small stitch.

Step 6
Then take another stitch, inserting your needle right behind the first stitch. Make sure you leave a decent amount of thread here.

Step 7
When your needle emerges, it should come up just past where the thread came up previously.

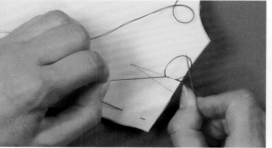

Step 8
Pull the thread through, but leave a loop. You should have a thread end and a decent-sized loop in the center.

Step 9
Now trim, leaving another end, so you have quite a lot of thread hanging free.

Step 10
Now do the same at the end of the dart, only this time you need to make a really tiny stitch.

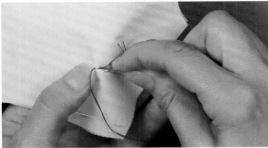

Step 11
Leave the thread dangling at the end and then make another stitch in pretty much in the same spot.

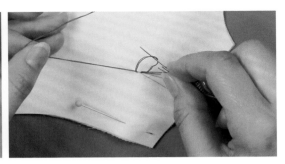

Step 12A
Once again, leave a loop.

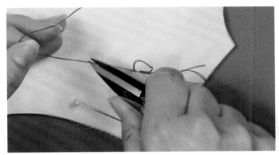

Step 12B
Trim the thread, leaving a decent amount of thread.

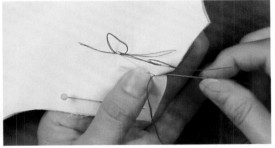

Step 13
Now you are going to stitch the top of the dart on the other side. Note how the instructor is stitching along the line, because that is what we are doing—transferring markings from the pattern onto the fabric. Leave your thread dangling, stitch close to it, and come up just past it.

Step 14
Leave your loop and trim. You have now finished your three single tailor's tacks.

Step 15
You will now be learning continuous tacking. We have rotated our back piece so that the bigger dart is on the right, enabling us to work from right to left.

Step 16
As before, stitch along the length of the dart. Come up, make a stitch, go down, and then come up again.

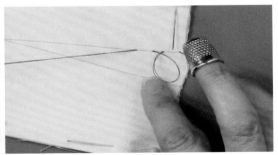

Step 17
Leave some thread hanging. A continuous tailor's tack is almost like a basting stitch—you are just going up and down—but instead of pulling your thread tight, you leave a loop each time.

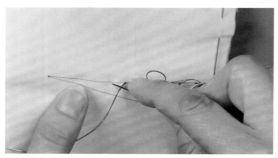

Step 18
Continue along the length of your dart, leaving loops as you go.

Step 19
If any of your loops looks a bit small, use your needle to guide and extend it.

Step 20
Rather than turn the piece around and continue down the other side, our instructor is choosing to tack this dart as two separate stitch lengths.

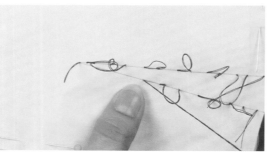

Step 21
The stitches here are about ¼" (6mm) long, and the spacing in between is also about ¼" (6mm) long. We have reached the last stitch here.

Step 22
Once you have made the last stitch, going to the point of the dart, trim the thread.

Step 23
The height of the loops we have created here is about ¾" (2cm).

Step 24
Now cut each of the loops.

Step 25
Next, take out the pins holding the layers together.

Step 26
After removing the pins, you will be ready to remove the pattern from the fabric layers. Pull it off very gently. It helps to put a finger or thumb on the threads and the fabric to make sure they remain in the fabric.

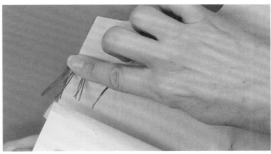

Step 27

Our instructor is holding some threads in place with her finger, just to make sure they are not removed along with the pattern. We are working here on the shoulder dart marked with single tailor's tacks.

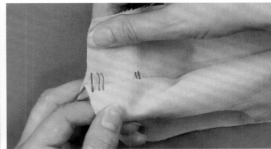

Step 28

Next, you will separate your fabric pieces. You want to pull them apart very gently, so that you leave an even amount of thread on each side.

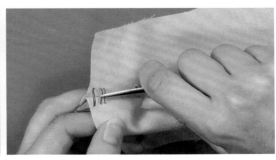

Step 29

The layers here have been pulled apart by about ¼" (6mm). Next, cut right in the middle of the threads.

Step 30

Do the same at the bottom of the dart.

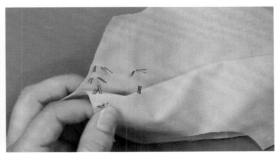

Step 31

Now carefully pull the fabric layers apart.

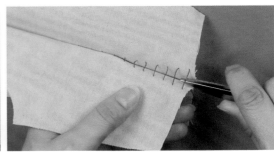

Step 32

Now do the same thing on the continuous tailor's tack on the other dart. Pull the layers apart by about ¼" (6mm) and then cut the threads right in the middle.

Step 33

Work right up to the top of the dart.

Step 34

Then continue cutting down the other side of the dart. The advantage of using a double thread is that, if you lose a thread, you will still have a second one in place.

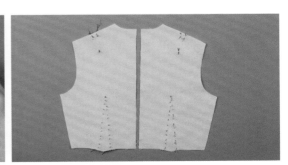

Step 35

As you can see, the pattern markings have been successfully transferred to both sides of our back bodice. You have now learned how to create a single tailor's tack and a continuous tailor's tack.

Hand Sewing

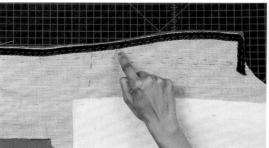

Step 1
The fell and pad stitch is used in the inner construction of tailored jackets. Here, we have pad-stitched hymo canvas to a jacket, but without the stitching going through to the other side. (We will demonstrate the pad stitch later.) The seam binding that secures the canvas at the edge has been basted down its center, and then fell-stitched on either side.

Step 2
To create a fell stitch, take your threaded and unknotted size 8 betweens needle and catch the top layer of fabric beneath only. Your needle should not go right through to the outside of the garment.

Step 3
Our stitches here are ³⁄₁₆" (5mm) in length, and diagonal. Make sure that you catch only the edge of the canvas, the seam binding, and the bottom layer of the fabric.

Step 4
As you can see here, the fabric remains clean and free of stitches on the other side.

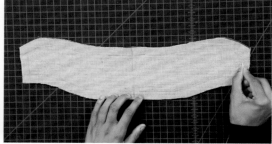

Step 5
We will now demonstrate the pad stitch on this under collar. We have already basted the hymo canvas to the fabric using a straight basting line.

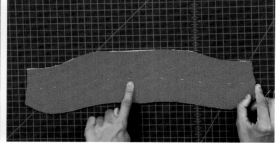

Step 6
Here are the basting stitches, as seen on the other side.

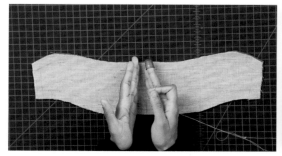

Step 7
You will start the pad stitching from the center, working out. One side here has already been completed, so we will demonstrate how to create the stitch on the other side.

Step 8
Thread your needle with a single strand of cotton thread, and knot the end. Our instructor is using a thimble. Start by making your first stitch perpendicular to, and ¼" (6mm) away from, the center-back line. Pass through the canvas but only partially through the fabric—the stitches should not be visible on the outside.

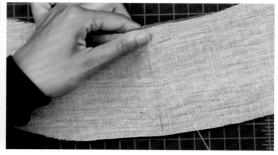

Step 9
The stitch will be ¼" (6mm) in width. Take a second stitch on top of the first to create a knot. In preparation for your next stitch, you may want to rotate your fabric for a better angle.

Step 10
Place your needle into the center-back line, and pick up another ¼" (6mm)-wide horizontal stitch, perpendicular to center back. Remember that your stitches should catch the hymo and the top wool layer only.

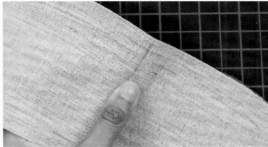

Step 11
Leave a ½" (1.3cm)-long length of thread before taking your next ¼" (6mm)-wide stitch at center back, as demonstrated.

Step 12
Note that by repeating these stitches you are creating a diagonal effect. Continue stitching until you reach the end of the row.

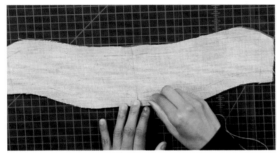

Step 13
Now reposition your work to start on the next diagonal row of stitches.

Step 14
The angled threads of pad stitching create a chevron pattern. To make sure that you end up with this pattern you need to angle your threads correctly, tilting your work to the angle that you think works best for you.

Step 15
You will be stitching the next row at a diagonal, repeating the stitching steps, but this time the diagonal stitches will be going in the opposite direction to form the chevron.

Step 16
Your stitch width is still ¼" (6mm) and the length of your stitches is ½" (1.3cm), the same as the first row. The distance between the two chevron lines is ⅛" (3mm). Make sure your stitches do not overlap or cross over each other at any time.

Step 17
When you reach the end of this row, reposition your work.

Step 18
Now begin the next diagonal row, repeating the same steps, but this time in the opposite direction from the previous row, taking a bit of the canvas and the fabric.

Step 19
Note that when we turn the collar to the right side, none of the pad stitches are visible.

Step 20
Continue to stitch your row. For demonstration purposes we are using contrasting thread, but for an actual garment you would use thread that matches the color of your fabric. Also, the distance between two rows would remain the same—that is, ⅛" (3mm)—for a pattern that was even overall.

Step 21
For illustration purposes, we will now continue with a black thread. Our needle is a size 8 betweens. The reason for using pad stitching in this exercise is that the canvas we are using is not fusible (it has no adhesive on it), so pad stitching helps fix it to the fabric.

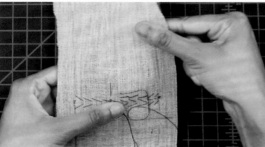

Step 22
Even when a canvas is fusible, sometimes the adhesive can ruin the fabric, which is why you might use pad stitching instead.

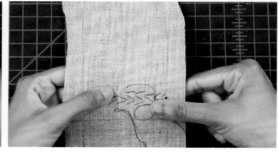

Step 23
Pad stitching also makes the fabric sturdy. For example, when you compare the weight of an unstitched portion to a stitched portion, you will feel the difference—the stitched area will be much firmer and sturdier.

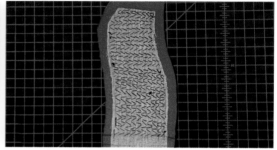

Step 24
Here is our under collar, with the pad stitching completed. You have now learned how to sew a fell stitch and a pad stitch.

Module 7:

Whipstitch

Step 1
We will now demonstrate how to do a whipstitch.

Step 2
A whipstitch is used to piece fabric together when you do not have much fabric width available for your seam allowance.

Step 3
Note how tiny the finished stitching is. It is almost invisible, which is exactly the idea—so that you cannot see that the fabric has been pieced together.

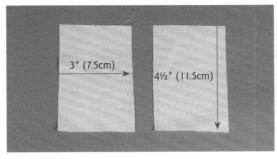

3" (7.5cm)

4½" (11.5cm)

Step 4
You will need to prepare two pieces of cotton, each measuring 3" (7.5cm) wide by 4½" (11.5cm) long.

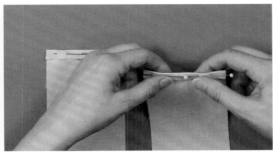

Step 5
First, turn the short edges down by about ¼" (6mm) to ⅜" (1cm) and pin them in place.

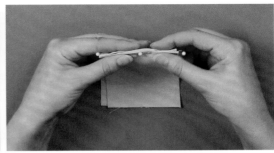

Step 6
Now take your pieces and put the right sides together, with the edges matching.

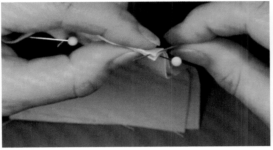

Step 7
Thread your needle with a single thread, with a knot at the end. Bring it up into the back piece, right up onto the fold, so that the knot is hidden underneath the fold. For this stitch it can be better to hold the edges together rather than pinning them—it gives you more control over keeping the edges together.

Step 8
Now go across into the next piece of fabric, taking just a small amount right on that fold and bringing the thread toward you. (The red thread here is for demonstration purposes; for an actual project you would choose a thread to match your fabric.)

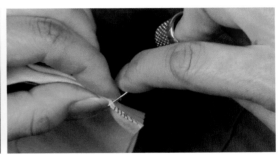

Step 9
Now take your thread across the top of the fold; the needle will go into the back piece of fabric and then into the front, right on that fold. You should catch just a very small amount of fabric. The stitches here are about ¹⁄₁₆" (2mm) apart. Note that the instructor is wearing a tailor's thimble.

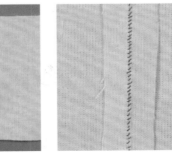

Step 10
Continue along the folds, taking just a small amount from each of the pieces. Note how it creates a diagonal stitch. Continue making stitches ¹⁄₁₆" (2mm) apart down the length of your fabric. The stitching "whips" over the edge of the fabric pieces, holding them together, which is why it is called a whipstitch.

Step 11
The finished row of whipstitch, from the right side (shown above left) and the wrong side (above right).

Slip Stitch Appliqué

Tools and supplies:

- #1 muslin (medium-weight calico)
- Cotton canvas (contrast color)
- Plastic or oaktag (card) template
- Size 8 sharps/appliqué needle
- Size 10 betweens needle
- 6-strand cotton embroidery floss (thread)

A slip stitch is a hidden stitch that can be used to stitch pockets, hems, quilts, and many other sewing projects.

Here you will be learning how to use slip stitch to sew an appliqué. We will show you how to create the stitches, and introduce you to a few tools and supplies that will help make the process easier.

Module 1:

Lesson Prep

Step 1A
For this lesson you will need to prepare a piece of cotton canvas measuring 8" (20.5cm) by 8" (20.5cm). Our canvas is brown.

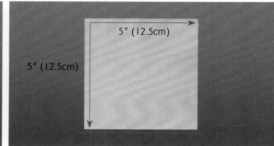

Step 1B
You will also need a piece of #1 cotton muslin measuring 5" (12.5cm) by 5" (12.5cm).

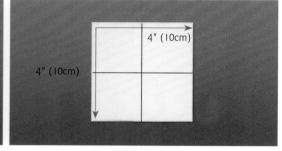

Step 1C
We have also created a plastic template that measures 4" (10cm) by 4" (10cm). You could also use a piece of oaktag paper. We marked the piece midway in the length and width.

Module 2:

Threading the Needle

Step 1
Begin by placing your open-top thimble on the middle finger that you will be sewing with. You will be using six-strand cotton embroidery floss for basting.

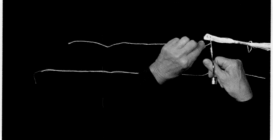

Step 2
Pull out a strand from the embroidery floss and cut a piece approximately 18" (45.5cm) in length.

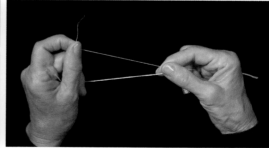

Step 3
Separate a single thread from the strand. We are using embroidery floss for basting because the stitches will not leave a mark when pressed on the fabric.

Step 4
Clip the end thread at an angle with small embroidery scissors.

Step 5A
Thread your size 8 sharps/appliqué needle by eye, or with the help of a needle threader.

Step 5B
Should your needle threader get tangled, you can separate it with the tip of your scissors.

Step 5C
Once the wire end of the needle threader has been opened up, you will be able to pass the thread through easily.

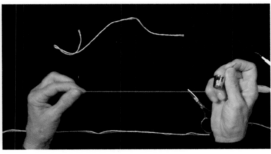

Step 5D
Insert the end of the needle threader into the eye of the needle and pull the thread through to thread the needle.

Step 6A
To knot the end of the thread, wrap the thread around the tip of the needle three times.

Step 6B
Then pull the twisted thread down along the needle with the tips of your fingers and then down along the thread to the end. This step will form a knot.

Step 1
Position your appliqué template on top of your muslin, allowing for a ½" (1.3cm) seam allowance around the four sides. The template lines are there to guide you with your grainlines.

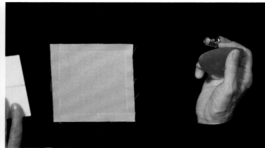

Step 2
Use your chalk marker to mark the four sides of the appliqué template onto the right side of the muslin fabric. Then remove the template.

Step 3A
To baste the appliqué stitching line, insert your threaded needle from underneath the middle of the chalk line. Be sure you have enough thread to go around the entire piece.

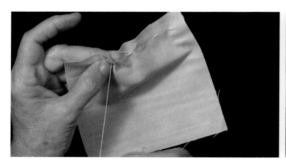

Step 3B
Now baste the appliqué along the chalk line, using a ¼" (6mm)-long running stitch.

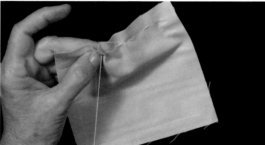

Step 3C
Do not pull the thread too tightly or it will cause gathers.

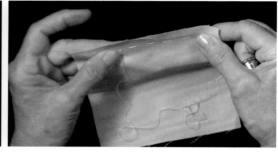

Step 3D
Pull the fabric edge with your fingers to help flatten the stitches as you sew.

Step 3E
A thimble can be used to help guide the needle through the fabric. Our instructor is using an open-top thimble, which is what tailors use. However, you could use a closed-top version if you prefer.

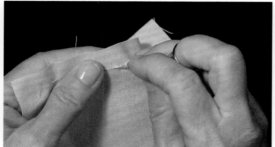

Step 4
Sew a backstitch when you reach the end.

Step 5
Push the needle to the other side, turn the appliqué over, and cut the end thread, leaving a ½" (1.3cm) tail.

  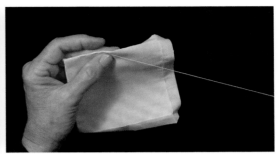

Step 6
Now clip the corners of the appliqué to help eliminate bulk. Here we are clipping off ¼" (6mm) from each of the four corners.

Step 7
Turn the seam allowance under and finger-press all four sides.

Step 8A
The next step is to baste the seam allowance under ⅛" (3mm) from the appliqué's edge. Start by inserting a newly threaded size 10 betweens needle underneath and in the middle of the appliqué's stitching line.

Step 8B
Sew a ¼" (6mm) running stitch. Be sure that your appliqué corners are nicely turned and basted. We are using a betweens needle for this step and not a sharps, because a betweens is shorter and therefore easier for sewing the corners.

Step 8C
When you reach the end, sew a backstitch and push the needle through to the underside. Then clip the end thread.

Step 1

In preparation for slip stitching the appliqué to your base fabric, thread your size 8 sharps/appliqué needle with silk thread and knot the end.

Step 2

The next step is to pass the thread across some Thread Heaven, a thread conditioner that will help the thread glide through the fabric much more easily. Unlike wax thread conditioners, this product does not leave behind any residue, so the thread does not require ironing before you sew.

Step 3A

Center your appliqué on the base cotton canvas, making sure that you align it on the correct grain.

Hand Sewing

Step 3B

Do not worry about the fact that the seam allowances are visible at the corners. You will hide them as you stitch.

Step 4A

Pin the appliqué to the base fabric in two places.

Step 4B

Now turn the base fabric over and pin the appliqué to the fabric in two places. Pinning on the back will keep the pins out of the way as you stitch on the right side.

Step 4C

Turn the base fabric back to the right side and remove the two top pins from the appliqué.

Step 5A

Now you are ready to slip stitch. Insert your needle into the appliqué from the back so that your knot will remain hidden underneath the fabric.

Step 5B

Pick up your first stitch in the base fabric directly underneath the appliqué stitch. Then come up and take a stitch ⅛" (3mm) from the first stitch, into the folded edge of the appliqué.

Step 5C
Now go back to the base fabric and take a stitch in the fold of the appliqué. Repeat the process of coming up, taking a ⅛" (3mm) stitch, and then passing into the folded edge of the appliqué. Hide your knot's thread tail underneath the appliqué.

Step 6
Continue to make your slip stitches. Untangle any threads with the tip of your needle as you sew.

Step 7A
When you get to the corner of the appliqué, use the tip of your needle to push the excess seam allowance underneath and then continue slip stitching.

Step 7B
As seen here, the stitches are very small, and are hidden. For demonstration purposes we are using red thread. However, for an actual garment you would use a matching color. If your garment was a two-tone, like our sample, you would match your thread color to the appliqué color and not to the base fabric.

Step 8A
When you reach the end, take a backstitch by going back into the last stitch.

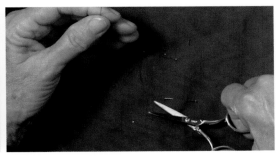

Step 8B
Then push the needle through to the back at the last stitch and turn the fabric over. Insert the needle through a single layer of the base fabric ½" (1.3cm) from the last stitch and then clip the end thread.

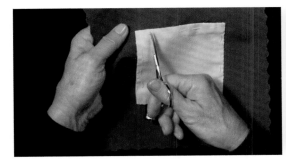

Step 9
Remove the pins, turn the fabric piece over to the right side, and clip the basting threads in sections. Lastly, remove the basting threads.

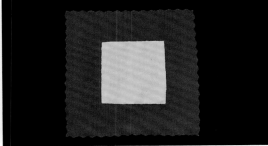

Step 10
You have now finished slip stitching an appliqué.

Catch Stitch

Tools and supplies:

- Wool melton
- Horsehair canvas
- Size 1 embroidery needle
- Pearl cotton thread

In this lesson we will demonstrate how to sew hair canvas to a piece of wool melton, using a catch stitch.

Used by bespoke tailors and couturiers, this technique will help you create garments that look professionally produced. You will also be able to use the technique on hems, seams, and when attaching interfacings and linings to jackets and coats.

Module 1:

Lesson Prep

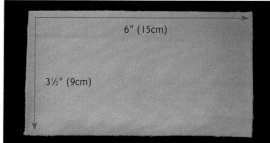

Step 1
For this lesson, you need to prepare a piece of wool melton fabric measuring 6" (15cm) wide by 3½" (9cm) long.

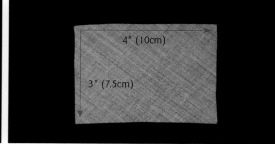

Step 2
You also need a piece of horsehair canvas cut on the bias, measuring 4" (10cm) wide by 3" (7.5cm) long.

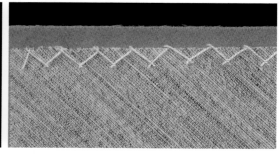

Step 3
We will demonstrate how to sew the horsehair canvas onto the wool melton using a catch stitch.

Step 4
For demo purposes only, we will be using a pearl cotton thread and a size 1 embroidery needle, so that you can really see the stitching. Pearl cotton is thicker than an all-purpose thread and is mostly used for embroidery or decorative stitching. For an actual garment, you would choose a fine sewing cotton thread or a silk thread and a size 8 sharps needle.

Step 5A
The first step is to center the horsehair canvas on the wool piece and then pin it in place, as demonstrated.

Step 5B
With your needle threaded and knotted at the end, sew a running stitch along the center, in the width of the piece, to hold the horsehair canvas in place.

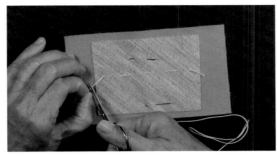

Step 5C
It is always easier to use basting stitches rather than pins when you are doing any fine hand sewing. Sew a backstitch when you reach the end and clip the end thread, leaving a ½" (1.3cm) thread tail. Then remove the pins.

Module 2:

Sewing the Catch Stitch

Step 1A
To begin the catch stitch, thread your needle. To make a knot at the end of the thread, a handy tailor's tip is to wrap your thread three times around the tip of the needle...

Step 1B
...then slide the thread down the needle and along the thread with your fingernail to form a knot.

Step 2
We will demonstrate how the catch stitch is sewn if you are right-handed—working from left to right. Start by inserting your needle under the horsehair canvas, ¼" (6mm) away from the edge, sandwiched between the canvas and the wool.

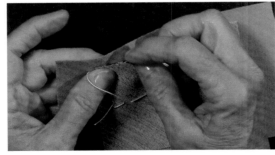

Step 3A
With your needle facing the left, pick up a thread from the wool.

Step 3B
Pull the thread through at a perpendicular angle to the stitch.

Step 3C
Then cross the stitch over and back onto the horsehair canvas, holding the thread down with your thumb.

Step 4

Now pick up another stitch ⅛" (3mm) wide, on the canvas only, and at about ⅜" (1cm) away from the first. Be sure not to pick up a thread from the wool for this stitch. Pull the thread through and to the right to form the next stitch.

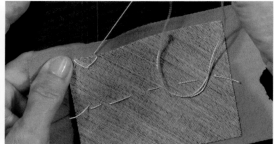

Step 5A

Now repeat the process to create the next stitch, holding the thread down with your thumb as you pick up a single thread from the wool, ⅜" (1cm) away from the last stitch.

Step 5B

As you can see you are, in effect, creating a series of little "X"s.

Step 5C

Repeat the steps of picking up a single thread from the wool, crossing at an angle, then picking up a stitch on the canvas. When picking up the canvas stitch it is important not to pick up any wool—and for the wool stitch, only pick up one thread, so that your stitches do not show on the right side of the fabric.

Step 6A

Turn the fabric over to the right side to check that none of your stitches are showing. If they are, then you will need to undo them and re-stitch.

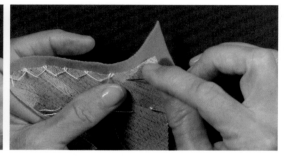

Step 6B

Note that by not having any pins here, the thread does not get tangled. This stitch is great for hems and for attaching the lining to the hem of jackets and coats. It is also used to hold down seams to a garment to keep them flat.

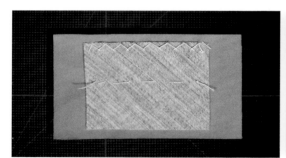

Step 7A

When you reach the end, sew a backstitch to the canvas.

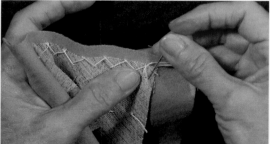

Step 7B

Then, to hide the end thread, insert the needle back into the canvas close to the last stitch.

Trim the thread. You have now finished sewing a hair canvas to a piece of wool using a catch stitch.

A dressmaker hand-basting a garment using a dome-top thimble.

Blind Stitch with a Double Overcast Stitch

Tools and supplies:

- Velvet
- Size 8 sharps needle
- 6-strand cotton embroidery floss
- Silk thread
- Open-top thimble
- Tiger Tape

This lesson will teach you how to sew a hem using blind stitch, with a double overcast edge.

This type of hem finish will add a couture touch to any fabric that has a tendency to fray. You will find that this finish soon becomes one of your favorites.

Module 1:

Lesson Prep

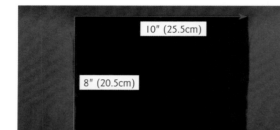

Step 1
For this lesson you will need to prepare a piece of velvet measuring 10" (25.5cm) wide by 8" (20.5cm) long.

Step 2
We will be using 6-strand cotton embroidery floss for demonstration purposes. If this were an actual garment, you would use matching cotton thread. We are also using an open-top thimble, but you could use a closed-top version if you prefer.

Step 3
Place your thimble on your middle finger and then cut a 15" (38cm) length of embroidery floss.

Step 4A
Now separate a single thread from the strand.

Step 4B
Thread your size 8 sharps needle, then create a knot at the end.

Step 5
With your velvet face up on the table, mark the hem at 2" (5cm) from the width edge, using a white pencil or tailor's chalk.

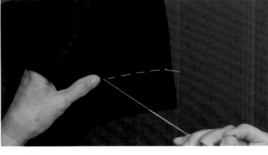

Step 6A
Now thread-trace the fold line of the hem from one end of the piece to the other. We are using an uneven thread-tracing stitch with a ½" (1.3cm) pickup and a ¾" (2cm)-long stitch.

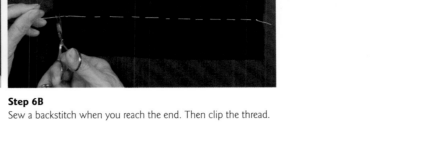

Step 6B
Sew a backstitch when you reach the end. Then clip the thread.

Module 2:

Sewing the Double
Overcast Stitch

Step 1
Start by threading your needle with a single strand of embroidery floss and creating a knot. To create the knot, twist your thread three times around the tip of the needle and then push the thread down along the needle to the end of the thread with your fingers.

Step 2
Now, with the wrong side of the velvet face up, fold the hem up along the fold line so that you can baste it in place.

Step 3A
Grab the fabric in one hand, as demonstrated, making sure that the hem is folded along the thread-tracing stitch so that, as you sew, you can see the stitching line.

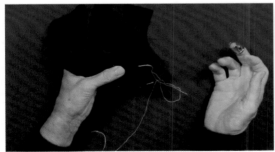

Step 3B
Next, uneven-baste the hem in place from right to left, sewing ¾" (2cm) away from the velvet's raw edge. (If you are left-handed, you should baste from left to right.)

Step 3C
Continue to uneven-baste the hem to the other side of the piece. We are avoiding using pins to hold the hem in place, as they may leave a mark on velvet. Working with velvet also requires additional basting, as the fabric has a tendency to slip.

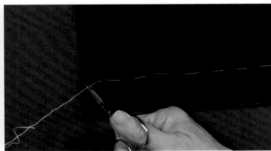

Step 3D
Sew a backstitch when you reach the end, and then clip the end thread.

Step 3E
Reposition the velvet piece so that the top raw edge of the hem is wrong side up and facing you.

Step 4A
Place your Tiger Tape ¼" (6mm) away from the width edge of your hem. Be sure that your tape is placed on the wrong side and not the right side, otherwise the fabric yarns will come out when the tape is removed. Be sure that it is flat and evenly spaced from the hem edge.

Trim the tape at both ends. Tiger Tape is used to help space your stitches as you sew. If you are an experienced sewer, then this step will not be necessary.

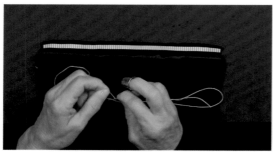

Step 4B
Thread and knot another single length of embroidery floss, approximately 18" (45.5cm) long. Right-handed sewers will sew the first part of the double overcast stitch from left to right.

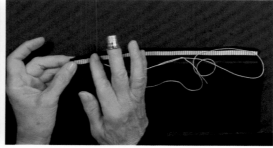

Step 4C
Start by inserting your needle into the hem on the left side, positioned next to the second line on the Tiger Tape.

Step 4D
Now wrap the thread around the hem edge and hold it in place with your forefinger.

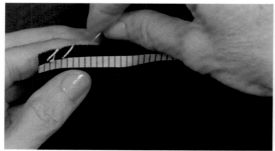

Step 5A
Pick up your next stitch two lines away from the last stitch. (Remember that here we are sewing from left to right.) Insert your needle from underneath at that line, come up, and pull the thread through to the top—again, wrapping the thread around the edge and holding it with your forefinger.

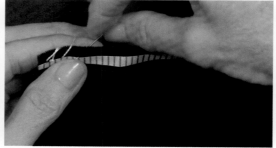

Step 5B
Repeat the process for the third stitch. Count across two lines, insert the needle from underneath at that line, and pull the thread to the top while wrapping the thread over the edge and holding it with your forefinger.

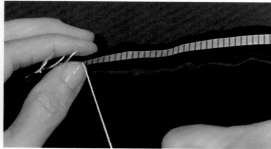

Step 5C
Continue to create your first series of overcast stitches. Note how the instructor has guided the stitches so that they are at an angle to the hem edge.

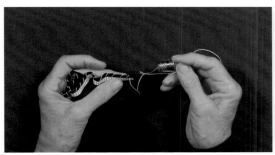

Step 6A
When you reach the end, you will reverse the stitch to start the second overcast stitch. You will now sew from right to left (unless you are left-handed, in which case you will be sewing from left to right).

Come up from underneath the fabric and take your first stitch, one line past the last stitch, as demonstrated.

Step 6B
Guide the thread as you pull it through the fabric to the top, so that you create an "X."

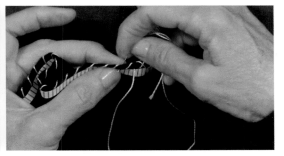

Step 6C
Create the next stitch by repeating the process of inserting your needle underneath the fabric at the next line on the tape and pulling the thread to the top.

The double overcast stitch is the perfect stitch for fabrics such as velvet, where the edges of the fabric have a tendency to unravel. You could also use this finish on seams, although in this case you would want to use silk thread to reduce the amount of bulk on the seam.

Step 6D
Continue stitching, following the lines on the tape.

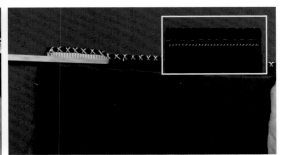

Step 6E
Note how the instructor uses the tip of the needle to redirect a stitch to create the "X" effect. You can also stop and redirect the stitches with your fingers to keep them even.

Step 6F
When you reach the end of the stitch, insert your needle underneath the fabric, come up to the top, and sew a backstitch. Then trim the end thread.

Step 7
Gently remove the Tiger Tape from the hem. This is how the double overcast stitch will look when you are finished sewing.

Step 1A

We will be using 100 percent silk thread for blind stitching the hem, as silk thread is thin, glides through fabric, and will not leave marks when removed or when pressed.

Step 1B

Passing your thread through some Thread Heaven before stitching will help keep the thread from tangling and breaking. Unlike other wax products, this thread conditioner does not require pressing after use to remove excess wax residue from the thread.

Step 1C

Thread your size 8 sharps needle and knot it by twisting the thread around the needle tip three times and sliding the thread down the needle and along the thread with your fingernail. We are using a contrast thread for demonstration purposes only. For an actual garment, you would use matching thread.

Step 2

To begin, grab the hem in your hands, just as you did when you basted your hem.

Step 3

Fold the top edge of the hem back by ⅜" (1cm) and hold it down with your thumb.

Step 4A

Take your first stitch into the folded-back edge of your hem allowance. We are working again from right to left.

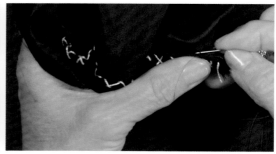

Step 4B

Take your next stitch in the base fabric, picking up only a few top threads and positioning the stitch directly in line with the first stitch. Be sure your stitch pickup does not go through to the right side, otherwise your stitches will show on the outside.

Step 4C

Your next stitch is taken on the folded-back hem edge. It is positioned ¼" (6mm) away from the last stitch and is ⅛" (3mm) in length.

Step 4D

Now repeat the process of picking up a few top threads from the base fabric in line with the last stitch and pulling the thread through each time.

Step 4E

Then move the needle into the hem-fold edge and continue the process of sewing the blind stitch.

Step 5A

You can see the thread on the wrong side of the hem because it is red. However, if it were a matching color you would barely see it, which is why it is called a blind stitch.

Step 5B

When you turn the fabric over to the right side, your stitches should not be visible.

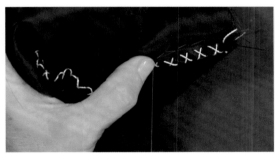

Step 5C

Continue blind stitching, taking care not to pull the thread too tightly, as this will cause the fabric to pucker. This is a very sturdy stitch and is often used on hems. However, you would never use it on a knit fabric, since it does not stretch the way a catch stitch would.

Step 5D

When you reach the end of the piece, sew two backstitches on the fold edge of the hem. Pass the needle through to the right side, then clip the end thread.

Step 6A

Turn the piece over to clip your basting threads and remove the threads in sections. Never pull your basting threads out in one length, as this will leave holes in the fabric.

Step 6B

Check the right side of the piece to be sure that none of your stitches are showing.

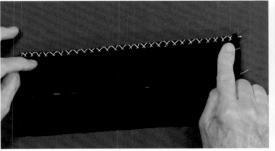

Step 6C

It does not matter as much if you can see the stitches on the wrong side, since this would be the inside of the garment. However, in couture you would not see any of the stitches on either side.

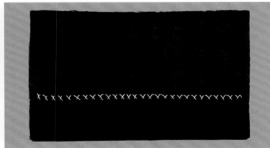

Step 6D

You have now finished sewing a velvet blind-stitch hem with a double overcast stitch.

Thread Bar & French Tack

Tools and supplies:

- Wool melton
- Size 5 sharps needle
- Pearl cotton thread
- Open-top thimble

You will learn two types of stitches in this lesson. The first one is a thread bar, which can be used as a loop for buttons, hooks, or lacings.

The second stitch is a French tack—also known as a French loop or thread chain. This can be used on a garment to hold a belt in place. It can also be used to hold lining in place, such as at the waist or underam of a jacket, or at the hem of a lined pant (trousers).

Module I:

Lesson Prep

Step I
For this lesson you will need to prepare a piece of wool melton measuring 4" (10cm) in the width grain of the fabric and 5" (12.5cm) in the length grain.

Step 2
Place your thimble on the middle finger of your sewing hand. Our instructor is using an open-top thimble, but you could use a closed-top version if you prefer.

Step 3
For demonstration purposes we will be using a pearl cotton, which is slightly heavier than regular sewing thread.

Step 4A
Cut an 18" (45.5cm) strand of thread and thread a size 5 sharps needle. To form a knot, wrap the thread twice around the point of the needle.

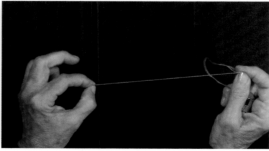

Step 4B
Hold the thread-wrapped needle with your thumb and forefinger as you push the needle up, and then slide the wrapped thread down the needle and along the thread to form the knot.

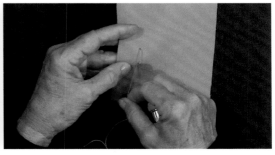

Step I
Start by inserting the needle from underneath the wrong side of the fabric. Then pull the thread through to the top.

Step 2
Now insert the needle from the top at I" (2.5cm) away and then emerge again at the point of the first stitch, as demonstrated.

Step 3
Pull the thread through, leaving a small thread loop with a slight amount of play. This is the basis of your thread bar.

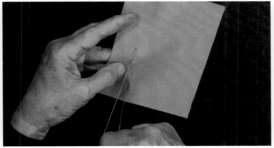

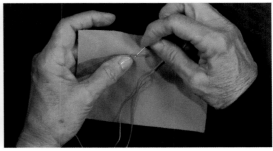

Step 4A
Repeat this step, taking another stitch through the same holes as the previous stitch.

Step 4B
Having two threads will reinforce the thread bar, making it a bit more sturdy.

Step 5A
Reposition the fabric so that the thread loops are horizontal. Now, starting on the left side of the loop, pass the needle under the thread loop.

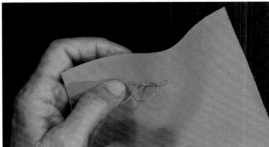

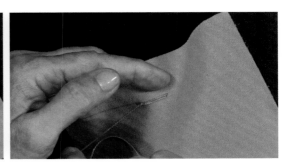

Step 5B
Pull the thread up and through the thread loop, as demonstrated.

Step 5C
Use your forefinger to guide the thread to create the first thread casing around the thread loops.

Step 5D
Then pull the thread tightly to the left to lock the stitch in place.

Step 6A

The next stitch is the same as the first. Pass the needle under the thread loops to form a loop.

Step 6B

Pull the thread tightly so that the second stitch is close to the first and so that it encases the thread loops.

Step 7A

Repeat these steps as you continue to wrap the entire width of the thread loops.

Step 7B

Be sure that you pull the thread tightly in the same direction and that you guide the thread so that your thread loops are thoroughly encased.

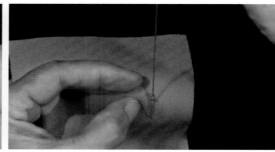

Step 7C

Note that by pulling the thread in the same direction a ridge will form on the edge of the thread loop.

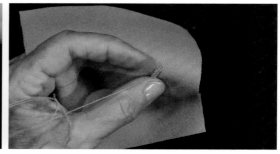

The result is a perfectly shaped thread bar.

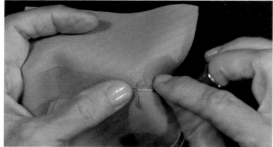

Step 7D

Also note that holding the thread down with your thumb as you create the loop helps guide the thread around the loop in the right direction. Thread bars can be any length, depending on their function—whether it is a button loop, a hook loop, or one of a series of loops used for lacing. A thread bar is stronger than a French tack.

Step 8A

When you reach the last stitch of the thread bar, pass the needle into the end of the thread loop.

Then pull the thread through to the back.

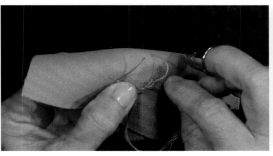

Step 8B
Turn the piece to the wrong side and create a loop by passing the needle under the thread loops and pulling it to form a knot.

If the thread becomes tangled, untangle it with the tip of your needle.

Then clip the end threads.

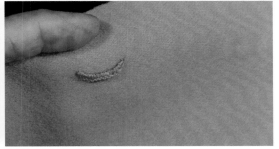

Step 8C
If you find that you have a space on your thread loop, you will be able to fix this by using the point of your needle to move the threads over to fill in the gap, as demonstrated.

Step 8D
You have now finished your thread bar.

Module 3:

Creating the French Tack

Tip
A French tack is sometimes known as a French loop or a thread chain.

Step I
To create a French tack, start by threading and knotting your needle, just as you did for the Thread Bar lesson. Use an 18" (46cm) length of pearl cotton.

Step 2
Insert your sewing needle into the underside of the fabric and pull the thread to the surface, to create the first stitch.

Step 3
Pass the needle back into the fabric and then come up $1/16$" (2mm) away from the first stitch, creating a small loop. For demonstration purposes, our stitch here is a bit wider.

Step 4A

Now pass the thread through the first loop.

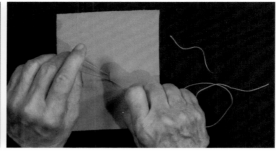

Grab it with the thumb and forefinger of your other hand.

Step 4B

As you pull the thread through the first loop, form a second loop with your thumb and forefinger.

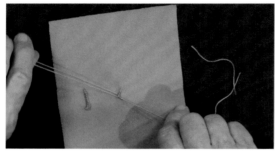

Step 5A

Now widen the second loop so that your thumb and forefinger can fit through the loop and then grab the thread.

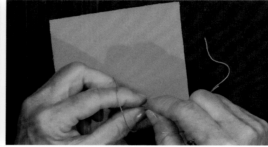

Step 5B

Hold the thread with one hand as you pull the loop to form a link on the chain at the base of the thread loop, which is basically a knot.

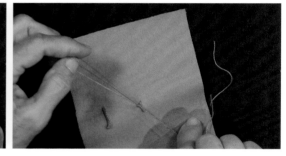

Leave another loop wide enough to form the next link.

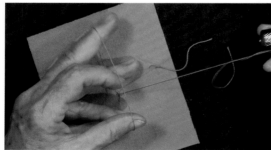

Step 6A

To form the next link, just repeat the process of grabbing the thread through the last loop, to create a new loop.

Step 6B

As you pull that loop to form the next link you will position it next to the previous link. Soon you will be able to see how the chain is formed. The process forms something like a crochet or macramé stitch.

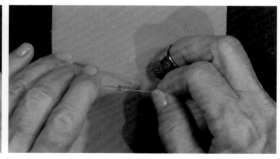

Step 6C

Repeat the process of looping and forming the links of your chain. Make sure that you pull the thread tightly as you go, until you have reached the length of chain that you desire.

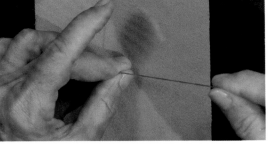

Step 7A
When you reach your desired length of thread chain, pass the needle through the last loop.

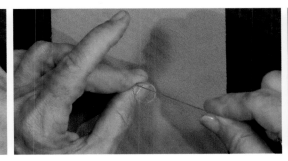

Step 7B
Pull the thread tightly through the loop...

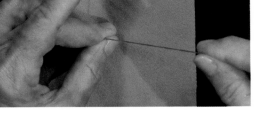

...to secure the knot.

Step 8A
Decide on the desired height of your loop—that is, the amount of space you will need for a belt to pass through if, for example, you are creating a belt loop.

Step 8B
Then hold the loop down with your thumb in that position as you take a holding stitch.

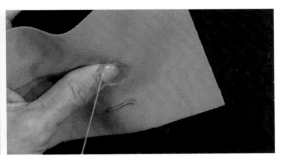

Step 8C
Take a small stitch on the right side of the fabric to secure the loop in place.

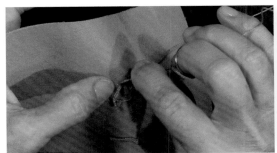

Step 8D
Pull the thread through and take another stitch to further secure the loop.

Step 9A
Pass the needle through to the underside and then clip the end threads.

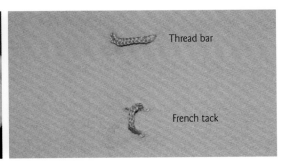

Thread bar

French tack

Step 9B
You have now finished sewing a French tack.

Overcast Stitch

Tools and supplies:

- Wool melton
- Size 8 sharps needle
- Pearl cotton thread
- Open-top thimble
- Tiger Tape

The hand stitch we are going to teach you in this lesson, the overcast stitch, is used to finish seams and hems, giving garments a couture finish.

If you are a less experienced sewer, you will find that our method of using Tiger Tape to create perfectly spaced stitches makes this a very easy exercise.

Module 1:

Lesson Prep

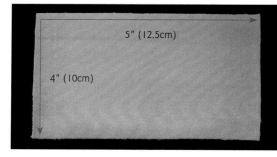

Step 1
For this lesson you will need to prepare a piece of wool melton measuring 5" (12.5cm) wide by 4" (10cm) long.

Step 2
You will be using an open-top thimble on the middle finger of your sewing hand. You will also be using pearl cotton thread and a size 8 sharps needle.

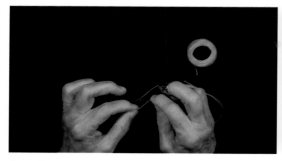

Step 3A
Begin by threading your needle. A tailor's tip for creating a knot at the end of your thread is to twist the thread around the needle tip three times...

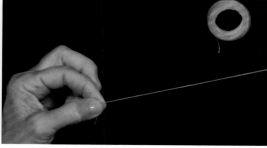

Step 3B
...then slide the thread down the needle and along the thread with your fingers to form the knot.

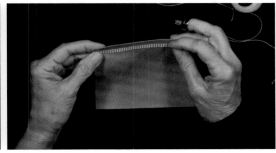

Step 1

Place your Tiger Tape ½" (1.3cm) from the length edge of your fabric piece. Be sure that your tape is placed parallel to the edge. Then trim the tape on both ends.

Step 2

We will begin the overcast stitch from the left side. (If you are left-handed, start from the right.)

Step 3A

Insert the needle from underneath the fabric level with the first line of the Tiger Tape.

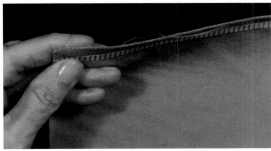

Step 3B

Wrap the thread around the edge of the fabric while holding the thread with your thumb and forefinger.

Step 3C

Looking at the lines on the tape, insert your needle level with the second line of the Tiger Tape from underneath to pick up your second stitch.

You could choose to make your stitches as long as you like, by choosing one of the other lines on the tape.

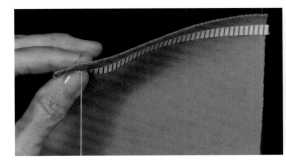

Note how we are angling the stitch as we sew.

Step 3D

Now create the third stitch by repeating the process of wrapping your thread around the edge, holding it with your thumb and forefinger, and then inserting your needle two lines along from the previous stitch.

Step 3E

Continue to make your overcast stitches. Note how the instructor is guiding the stitches so that they are angled and equally spaced along the edge. Do not pull the thread too tightly as you sew, or you will cause puckering. The overcast stitch can be used on seams and hems to keep them from fraying.

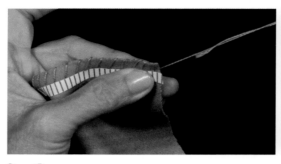

Step 4A
When you reach the end, sew a backstitch, push the needle to the underside, and then trim the end thread.

Step 4B
Manipulate the stitches with your fingers to space them evenly.

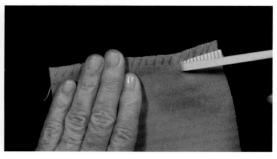

Step 4C
Remove the Tiger Tape and smooth the nap of the fabric with your hands.

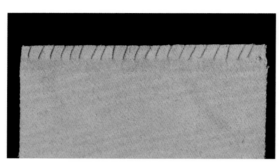

Step 4D
You have now finished sewing an overcast stitch.

Blanket Stitch

Tools and supplies:

- Wool melton
- Size 1 embroidery needle
- Pearl cotton thread
- Thimble
- Triangular chalk marker
- Tiger Tape

A blanket stitch is used as an embellishment on the edges of jackets, coats, sleeves, or pockets—or anywhere that a special touch is required.

We will demonstrate an easy technique for creating this decorative stitch, using Tiger Tape to ensure that your stitch will turn out perfect every time. The tape will also enable you to complete it in no time at all!

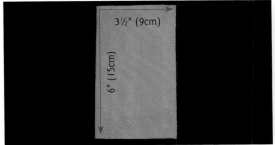

Step 1
For this lesson you will need to prepare a piece of wool melton measuring 3½" (9cm) in the width grain by 6" (15cm) in the length grain.

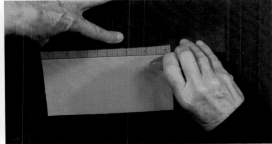

Step 2A
Mark the fabric with your triangular chalk marker at ⅜" (1cm) away from the length edge of your fabric.

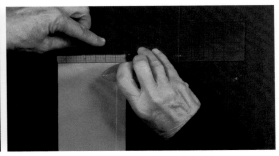

Step 2B
Then reposition the swatch and chalk the width edge at ⅜" (1cm) away.

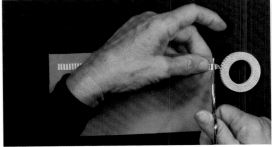

Step 3A
Next, apply your Tiger Tape along the chalk-marked length edge. Then trim the excess tape with your small embroidery scissors.

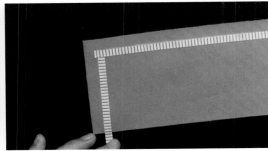

Step 3B
Now apply Tiger Tape to the width edge of the fabric. Again, trim away the excess tape.

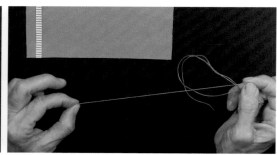

Step 1A

Place your thimble on the middle finger of your sewing hand. We will be using pearl cotton thread in a contrasting color. This thread is thicker than all-purpose thread and is mostly used for embroidery or decorative stitching.

Step 1B

Thread your size 1 embroidery needle with an 18" (46cm) length of thread. A tailor's tip for knotting the thread is to wrap the thread three times around the tip of the needle...

...and then slide it down along the needle and the thread with your fingernails, to form the knot.

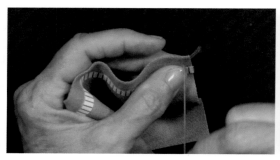

Step 2A

Start the blanket stitch by inserting your needle from underneath the fabric at the second line on the Tiger Tape, then pull the thread through to the top.

Step 2B

Now, insert the needle 1/8" (3mm) away from the first stitch at a right angle to the Tiger Tape.

Pull the thread through, but leave a small loop.

Step 2C

Insert the needle through the loop, as demonstrated.

Then pull the thread through, with the thread facing the edge.

Step 3A

Hold the thread between your forefinger and middle finger as you insert the needle back into the fabric from underneath, two lines on the Tiger Tape past the first, to create the first stitch.

Step 3B

Now you will repeat the process of inserting the needle into the thread loop and then pulling the thread through at the third line on the Tiger Tape.

Note how your stitch forms a blanket-like finish on the edge of the fabric.

Step 4A

Continue the process of counting along three lines on the Tiger Tape, inserting the needle from underneath, and then inserting the needle into the thread loop to create the next stitch.

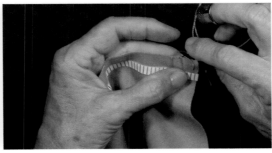

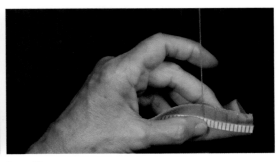

You can choose to make your stitches any length you desire. They simply need to remain a regular distance apart. It is also important to hold the thread so that you can create a slight amount of tension.

You must be able to direct the thread loop so that it aligns with the edge of the fabric. Use the tip of your needle to guide the thread loop in place along the edge.

Step 4B

Once you have sewn a few stitches, you can start making your stitches from the top instead, if you find that position more convenient. Note how your needle will be on top of the thread as you loop it through to form the blanket stitch edge.

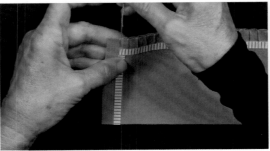

Step 4C

The blanket stitch can be used on the edges of jackets, coats, ponchos, pockets, sleeve openings, or any place where you are looking to create a decorative edge finish. It is also used to cover hooks and eyes, although the stitches need to be much tighter in that case. You can also use silk thread, cotton thread, or even wool yarn for a sportier look.

Step 4D

If you find that you do not have enough thread to finish the piece, leave enough thread so that you can turn the piece to the wrong side.

Inserting the needle at the base of the final stitch...

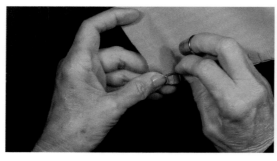

...sew a small backstitch to secure the thread.

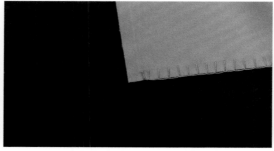

Then trim the end thread.

Step 5A
Use the tip of your needle to realign the last stitch.

Step 5B
Then begin again on the edge, by inserting your needle underneath the fabric, ⅛" (3mm) away from the last stitch.

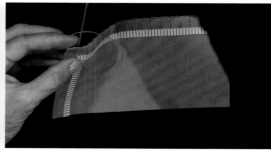

Insert your needle again below this stitch, leaving a loop, and then emerge underneath the fabric, passing your needle through this loop and pulling it upward.

Step 5C
Pull the thread up and take the next stitch from on top of the fabric—in our case, that happens to be at the corner of the fabric piece. Then, pull the thread through the loop to complete the stitch, as demonstrated.

Step 5D
Because you are working the corner now, you need to create your stitches so that they emanate from the inside corner...

...as shown.

Guide the stitches with your needle and fingers so that they are evenly spaced.

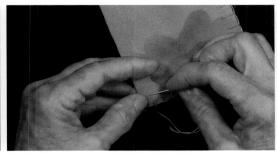

Step 5E
Your next stitch will be from underneath, but then you can change back to taking your stitches from the top. It is completely your choice and depends on what feels most comfortable.

Step 5F
When you reach the end, turn the piece to the wrong side and sew a backstitch.

Then clip the end thread.

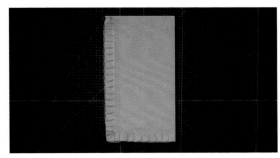

Step 5G
You have now finished sewing a blanket stitch.

Pick Stitch

Tools and supplies:

- Wool melton
- Size 1 embroidery needle
- Pearl cotton thread
- Tiger Tape

We will now teach you how to sew a pick stitch using a technique that is both easy and guarantees the best results.

The pick stitch can be applied to any fabric. It is most often used to add a decorative touch to the edges of jacket and coat collars and lapels, as well as pocket and sleeve trims.

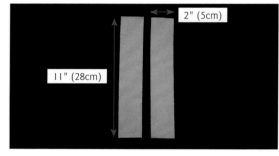

Step 1
For this lesson you will need to prepare two strips of wool melton, each measuring 2" (5cm) wide by 11" (28cm) long.

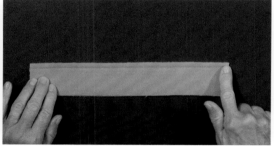

Step 2
We have already stitched the two wool strips together in the length with a ¼" (6mm) seam allowance.

Step 3A
Open the seam up with your fingers.

Step 3B
Place a pressing cloth on top of the seam and press the seam open and flat, using steam. Let it cool before removing the pressing cloth.

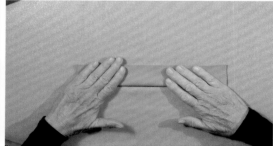

Step 4
Now, fold the piece back so that the wrong sides are facing each other and the seam edge is centered and flush with the edge.

Step 5A
Once the seam is centered and flush with the edge, use your pressing cloth to press the seam flat with your iron, using steam.

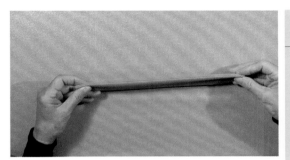

Step 5B
Allow the piece to cool, then remove the pressing cloth. Check to make sure that the seam is centered. If it is not, reposition it and repeat the pressing step.

Self-evaluation

☐ Is my needle the correct type and size for my project?
☐ Would a thimble assist me when sewing my project?
☐ Are my pins and needles sharp?
☐ Is my thread weight compatible with my fabric?
☐ Are my hand stitches spaced accurately?

Module 2:

Sewing a Running Stitch

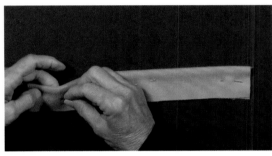

Step I
You now need to pin the layers together at ¾" (2cm) from the edge. Make sure that the seam is centered as you pin.

Step 2
Next, you will use some pearl cotton thread and a size 1 embroidery needle to baste (tack) the pieces together at ½" (1.3cm) from the edge.

Step 3A
The stitch you are using here is called a running stitch. Place your stitches approximately ½" (1.3cm) to ¾" (2cm) apart and remove the pins as you sew.

Step 3B
Make sure that the seam is centered.

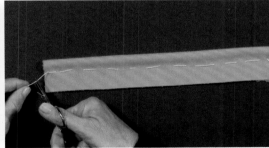

Step 3C
Continue to baste until you reach the end. End the basting stitches with a backstitch and then clip the end thread.

Step 4
Once again, make sure that the seam is centered. If it is not, remove the basting stitches and correct the position of the seam so that it is centered.

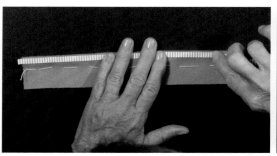

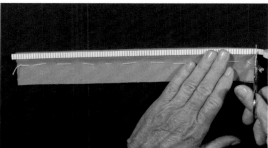

Step 1A

Now you will position your Tiger Tape along the edge of the fabric, as demonstrated. Make sure that the tape is placed right on the edge. This will provide a guide for you when sewing the pick stitch. This tape works better than chalking the edge to create a guide.

Step 1B

Once the tape is affixed to the edge of the fabric, trim the ends of the tape.

Step 2

For demonstration purposes we will be using pearl cotton thread in a contrasting color. This is a thicker type of thread. You could also use another heavy thread or even buttonhole twist, and your thread could be matching or contrast.

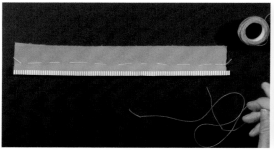

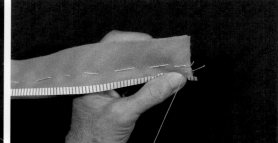

Step 3

To begin, thread your needle. Form a knot by twisting the thread around the tip of the needle three times and then pulling it down along the needle and thread with your fingers. Be sure that you have threaded the needle with enough thread to sew the length of the piece.

Step 4A

Using the tape as a guideline, start at the end of the piece by placing your needle in between the fabric layers. Since the instructor is right-handed, she will be working from right to left.

Step 4B

Come up with your needle at about ½" (1.3cm) from the right side to the nearest line on the tape and pull the thread through to the top. This will hide your knot in between the layers.

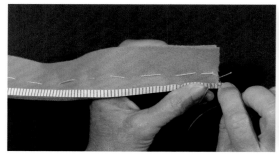

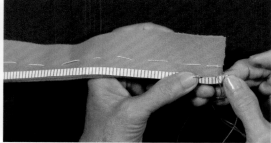

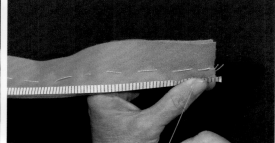

Step 5A

Next you will take a backstitch. The lines are now going to indicate exactly where your stitches should go. So, go back one line to create your backstitch, inserting your needle through the top layer of fabric only.

Step 5B

Depending on how long you want your pick stitches to be, you want to come up that amount. In our case, the needle is coming up at the third line.

Step 5C

Pull the thread through and that will be the length of your first stitch.

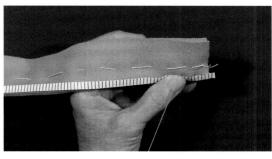

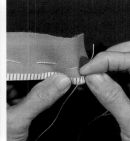

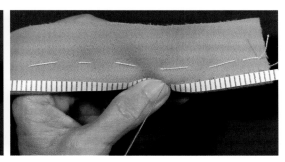

Step 5D

Now come back one line and insert the needle to finish the first stitch. Remember not to pass your stitch through to the lower layer. All of your stitches will be taken on the top layer only.

Step 6

Repeat the process of bringing your needle back up and out at the third line to start the second stitch. Pull the thread through to the top. Again, the stitches are only made on the top layer; this is not topstitching, which would be stitching through both layers of fabric. Do not pull the thread too tight.

Step 7A

Continue pick stitching, repeating the process of coming back one line, inserting the needle into the single layer at that point, then emerging on the third line and pulling the thread through to the top. Each of our stitches is ⅛" (3mm) long and ⅜" (1cm) apart, but you can make them as long as you like.

Tip

A graded seam has one layer of seam allowance trimmed smaller than the other.

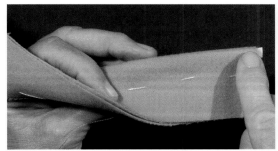

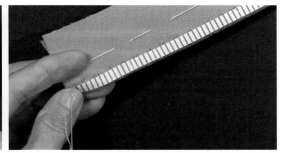

Step 7B

Turn the piece over to check that none of your stitches have gone through to the underside of the fabric.

Step 7C

As you can see, the stitches are sitting right on top of the fabric. This stitch can be applied to any fabric and, as mentioned earlier, can be added to collars, lapels, and pockets—or anywhere where you are looking to add a decorative touch.

Step 7D

Our sample does not use interfacing, but an actual garment would. Your stitches would include the interfacing layer. And if you were looking for a more pronounced stitch effect, you would leave your seam allowance wider on the top layer and include the top seam-allowance layer in your stitch.

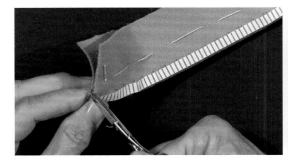

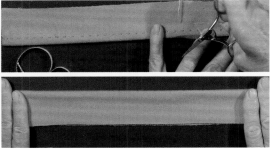

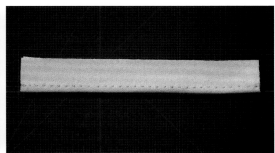

Step 8A

Sew a backstitch when you reach the end, and then trim the end thread.

Step 8B

Remove the Tiger Tape, then clip and remove your basting thread. Turn the piece over and check that none of your pick stitches is showing on the other side.

Step 8C

You have now finished sewing a pick stitch.

2 Pressing

The secret to a truly professional-looking garment lies in pressing your seams during the construction process. In this chapter you will learn **pressing techniques** for a variety of fabrics, including leather, and how to press garment details. You also learn about **pressing cloths and tools**, including those specific to napped fabrics, such as velvet and corduroy.

You will learn how to use other tools, too, such as a seam roll, clapper (a tool no tailor can live without), sleeve board, ham, and a mitt for spot pressing. We will also show you tricks to make pointed collars and cuffs come out perfect every time.

Introduction to Pressing Tools & Techniques

Learning objectives

☐ Discover how to press lightweight, napped, and heavyweight fabrics, and how to press leather

☐ Understand when and how to press straight and curved seams without leaving marks

☐ Know the correct pressing techniques for tailored garments, points, and sleeves, and how to spot press

Pressing a seam during construction.

Tools and supplies:

- Iron and ironing board
- Pressing cloths including:
- Heavyweight cotton drill fabric
- Silk organza
- Terry toweling (terry cloth)
- Brown paper
- Oaktag (card)

- Needle (velvet) board
- Seam (pressing) roll
- Clapper
- Pointer
- Pressing (tailor's) ham
- Sleeve board
- Pressing (sleeve) mitt

Module 1:

Pressing Lightweight Fabrics

Step 1
Start by testing the steam from your iron and making sure it is not too hot. Try it on a sample of your fabric before pressing your garment.

Step 2
A very light organza pressing cloth is useful for any lightweight or silk fabric, because you can see through the organza. Press very lightly, with some steam.

Module 2:

Pressing Napped Fabrics

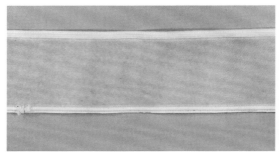

Step 1
When sewing with napped fabrics, such as velvet and corduroy, you need to use a needle board (sometimes referred to as a velvet board).

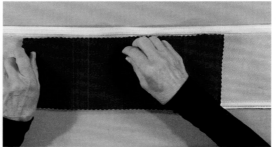

Step 2A
Lay the napped fabric face down on top of the board.

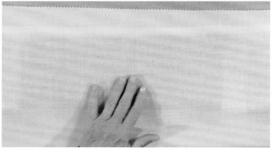

Step 2B
Press with a medium-weight pressing cloth. Again, you can see right through this cloth.

Step 2C
Steam the fabric, making sure not to press down on it directly.

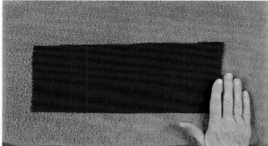

Step 3
If you do not have a needle board, you can use a towel as a substitute.

Steam the fabric as before.

Step 1
When pressing wool, or any heavyweight fabric, you need to use a heavyweight pressing cloth.

Step 2
A pressing cloth made of drill, such as this one, is a good choice.

Step 3
Press using a good amount of steam.

Step 1A
To press leather, use brown paper instead of a cloth.

Step 1B
Cover the leather with the paper and use a dry iron.

Step 2A
If you do need to use steam, first turn the leather over, with the wrong side uppermost.

Step 2B
Cover with the brown paper, and apply the steam.

Tip
Leather garment seams can be pressed open and then glued flat, or pressed open and topstitched down. Always use brown paper when pressing the right side of any leather garment.

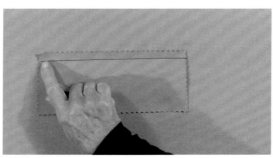

Step 1
Make sure you always press your seams after sewing.

Always press the stitch line on the wrong side of the fabric.

Step 2
Use a seam roll (also called a pressing roll) to flatten a seam without leaving marks on the right side of the fabric.

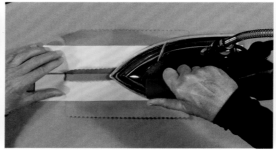

Step 3
Finger-press the seam open over the seam roll, and apply steam.

Step 4
If you do not have a seam roll, place two pieces of oaktag (card) in the seam allowance before pressing.

The pressed seam, without any marks on the right side.

Tip
Pressing your garment, especially the seams, during construction is crucial to a professional-looking end result. It also makes sewing the project a lot easier. Once the garment is finished, it is almost impossible to press areas such as seams, collars, and pockets.

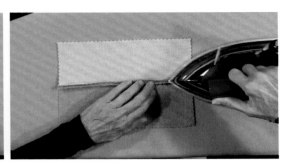

Step 1
When you are making a tailored garment, such as a coat or jacket, all seam lines must be pressed flat with steam on the wrong side of the fabric after sewing.

Step 2
Now finger-press the seam open.

Then apply steam.

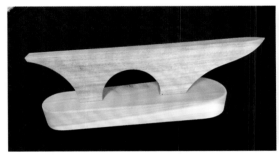

Step 3
Make sure you also have a clapper at hand. This wooden block smooths seams and absorbs moisture from steam.

Step 4
First turn your seam, perhaps a lapel or the edge of a jacket, to the inside.

Step 5
Place a heavyweight pressing cloth on top and press with quite a bit of steam.

Step 6
Now press down hard with the clapper until the fabric is dry.

Tip
A clapper with a point presser is an invaluable tool that can be used to press hard-to-reach seams or any area of a garment such as pockets, hems, and collars. Apply plenty of steam and hold the clapper on the area until it cools.

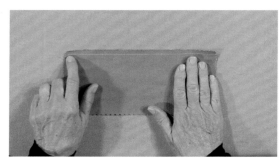

Step 1

When making cuffs, collars, or any garment piece with a point, it is important to press seams as you go.

Press all seams on the wrong side using steam.

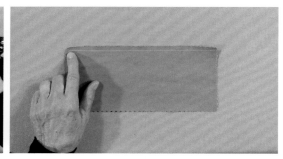

Step 2A

You will need a pointer to get into a corner like this.

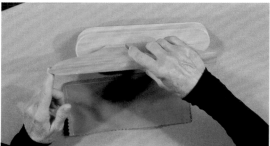

Step 2B

You will find a pointer at the edge of your clapper.

Step 3A

Slide your fabric point onto the pointer and finger-press.

Step 3B

Now apply steam with your iron.

Apply steam along the entire seam.

Step 3C

Work your way along all the seams of your pointed piece, sliding them onto the pointer...

...and applying steam with your iron.

Step 4A
When making any piece with a right-angled corner, you will need to press it on the right side.

Step 4B
Clip the corner to reduce bulk—not too close, but just enough.

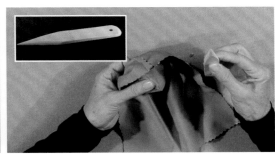

Step 4C
Take a small pointer, such as this.

Step 4D
Press it into the corner to make your point nice and sharp.

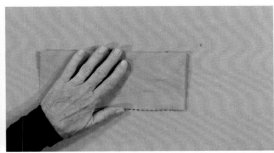

Step 4E
Turn your piece right side out.

Step 4F
Press using a pressing cloth and steam.

Module 8:

Pressing Curved Seams

Tip
A ham can be used for pressing other curved seams such as armholes, hems, and crotch seams.

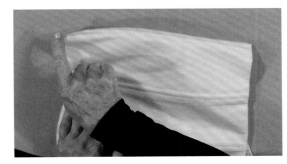

Step 1
To press a curved seam, such as the princess seam in this bustier, you will need a ham.

Step 2
The curved form of a ham provides support for contoured seams. Place your curved seam right over the ham.

Introduction to Pressing Tools & Techniques

Step 3
Press using steam. The fabric shown here was muslin (calico), so did not require a pressing cloth.

Step 4
Make sure to use a pressing cloth over any fine fabric.

Module 9:

Pressing Sleeves

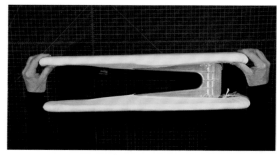

Step 1
When pressing sleeves, or any part of a garment that you do not want to have a crease line, use a sleeve board.

Step 2A
Insert the board into the sleeve or wherever the seam is.

Step 2B
Use a pressing cloth, and press using steam.

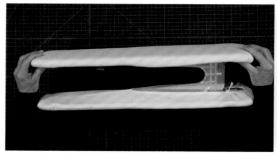

Step 3
A sleeve board has two sides, with one side usually narrower than the other.

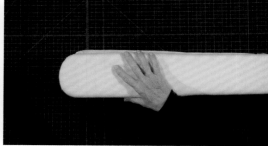

Step 4A
The wider section of the sleeve board is useful for the cap of the sleeve.

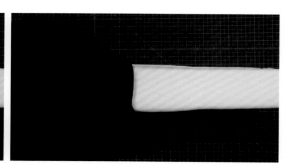

Position the sleeve cap over the wide edge of the board.

Tip
Both ends of the sleeve board are useful. The small end can be used for pressing narrow areas such as sleeve hem openings and necklines. The wider end is used for pressing sleeve caps or any other area on a garment that has a curved seam.

Step 4B
Press with steam—again, using a pressing cloth.

Module 10:

Spot Pressing

Step 1A
There will be times when you need to spot-press a small area on a garment.

Step 1B
A pressing or sleeve mitt is useful here. Slide your hand into the mitt.

Step 2A
A sleeve mitt is padded on one side. Insert the mitt beneath the garment area to be pressed, with the padded side uppermost.

Step 2B
Without touching the garment, go over it lightly with a little bit of steam.

Self-evaluation

☐ Did I accurately determine the proper iron temperature for pressing my fabric?

☐ Did I apply enough steam and pressure when using the clapper?

☐ Were my seams opened and pressed flat as I used the ham?

☐ Did I use a pressing cloth with my sleeve board and pressing mitt?

3 Interfacings, Underlinings, Interlinings, & Linings

This chapter will introduce you to interfacings, underlinings, interlinings, and linings, explaining the difference between them and how and why they are used in garment construction.

Interfacing is used in specific areas of a garment to provide structure and support. You will learn about the many types of interfacing available, and how to choose the right one for your garment. We will also clarify the distinction between an **interlining** and an **underlining**—and, again, introduce you to the various types available.

When it comes to inserting a standard **lining**, choosing the right fabric is crucial, so here we cover a wide array of options, enabling you to make an informed choice every time.

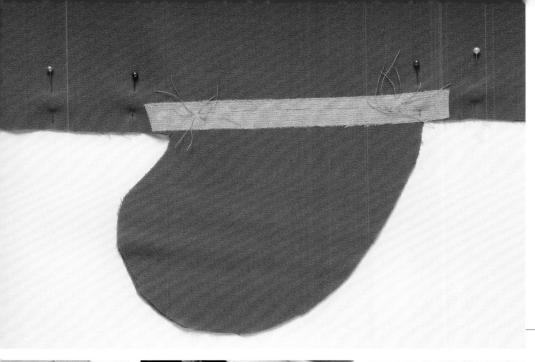

Introduction to Interfacings, Underlinings, Interlinings, & Linings

Learning objectives

☐ Understand what interfacing is, all the different types that are available, and what they are used for

☐ Prepare interfacing by testing for shrinkage and pre-shrinking

☐ Compare and use the different types of underlining

☐ Add warmth with interlining, and identify the main types

☐ Choose a lining from the different options available, including specialized linings

Areas on a garment where interfacing, underlining, interlinings, and linings are used.

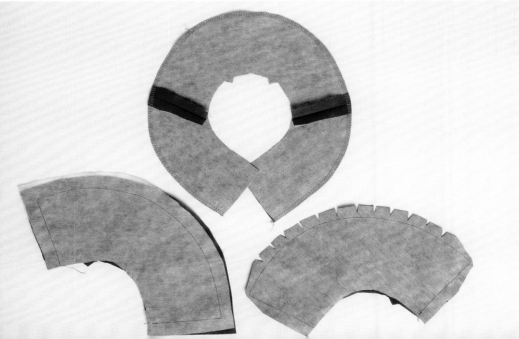

Interfacings, Underlinings, Interlinings, & Linings

What is Interfacing?

Interfacing is a material applied to specific areas
on the inside of a garment. It adds shape and
structure to features such as collars, cuffs,
and pockets, or acts as a stabilizer in areas
such as seams, necklines, and facings.
The most suitable interfacing will add body,
not bulk, to a garment.

Areas commonly interfaced

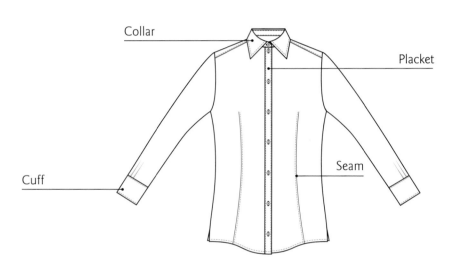

Collar

Placket

Seam

Cuff

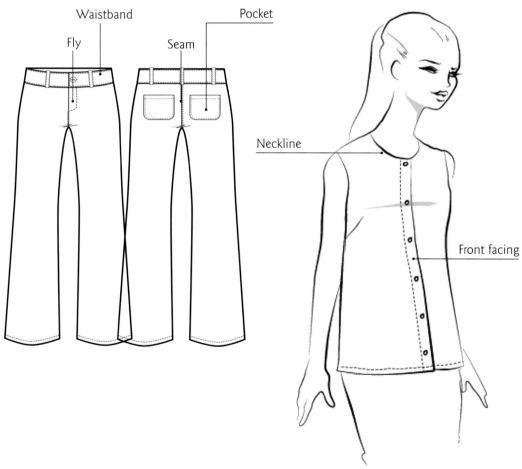

Waistband

Fly

Pocket

Seam

Neckline

Front facing

Tip
Fusible interfacing is the preferred stabilizer for beginners, because it has a glue backing and can be ironed onto a garment easily. It is available in many weights and colors.

Types of Interfacing

Interfacing can be woven, nonwoven, or knitted, and the fiber content used in its manufacture can vary. It also comes in different widths. You can purchase either fusible or non-fusible interfacing. (The latter must be sewn in.)

Woven interfacing

Nonwoven interfacing

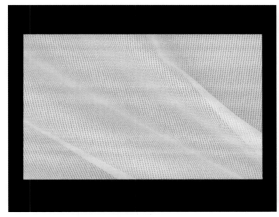

Knit-tricot interfacing

Knit-weft interfacing

Most interfacing is offered in black, charcoal, or white, but some options are available in other colors, too. Choose one that most closely matches your garment fabric. Interfacing also comes in different weights, from sheer to heavyweight, so again, choose what will be most compatible with your garment fabric.

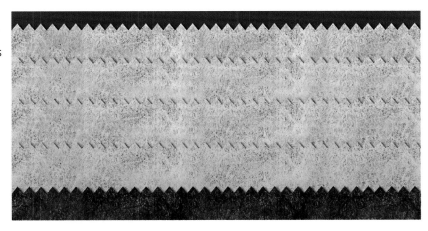

Interfacing Strips

Interfacing and stabilizer are also available by the yard in strips, purchased on rolls. These are much more convenient than strips cut from a larger piece. They come in different widths and colors, and in woven/nonwoven and fusible/non-fusible versions. These are used to reinforce seams, hems, pockets, zippers, buttonholes, or other areas needing stability.

Pellon® fusible interfacing

Non-fusible (sew-in) bias-cut tailoring interfacing

Choosing an Interfacing

A general rule when choosing interfacing is to go lighter than the fabric being interfaced. Also, a fusible interfacing will generally provide more body and stiffness than a non-fusible one.

You also need to consider the fiber content, care instructions, and construction type of both the interfacing and the garment fabric. Do not, for example, use a woven interfacing on a knit garment, as it will restrict the stretch. However, you may use a knit interfacing on a woven garment.

Always test several different interfacing options to find the one that best suits the desired drape and hand (feel) of your garment. Hold both the fabric and the interfacing in your hands to get an idea of how they will feel when combined. Remember, too, that fusible interfacings will add a bit of stiffness when pressed.

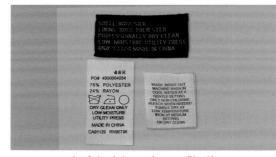

Interfacing choice must be compatible with
fabric fiber content and care instructions

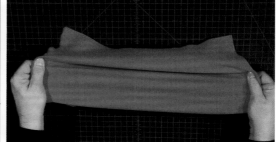

Never use woven interfacing on stretch knits

Testing interfacings for compatibility

Testing for Shrinkage

You should always test any interfacing for shrinkage before use—some will shrink when pressed, laundered, or dry-cleaned. Do not rely on the care instructions alone.

Here we have prepared two pieces of preshrunk fabric, each measuring 4" (10cm) wide by 5" (12.5cm) long, and one piece of interfacing, also 4" (10cm) wide by 5" (12.5cm) long.

Preshrunk fabric   Interfacing

Now we will iron our interfacing to one of the preshrunk fabric swatches, using a medium to high heat and a pressing cloth. If you are testing a fusible interfacing, make sure that the glue side is facing down, on the wrong side of the fabric, so that it adheres to the fabric and not the iron.

We will now compare the unpressed fabric swatch to the pressed and interfaced swatch to check for shrinkage. Here our interfacing has shrunk the fabric, so we would need to preshrink this interfacing before cutting it. You should perform this test on all interfacings, whether they are woven, nonwoven, or knit, and for both fusible and non-fusible types. Make sure, too, that you only perform this test on preshrunk fabric.

Preshrinking Interfacing

To preshrink a non-fusible interfacing, wash the material by hand in hot water, and then either line-dry it or dry it in a clothes dryer.

Although fusibles are less likely to shrink, if you do need to preshrink your fusible interfacing, then soak it in warm water and line-dry it only. Avoid excessive heat when preshrinking a fusible or you will deactivate the adhesive backing.

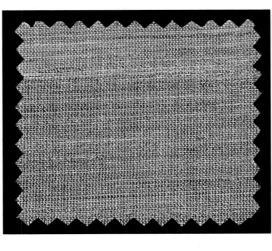

What is Woven Interfacing?

Woven interfacing is a material that, like fabric, has a lengthwise and a crosswise grain. Woven interfacing is most often cut in the same direction as the garment grain, although sometimes it may be cut on the bias for a softer effect.

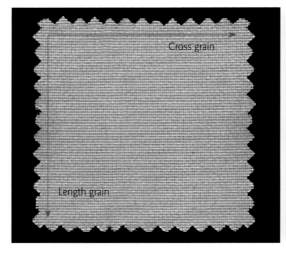

Types of Woven Interfacing

There are many weights, textures, and fiber compositions to choose from when selecting interfacing, so focus on the degree of shape, structure, or reinforcement you want to achieve, and the interfacing's compatibility with the garment fabric.

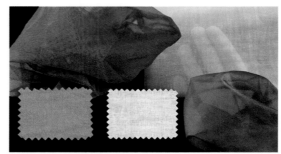

Lightweight Woven Interfacings for Lightweight Fabrics

If you are interfacing a lightweight or sheer fabric, you can either self-face (in other words, use the same fabric as the garment itself), or choose netting, organdy, silk organza, cotton voile, or cotton batiste.

Tip

Using the outer shell fabric as your garment interfacing can only be done if your fabric is not thick or bulky, since interfacing is most often a lighter material than the outer shell. The exception is sheer fabrics, where self-interfacing is preferred.

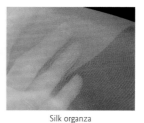

Netting   Cotton organdy   Silk organza

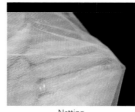

Cotton voile   Cotton batiste

Lightweight Woven Interfacings for Medium-weight Fabrics

For medium-weight fabrics, and depending upon the level of stiffness you are looking for, you can choose a batiste, broadcloth, or even a soft siri (shirting interfacing), soft haro, or a soft muslin (calico). Always test several interfacings before making your final decision.

Cotton batiste

Cotton broadcloth

Soft siri

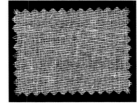
Soft haro

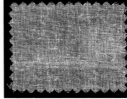
Soft muslin

Medium-weight Interfacings

There are a number of medium-weight interfacing options to choose from, including medium-weight siri and haro, #1 muslin (medium-weight calico), lightweight Irish linen, and lightweight hymo (a tailoring canvas, see below).

Medium siri

Medium haro

#1 muslin

Lightweight Irish linen

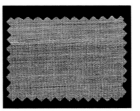
Light- to medium-weight hymo

Tailoring Canvas

Tailoring canvas, including hair and horsehair canvas, is used to interface areas of jackets and coats, and is available in a variety of weights and fibers. Hymo, traditionally a blend of mohair and linen, is today used to describe all hair canvases.

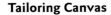

Hair Canvas

Hair canvas ranges in width from 30 to 74" (76 to 188cm). It comes in a variety of blends. One of the fibers is animal hair (usually goat hair), which is woven into the weft. This provides a certain springiness that helps to retain shape and add stiffness to a garment.

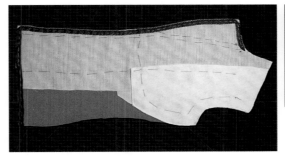

Mohair/Linen

Some hair canvas blends, like the medium-weight version shown here, are composed of rayon, cotton, goat hair, polyester, and wool. The heavyweight alternative—known as "red line" or "orange line"—is a blend of rayon, goat hair, cotton, and polyester. Note the fine hairs along the selvage, on the red-line interfacing.

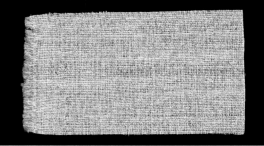

Medium-weight hair canvas
(39% rayon, 26% cotton, 20% goat hair, 11% polyester, 4% wool)

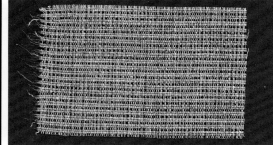

Heavyweight red-line/orange-line hair canvas
(43% rayon, 26% goat hair, 23% cotton, 8% polyester)

Horsehair Canvas

Horsehair canvas—or haircloth, as it is sometimes called—is a blend of wool or cotton and horse mane and tail. The horsehair, which is woven into the weft, is the reason why this type of canvas only comes in widths of up to 22" (56cm). The coarseness of the hair results in increased springiness. Note the horsehair fibers on both sides of the selvage in this example.

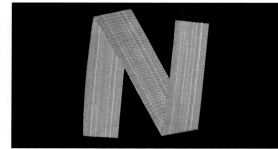

Horsehair canvas

Other Heavyweight Woven Interfacings

In addition to tailoring canvas, other heavyweight interfacing choices include firmer versions of siri and haro. You can also interface with duck, drill, or heavyweight Irish linen. These are especially popular for interfacing coats.

Hard siri

Hard haro

Duck

Drill

Heavyweight Irish linen

Stiff Woven Interfacings

If you are seeking a very stiff look, then choose a medium-weight or very stiff buckram. Buckram is a coarsely woven material, produced with a certain amount of sizing for added stiffness.

Medium-weight buckram

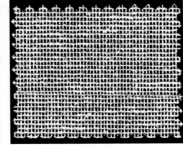
Stiff buckram

What is Nonwoven Interfacing?

Nonwoven interfacings are manufactured by bonding or felting man-made fibers to create by-the-yard interfacing. Nonwoven interfacing creates a crisper look than woven or knit interfacing, and can be dry-cleaned or machine-washed. Pellon® is an example of a nonwoven interfacing. While Pellon® has no grain, versions are available with cross, length, and/or bias stretch.

Pellon® nonwoven interfacing

Tip
Double-sided fusible interfacing bonds two layers of fabric together and is most often used on hems, in quilting, and for making accessories.

Types of Nonwoven Interfacing

Nonwoven interfacing comes in a variety of textures and weights, ranging from featherweight to lightweight, medium-weight, heavyweight, and rigid. Nonwoven is the easiest type of interfacing to use, particularly for beginners, and is most popular in fusible form; double-sided fusible options are even available.

Featherweight nonwoven interfacing: double-sided fusible

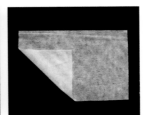
Lightweight nonwoven interfacing: fusible

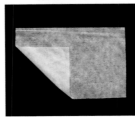
Medium-weight nonwoven interfacing: fusible

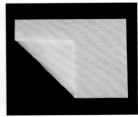
Heavy/rigid nonwoven interfacing: fusible

What is Knitted Interfacing?

This type of interfacing is made on knit machinery, so has stretch incorporated. It is therefore used for stretch fabrics. Tricot interfacing has the greatest amount of stretch, and weft interfacing has the greatest amount of stretch when cut on the bias. As with woven and nonwoven interfacings, there are also different weights to choose from.

Tricot interfacing

Weft interfacing

Choosing a Knitted Interfacing

Although used generally for stretch fabrics, knitted interfacing can also be used on woven fabrics and leather for a softer end result. It is also available fusible and non-fusible.

What is Fusible Interfacing?

Woven, nonwoven, and knitted interfacings can all be manufactured as fusible. The process involves adding a heat-activated adhesive to one side (or both sides, in the case of doubled-sided fusibles). The side with added adhesive will have small bumps or a rough feel on its surface.

Fusibles have little to no shrinkage and they do not unravel like a woven interfacing. A garment containing a fusible interfacing can also be washed or dry-cleaned. Fusibles are available in different weights, from featherweight to heavyweight.

Tips for Fusibles

Always do a pre-test on a swatch before applying a fusible interfacing to your garment. This is so that you can gauge the correct temperature for your iron. Too much heat will damage the fabric (even with a pressing cloth); too little heat will mean that the adhesive will not bond.

Rather than cutting individual pieces of interfacing, it can sometimes be easier to block-press the interfacing to the fabric first, or fuse the cut garment pieces directly onto the interfacing and then cut them out.

Applying Fusibles

Apply the fusible interfacing, adhesive side down, on the wrong side of your garment fabric. (You may wish to use a pressing cloth to prevent any adhesive damaging your iron.)

Now, using moderate heat, steam, and pressure, press the fusible onto the fabric, working from the inside out, in an even motion. Exert pressure as you press to secure the bond. Always allow the interfacing to cool before lifting the fabric from the ironing board.

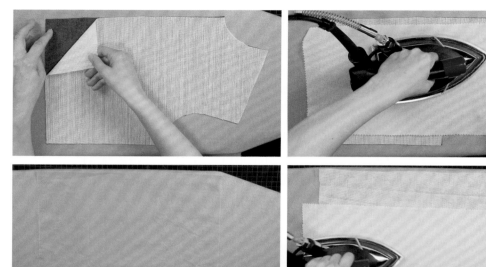

When to Avoid Fusibles

When deciding whether or not to use a fusible interfacing, there are a few things to consider.

Never use a fusible on a garment that is heat sensitive. This includes fabrics finished with beads or sequins; fabrics such as vinyl or faux leather; and fabrics that have a nap, such as velvet, velveteen, and corduroy. You will not be able to press hard enough for the adhesive to bond, and you will damage the fabric.

Never use a nonwoven or woven fusible on a stretch knit fabric, or on any open or loosely woven fabric such as lace. Do not use a fusible on a garment that requires excessive laundering or dry cleaning, either. This will cause the adhesive to disintegrate. Bear in mind, too, that a fusible interfacing will become slightly stiffer when applied to fabric, so this may not be appropriate for your particular gament.

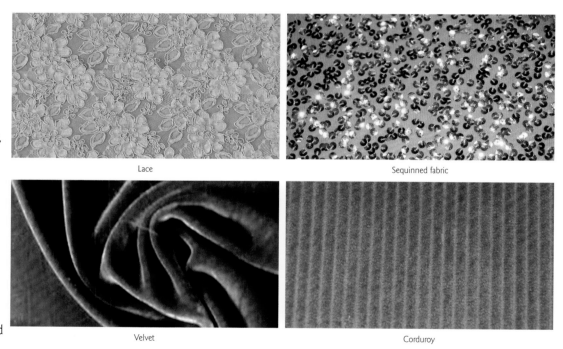

Lace

Sequinned fabric

Velvet

Corduroy

What is Underlining?

Underlining is a material that is used on the underside of a garment's outer-shell fabric. It can be used for one or more of the following reasons: to provide a lightweight fabric with additional body, to stabilize a loosely woven fabric, to hide construction details, to reduce transparency on a sheer fabric, or to add structure to certain areas of a garment. Underlinings are also used on high-end garments to reduce wrinkling. As with interfacings, underlining fabrics come in a variety of weights and textures.

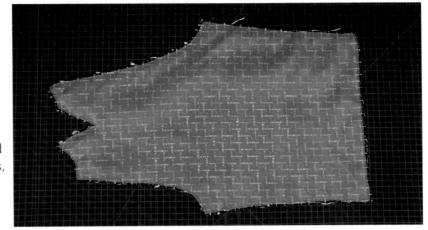

Choosing an Underlining

If you decide to add an underlining to a garment, there are several things you must consider. As with interfacing, the general rule is to choose an underlining that is lighter in weight than the fabric being underlined. The exception to this rule is when you are looking to provide a garment with additional shape, as you would with buckram.

You also need to consider the compatibility of the underlining to the fabric in terms of fiber content, fabric care, and construction, and whether the underlining will shrink when pressed, washed, or dry-cleaned.

Choosing a fusible underlining will stiffen the hand of your fabric, just as with interfacing. And you should always test your underlining before making a final decision. Always preshrink both your garment fabric and your underlining before cutting.

Underlining Tips

Because your underlining essentially constitutes a second layer to your garment, you can cut it out using the same pattern that you used for the garment itself.

If you are using a fusible underlining, refer to the steps outlined for applying fusible interfacing (see opposite). If you are attaching a non-fusible, or "sew-in," underlining, recess the underlining by ⅛" (3mm) all the way around the garment for ease.

Always use a knitted underlining on a knit fabric—for example, select a power mesh if your garment is made from a stretch knit lace. As with interfacing, you should never use a woven underlining on a stretch garment, but you can opt to use a knitted underlining on a woven outer fabric.

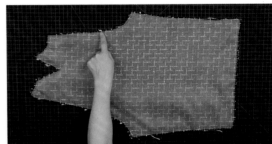

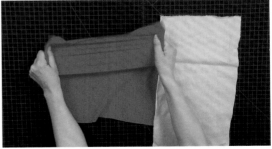

Featherweight Underlinings

There are many different options if you are looking for a featherweight underlining.

For sheer fabrics such as organza, you may wish to use self fabric, which solves the problem of finding a good color match. For sheers you could also use a soft English or silk tulle, in nude, black or white, or a matching color. For extra shape, nylon netting or silk organza are good choices. Since they do not add bulk, these fabrics are also good underlining choices for stabilizing loosely woven fabrics.

A featherweight Pellon® and featherweight tricot, both fusible or non-fusible, are other possibilities. However, do not use a fusible underlining on sheers or other fabrics where the adhesive will show through.

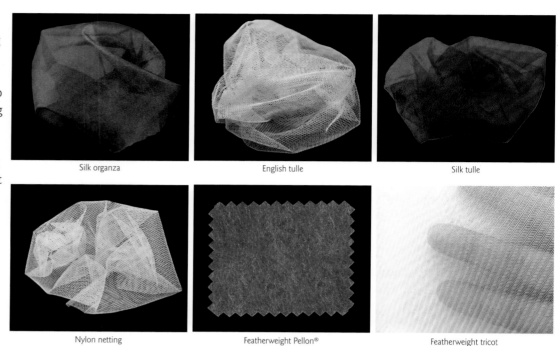

Silk organza   English tulle   Silk tulle

Nylon netting

Featherweight Pellon®

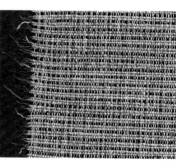

Featherweight tricot

Tip
Hair canvas works well for underlining portions of a blazer or jacket.

Lightweight to Medium-weight Underlinings

The correct choice when underlining a lightweight or medium-weight fabric depends on fabric compatibility and the level of stiffness required. Refer to Modules 2, 3, and 4 in this chapter when deciding whether to opt for a fusible or non-fusible, and when choosing between woven, nonwoven, or knitted.

Fusible woven interfacing (folded)   Tricot knit interfacing   Jacket hair canvas

Heavyweight Underlinings

Due to their inherent composition, heavyweight fabrics do not often need underlining. However, if a heavy fabric does needs stabilizing, a lightweight underlining such as organza or tulle is a good choice because it will not add bulk.

Organza

Tulle

Module 7:

Interlining

What is Interlining?

Interlining is an underlining that is used for warmth, inserted between the outer-shell fabric and the lining of a garment. An interlining can also be attached to the garment lining for additional warmth.

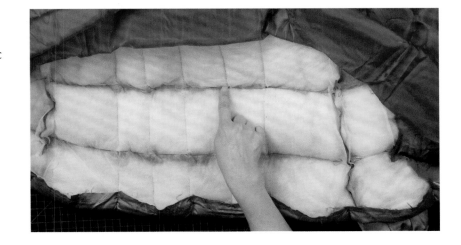

Lightweight to Medium-warmth Fabric Interlinings

There is a wide selection of interlinings available, depending upon how warm you want your finished garment to be. For a minimal amount of warmth you could use a cotton flannelette or a soft knitted French wool. Or, for intermediate warmth, choose a low-loft fleece (also available in fusible form) or a lightweight wool.

Cotton flannelette

French wool

Low-loft fleece: fusible

Lightweight wool

Down, Feather, & Down/Feather Blends

Other options for warmth are down fillings, feather fillings, and down/feather blends. Down is the fluffy undercoating of waterfowl, usually taken from a goose, duck, or swan. Feather fillings are made from feathers taken from the outer coverings of waterfowl or landfowl. Down and feather blends might consist of 90 percent down and 10 percent waterfowl feathers; down and crushed feathers; or a blend of down, polyester, and/or other fibers.

Goose down filament   Goose feather filling

Down/Feather Construction

Garments made with down and down blends are lightweight, breathable, easily compressed, have great recovery, provide excellent warmth, and are machine washable and dryable. Working with down and feathers, however, can be a challenge. They are sold in bags and are hard to control once the bag is open. Down and feathers are sandwiched in between prestitched quilted channels in the outer shell and underlining layer for a garment, prior to its construction. At the industrial level, a special machine is used to infuse the feathers into these channels.

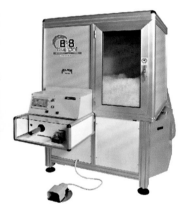

Synthetic Insulation Products

Other underlining materials used for warmth include man-made insulation products marketed under the brand names Thinsulate, Poly-Fil, and PrimaLoft. These are available in different weights, thicknesses, and levels of thermal resistance. Thermal resistance describes the degree to which insulation impedes the flow of heat and moisture away from the body. These materials are moisture resistant, so they can be used for outerwear and do not need to be preshrunk. They are also machine washable/dryable and can be dry-cleaned.

Thermal Insulation and Resistance Chart

Typical Values	3M™ Thinsulate™ Insulation Types C/CS/CDS							
Product Designation	Basis Weight		Thickness		Thermal Resistance (R$_{cf}$) ASTM F 1868			Roll Length (CDS lengths in parentheses)	
	g/m²	oz/yd²	cm	inch	clo	R-value	m² °K/W	yd	m
C/CS/CDS40	43	1.3	0.30	0.12	0.7	0.6	0.11	350 (348)	320 (318)
C/CS/CDS70	74	2.2	0.50	0.20	1.0	0.9	0.15	200 (198)	183 (181)
C/CS/CDS100	105	3.1	0.70	0.28	1.3	1.1	0.20	140 (138)	128 (126)
C/CS/CDS150	157	4.6	1.1	0.41	1.9	1.7	0.29	100 (98)	91 (89)
C/CS/CDS200	210	6.2	1.4	0.55	2.5	2.2	0.39	70 (68)	64 (62)

3M
Thinsulate™
INSULATION
thin, light, warm

Choosing Synthetic Insulation

The fiber composition of insulation materials varies from those that are 100 percent polyester, through to blends that include combinations of other man-made fibers such as olefin, polypropylene, modacrylic, and aramid. Weight and loft thickness vary, too, with some options being lighter and thinner than others. Some products have four-way stretch, while others are perfect for quilting. Mid-loft and high-loft insulation products are perfect for outerwear. Poly-Fil Fiber Fill and 3M's Thinsulate Featherless Insulation mimic the effect of down when the fill is inserted into quilted channels.

Lightweight loft

Medium-weight loft Poly-Fil

High-loft insulation

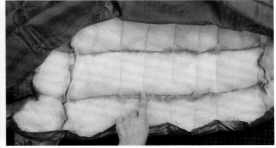

Synthetic down-filled insulation channels

Working with Synthetic Insulation

Whether you choose a by-the-yard factory-quilted fabric or you plan to quilt your fabric manually in sections, you must allow extra ease at the pattern-making stage of your project.

The amount of ease will depend on the amount of loft. The higher the loft, the more ease you will need to add in both the length and the width. Sewing a test sample is always advisable.

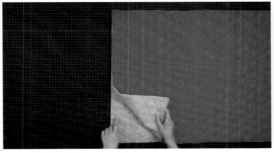

By-the-yard quilted insulation fabric

Allow extra ease to a pattern before cutting quilted fabric

Quilting Synthetic Insulation

Trying to machine-quilt yard goods (fabric sold by the yard) is virtually impossible, so it is best if you pre-quilt sections of your garment before you sew the garment together. A tip is to cut each fabric and insulation block 3" (7.5cm) bigger than your garment pattern. Then do your quilt stitching. Remember to plan where you want your quilting lines to sit on the garment.

Place your pattern piece on the quilted fabric block and trace your pattern with chalk. Add a 2" (5cm) seam allowance all around the pattern, then cut out the pattern piece. The extra 2" (5cm) are in case more width and length are needed when fitting the garment. Repeat this for all of your pattern pieces.

Fabric block cut 3" (7.5cm) larger than the pattern piece

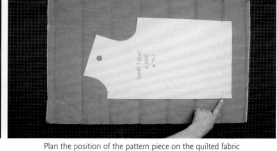

Plan the position of the pattern piece on the quilted fabric

Add 2" (5cm) seam allowance as you chalk each pattern piece

Module 8:

Lining

What is Lining?

Lining is a material that, as the name suggests, "lines" a garment. It can be attached to the garment's neck, waistband, or sleeves; it can also be attached at the hem, or left to hang freely. Linings are generally smooth, lustrous fabrics that enable the wearer to slip in and out of the garment with ease.

The Purpose of a Lining

There are many reasons to provide a garment with a lining. Sometimes a lining is added for warmth, although generally, when choosing a lining, the rule is that it should be lighter than the outer garment shell. A lining can also be used to hide the inner construction of a garment, and for the wearer's comfort. It can keep the outer shell fabric from wrinkling, too, and can help the garment keep its shape, while also prolonging the life of the garment. Linings made from printed, patterned, or contrast fabrics can also be added as a deliberate design detail.

Choosing & Working with Lining

Always check the fiber content and care instructions of your lining choice to make sure that they are compatible with the outer shell fabric. Perform the same shrink test on your outer shell and lining fabric as you did in Module 1, and preshrink both fabrics if necessary. Be sure to add wearing ease, too, when you pattern your lining.

Always make sure that your lining choice is functionally appropriate for the garment. For example, choose a heavyweight lining for a coat, and never use a woven lining for a knit garment. However, you can use a knitted lining for a woven garment.

Choose a lining that is breathable and comfortable. And avoid fabrics that will make it difficult for the wearer when getting in and out of the garment. For example, the coat shown here uses a smooth lining that will slip easily over any clothes worn underneath it.

Sheer Linings

Sheer garments are either unlined or self-lined. Lightweight garments can be lined with cotton voile, organdy, organza, tulle, or Chantilly lace, although these fabrics, along with silk chiffon, poly chiffon, and poly double georgette, do not allow arms to glide in and out easily. A smooth alternative fabric for the sleeves is recommended.

Cotton voile

Cotton organdy

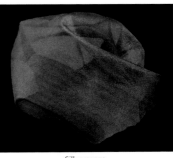

Silk organza

Cotton tulle

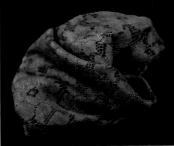

Chantilly lace

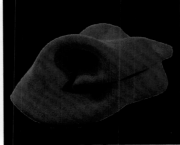

Silk chiffon

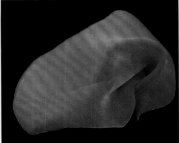

Poly chiffon

Poly double georgette

Lightweight Linings

Cotton batiste and cotton broadcloth are popular lining choices, especially when printed, but they also share the non-glide issue. China silk and silk habotai, which are measured in weight in terms of mommes (mm), are a perfect lightweight lining choice at 8mm. The higher the mommes, the heavier the weight. Poly China silk and poly habotai are also good choices, as is a 1.5-oz (50gsm) tissue lamé.

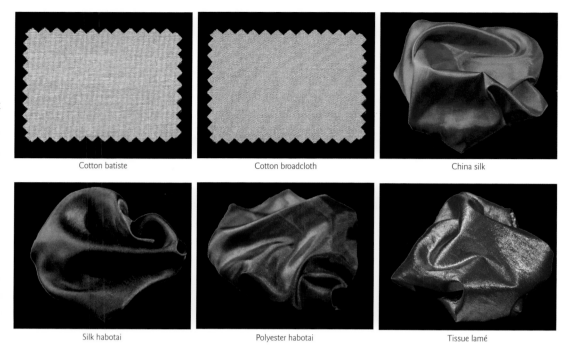

Cotton batiste

Cotton broadcloth

China silk

Silk habotai

Polyester habotai

Tissue lamé

Medium-weight Linings

Medium-weight linings are the most popular and are used in dresses, pants (trousers), skirts, and jackets. Choices include silk crêpe de chine, micro-poly crêpe de chine, silk dupioni, faux dupioni, silk shantung, silk charmeuse, and poly satin charmeuse. A 4-oz (135gsm) poly twill is also an option when you are looking for a more durable lining for jackets.

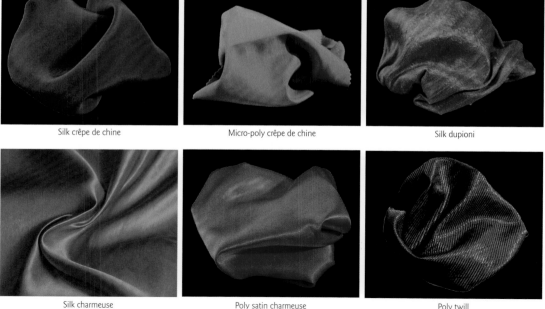

Silk crêpe de chine

Micro-poly crêpe de chine

Silk dupioni

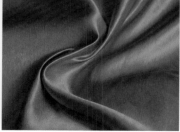

Faux dupioni

Silk shantung

Silk charmeuse

Poly satin charmeuse

Poly twill

Taffetas & Medium-weight Linings

Taffeta is a crisp, smooth, plain-weave textile and can be used as a medium-weight lining. A silk taffeta is a great choice for high-end garments. A 100 percent acetate taffeta, though much less expensive than silk, is not as durable. Other medium-weight lining choices—and perhaps the most popular and affordable—are rayon/acetate blends and nylon/acetate blends. Nylon improves a lining's elasticity and makes it stronger and more resistant to wrinkling. Polyester taffeta and linings made with polyester blends, while durable and affordable, are not as breathable as rayon and viscose/acetate blends.

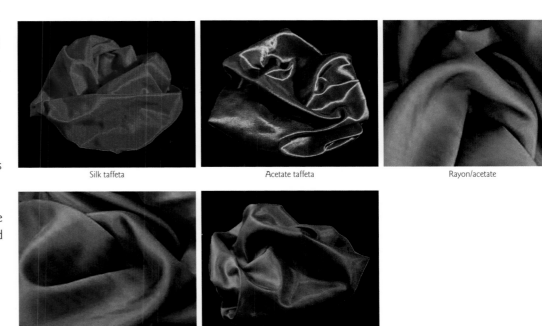

Silk taffeta   Acetate taffeta   Rayon/acetate

Polyester blend   Nylon/acetate blend

Rayon, Viscose/Acetate & Jacquard Linings

Bemberg (cupro) lining is a rayon cellulose filament fiber derived from cotton linter and made by the cuprammonium process. Due to the high manufacturing costs and the impact that this process has had on the environment, cuprammonium rayon is no longer manufactured in the U.S.

Viscose and acetate made from wood pulp are used in blends that have become more popular. They are available in solids as well as jacquards, such as the paisley and novelty dot examples shown here. Printed linings are also popular.

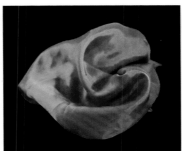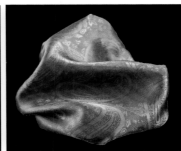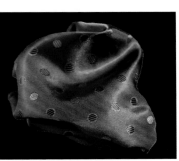

Bemberg cuprammonium rayon: 100% (3oz/102gsm)   Jacquard paisley: 60% viscose, 40% acetate   Jacquard dot: 60% viscose, 40% acetate

Heavyweight Linings

Depending upon the amount of warmth you are looking for, there are several lining fabrics to choose from, in just about every blend. A twill weave in a blend of rayon, poly, or nylon is your best bet, since it is durable and has just the right amount of warmth for a medium- to heavyweight jacket or coat. For additional warmth you could add a second layer to the lining, perhaps out of French wool. Or you could choose a satin weave like the flannel-back satin shown here. For maximum warmth, consider using a quilted lining, such as quilted nylon acetate lining, or a knitted fleece. Never line sleeves with fleece, though—use a quilted lining for them instead.

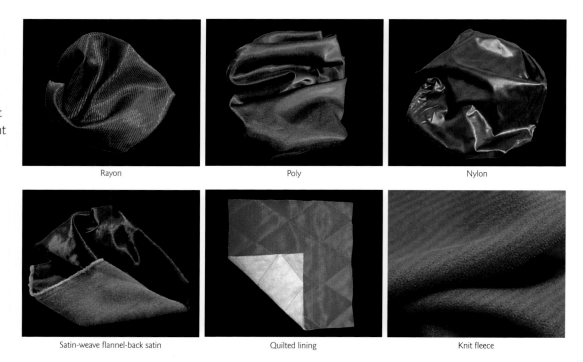

Rayon

Poly

Nylon

Satin-weave flannel-back satin

Quilted lining

Knit fleece

Stretch Linings

Though stretch linings are usually more expensive, they do offer the wearer the most comfort. Some stretch-fabric options are power mesh, stretch lace, polyester microfiber jersey, and silk stretch charmeuse. Outerwear fleece is a good choice as long as it is used for the body and not the sleeves.

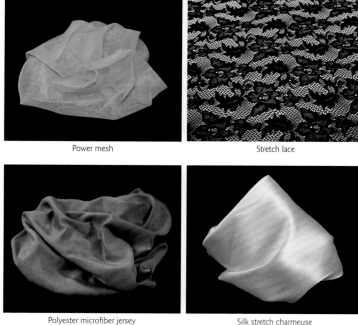

Power mesh

Stretch lace

Polyester microfiber jersey

Silk stretch charmeuse

Specialty Linings

Specialty linings are available for specific end uses, such as a fusible softener lining, which can be used to stabilize or add body to a lining. In activewear, athletic mesh is used to line vests and jackets. And specialty fabrics such as moisture- and allergen-barrier fabrics, as well as thermal-barrier fabrics, are used in performance apparel.

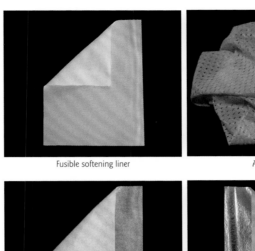

Fusible softening liner

Athletic mesh

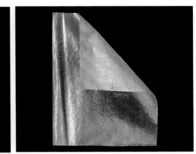

Moisture- and allergy-barrier fabric

Thermal-barrier fabric

Self-evaluation

- ☐ Do I know how to test interfacing before using it?
- ☐ Can I describe which interfacing to use and why for a particular project?
- ☐ Did I test my interlining for shrinkage before constructing my garment?
- ☐ Is my underlining the best choice for the design?
- ☐ Is my lining compatible with my outer shell fabric in terms of weight, look, and care instructions?

4 Seam Finishes

Choosing the correct seam finish will help your garment hang better, last longer, and also add value. Unfinished seams have a tendency to curl and fray, and will shorten the life of the garment. We begin by suggesting **seam finishes for sheer and lightweight fabrics**. Whether you are sewing a very full sheer skirt with no stress on the seams, or a sheer sleeve where a stronger seam finish is required, you could choose a single edge-stitch seam or a double-stitched seam, based on the type of garment, its end use, and the look you are trying to achieve. For a clean edge use a French seam, or a mock French seam to achieve a similar effect quickly.

A majority of clothing is made in **medium-weight fabrics**. We demonstrate a wide variety of seams for garments in medium-weight wool, double-face wool, and cotton. You will learn the easiest pinked and open seam finish, an overlocked and open seam for a clean finish, and how to sew a flat-felled seam, used on jeans. Specialty seams such as the slot seam, the double-faced seam, the lapped seam and the Hong Kong seam are all functional and decorative finishes that add extra value to a garment.

Lightweight Seam Finishes

Learning objectives

☐ Work a basic single edge-stitch seam, and know when to use it

☐ Create a double-stitched seam for areas of stress in the garment, and understand when it is needed

☐ Use enclosed seams: work a French seam and a mock French seam on sheer fabrics

In this section:

- Single Edge-stitch Seam
- Double-stitched Seam
- French Seam
- Mock French Seam

Single Edge-stitch Seam

Tools and supplies:

- Silk chiffon
- Matching cotton thread
- Silk pins

A single edge-stitch seam is used on sheer fabrics such as organza, voile, chiffon, and georgette.

This finish is most commonly used for sheer seams that will bear no stress, such as those on very full skirts and dresses with many layers of fabric. This seam finish is also a great choice when you want the seam allowance on your design to be as invisible as possible.

Seam Finishes

Module 1:

Lesson Prep

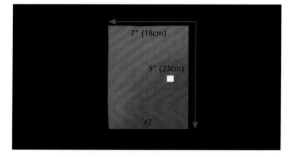

For this lesson you will need to prepare:
Two pieces of silk chiffon, each measuring 7" (18cm) wide by 9" (23cm) long. Use a sticker to denote the wrong side of the fabric.

Module 2:

Creating the Single Edge-stitch Seam

Step 1
Begin by aligning your pieces lengthwise, right sides together, and pinning them in place.

Step 2
Stitch the seam with a ½" (1.3cm) seam allowance, removing the pins as you sew. With your right hand, gently guide the piece through the machine, but be careful not to pull as this will cause the fabric to stretch. Note that, for demonstration purposes, contrast thread is used here.

Step 3
With your fabric shears, trim the seam ⅛" (3mm) away from the stitched edge.

Step 4
Before pressing, stabilize the seam by inserting a pin through one end, securing it to your ironing board. This will help the seam remain straight as you press.

Step 5
Turn to the right side and press the seam in one direction.

Step 6
The finished single edge-stitch seam.

Double-stitched Seam

Tools and supplies:

- Silk chiffon
- Matching cotton thread
- Silk pins

This seam finish is appropriate for sheer fabrics such as organza, voile, chiffon, and georgette.

A double-stitched seam is a great choice for sheer garments, especially in areas where there may be some stress, and where you do not want the seam allowance to be too visible.

Module 1:

Lesson Prep

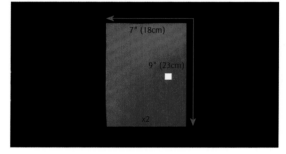

For this lesson you will need to prepare:
Two pieces of silk chiffon, each measuring 7" (18cm) wide by 9" (23cm) long. Use a sticker to denote the wrong side of the fabric.

Module 2:

Creating the Double-stitched Seam

Step 1
Begin your double-stitched seam by aligning your pieces lengthwise, right sides together, and pinning them in place.

Step 2
Stitch the seam with a ½" (1.3cm) seam allowance, removing the pins as you sew. With your right hand, gently guide the piece through the machine, but be careful not to pull as this will cause the fabric to stretch. Note that, for demonstration purposes, contrast thread is used here.

Step 3
Now place another stitch ⅛" (2mm) away from the first. Again, gently guide the piece through the machine as you sew.

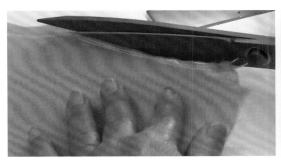

Step 4
The next step is to trim the seam allowance close to the second row of stitches.

Step 5
Before pressing, stabilize the seam by inserting a pin through one end, securing it to your ironing board. This will help the seam remain straight as you press.

Step 6
Turn to the right side and press the seam in one direction.

Step 7
The finished double-stitched seam.

French Seam

Tools and supplies:

- Silk chiffon
- Matching cotton thread
- Silk pins

A French seam is one of the most important seam finishes to know, and one of the nicest looking, too, because the raw edges are hidden. It is ideal for use on sheer fabrics, or on any other lightweight material.

We will teach you how to create this seam using our easy-to-follow technique. Once you've mastered the French seam, you will understand why it is the most popular seam finish in couture dressmaking.

Module 1:

Lesson Prep

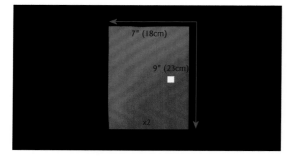

For this lesson you will need to prepare:
Two pieces of silk chiffon, each measuring 7" (18cm) wide by 9" (23cm) long. Use a sticker to denote the wrong side of the fabric.

Module 2:

Creating the French Seam

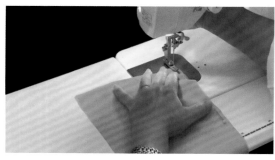

Step 1
Begin by aligning your pieces lengthwise, wrong sides together, and pinning them in place.

Step 2
Stitch the seam with a ½" (1.3cm) seam allowance, removing the pins as you sew. With your right hand, gently guide the piece through the machine, but be careful not to pull as this will cause the fabric to stretch. Note that, for demonstration purposes, contrast thread is used here.

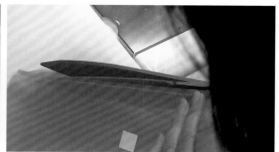

Step 3
Trim the seam allowance to ⅟₁₆" (2mm).

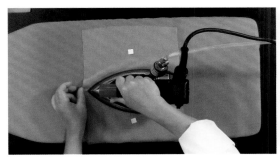  

Step 4
Press the seam allowance on the wrong side and then turn to the right side. Press the seam allowance in one direction.

Step 5
Now press the seam on the wrong side, with the seam allowance sandwiched in between the pieces and the stitching line exactly on the fold. Press carefully so that the seam edge is straight.

Step 6
Stitch a seamline on the wrong side, ³⁄₁₆" (5mm) away from the edge, sandwiching the seam allowance inside the seam. Gently guide the piece through the machine with your right hand.

 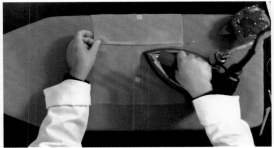 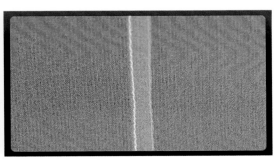

Step 7
Before pressing on the wrong side, stabilize the seam by inserting a pin through one end, securing it to your ironing board. This will help the seam remain straight as you press.

Step 8
Turn to the right side and press the seam allowance in one direction.

Step 9
Wrong side of the finished French seam.

Mock French Seam

Tools and supplies:

- Silk chiffon
- Matching cotton thread
- Silk pins

A mock French seam finish creates a clean fabric edge without the labor involved in creating a French seam. Use it on sheer fabrics such as organza, voile, chiffon, and georgette.

As with the previous seams in this lesson, we will demonstrate the trade techniques (such as how to control the fabric at the sewing machine) involved in sewing and pressing this seam finish successfully.

Module 1:

Lesson Prep

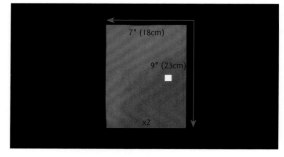

For this lesson you will need to prepare:
Two pieces of silk chiffon, each measuring 7" (18cm) wide by 9" (23cm) long. Use a sticker to denote the wrong side of the fabric.

Module 2:

Creating the Mock French Seam

Step 1
Align your pieces lengthwise, right sides together, then pin them in place. Stitch the seam with a ½" (1.3cm) seam allowance, removing the pins as you sew. With your right hand, gently guide the piece through the machine, but be careful not to pull as this will cause the fabric to stretch.

Step 2
Trim the seam allowance on the top side only to ⅛" (3mm) and press the seam flat.

Zhang Wei demonstrating a sheer seam finish, 2014.

Step 3
Fold the large seam allowance over the small seam allowance, then turn your piece to the wrong side and stitch the folded seam allowance in place, close to the original stitching line. Fold the seam allowance carefully as you sew to avoid twisting.

Step 4
Before pressing, stabilize the seam by inserting a pin through one end to secure it to your ironing board. This will help the seam remain straight as you press.

Step 5
Turn to the right side and press the seam allowance in one direction.

Step 6
The finished mock French seam.

Medium-weight Seam Finishes

Learning objectives

☐ Use enclosed seams: work a flat-felled seam and a Hong Kong seam

☐ Create seams for non-fraying fabric: the pinked and open seam, and the lapped seam

☐ Sew an overlocked and open seam and know when to use it

☐ Understand specialist seams and work a double-faced seam, and a slot seam

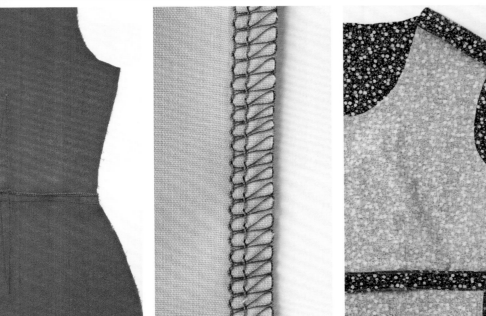

Medium-weight seam finishes: flat-felled (top) and overlocked and open (bottom row).

In this section:

- Flat-felled Seam
- Hong Kong Seam
- Pinked & Open Seam
- Overlocked & Open Seam
- Double-faced Seam
- Slot Seam
- Lapped Seam

Flat-felled Seam

Tools and supplies:

- Worsted wool fabric
- Matching cotton thread
- Pressing cloth

Here, we show you how easy it is to sew a flat-felled seam. This is used on sportswear and outerwear because it provides such a durable finish.

A flat-felled seam is commonly used on denim jeans and made using a flat-felling machine. A hand-made flat-felled seam can be used on wools and other medium-weight fabrics. If you want an even sportier look, you can always complete the topstitching in a contrasting color.

Module 1:

Lesson Prep

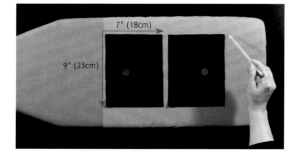

For this lesson you will need to prepare:
Two pieces of wool fabric, each measuring 7" (18cm) wide by 9" (23cm) long. Use stickers to denote the wrong side of the fabric.

Module 2:

Creating the
Flat-felled Seam

Step 1
Join your fabric pieces, stitching right sides together with a ¾" (2cm) seam allowance.

Step 2
Separate the seam allowance and trim it on the left side to within ¼" (6mm) of the stitching line.

Step 3
Turn the fabric over onto the right side and, using a pressing cloth, press the seam allowance in one direction. Gently pull the fabric so that your seam is flat.

Step 4A
Turn the fabric back over to the wrong side, then fold the larger seam allowance over to encase the smaller seam allowance.

Step 4B
Use your finger to guide the seam allowance under as you topstitch the folded edge.

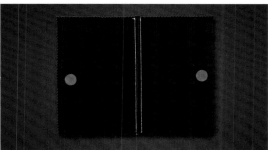

Step 5
Press your seam flat on the wrong side. Then turn the sampler to the right side and press with a pressing cloth.

Step 6
The finished flat-felled seam.

Hong Kong Seam

Tools and supplies:

- Worsted wool fabric
- Silk organza
- Matching cotton thread
- Pressing cloth

The Hong Kong seam is one of the nicest ways to finish a seam. It can be used to create a neat finish on an unlined garment, including unlined jackets or coats made in a heavyweight fabric.

We begin by demonstrating how to join the seams of a wool sampler. Then, using silk organza bias strips, we show you how to encase the seam to produce a clean finish, the way they do it in couture dressmaking.

Module 1:

Lesson Prep

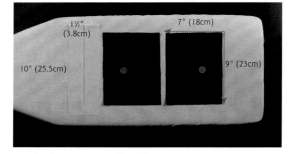

For this lesson you will need to prepare:
Two pieces of wool fabric, each measuring 7" (18cm) wide by 9" (23cm) long, and two bias organza strips, each 1½" (3.8cm) wide by 10" (25.5cm) long. Use stickers to denote the wrong side of the wool fabric.

Module 2:

Creating the Hong Kong Seam

Step 1
Join your fabric pieces, stitching right sides together with a 1" (2.5cm) seam allowance.

Step 2
Sew one of your bias strips to the fabric at ¼" (6mm) from the raw edge on each side of the seam allowance. Take care not to pull the bias strip while sewing, as this will cause it to twist. You may find that using 100 percent polyester for the strips is much harder to handle. Lining material is an acceptable substitute for the organza.

Step 3
Using your fingernail, finger-press the bias strip in the direction of the seam allowance.

Step 4A
Fold the bias strip back over the ¼" (6mm) stitching line. Be sure not to pull the strip as you sew, to avoid twisting. Then carefully stitch in the ditch, which means stitch as close to the stitching line as you can.

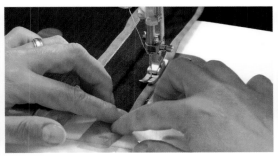

Step 4B
Repeat this process on the other side.

Step 5
Turn the seam to the wrong side and trim the bias strip excess to ⅛" (3mm) away from the stitching line. Do the same thing on the other side.

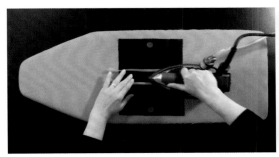

Step 6A
Open the seam allowance and press the seam flat.

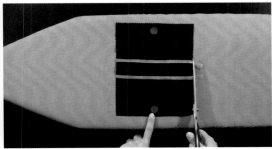

Step 6B
Trim the organza ends.

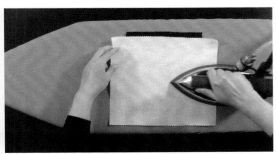

Step 7
Use a pressing cloth to press the seam open on the right side.

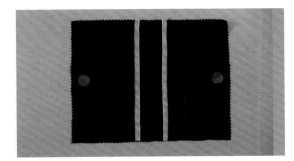

Step 8
The finished Hong Kong seam.

Pinked & Open Seam

Tools and supplies:

- Worsted wool fabric
- Matching cotton thread
- Pinking shears
- Pressing cloth

A pinked and open seam finish is most often used on wools and fabrics that do not fray excessively.

In this lesson we introduce you to the use of pinking shears to trim back your fabric edges. Compared to other, more labor-intensive seam finishes, you will find this one a breeze!

Module 1:

Lesson Prep

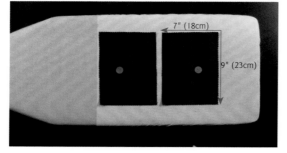

For this lesson you will need to prepare:
Two pieces of wool fabric, each measuring 7" (18cm) wide by 9" (23cm) long. Use stickers to denote the wrong side of the fabric.

Module 2:

Creating the Pinked & Open Seam

Step 1
Join your fabric pieces, right sides together, with a 1" (2.5cm) seam allowance.

Step 2
Using pinking shears, trim away ¼" (6mm) from the raw edge of both sides of the seam allowance. You may want to mark this with a ruler for accuracy.

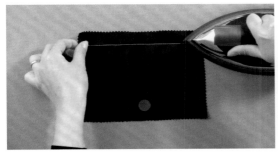

Step 3
Press the seam flat.

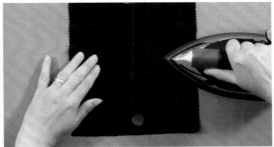

Step 4
Turn the sampler to the wrong side and press the seam open.

Step 5
Then turn the sampler over to the right side and use a pressing cloth for a final pressing.

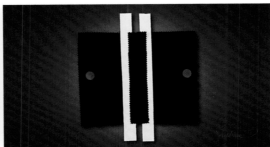

Step 6
The finished pinked and open seam.

Overlocked & Open Seam

Tools and supplies:

- Worsted wool fabric
- Matching cotton thread
- Pressing cloth

For this seam finish, you will use your serger, or overlocker, to clean finish the edges of your fabric. This finish is suited to medium- to lightweight fabrics.

Using an overlocker is a great way to finish seams, particularly on fabrics that fray, and it is a technique commonly used in garment manufacture.

Module 1:

Lesson Prep

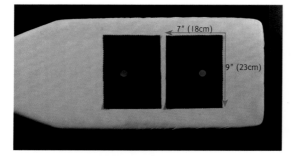

For this lesson you will need to prepare:
Two pieces of wool fabric, each measuring 7" (18cm) wide by 9" (23cm) long. Use stickers to denote the wrong side of the fabric.

Module 2:

Creating the Overlocked & Open Seam

Step 1
Overlock both edges of the wool fabric, wrong side up, using your overlocker machine. Trim your end threads.

Step 2
At your sewing machine, join your fabric pieces, stitching right sides together with a ¾" (2cm) seam allowance. Here, this has been chalked for demonstration purposes.

Step 3A
Next, press the seam flat.

Step 3B
Open the seam and press again.

Step 3C
Turn to the right side and press with a pressing cloth.

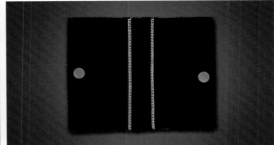

Step 4
The finished overlocked and open seam.

Double-faced Seam

Tools and supplies:

- Double-faced wool fabric
- Size 8 needles: betweens & sharps
- 6-strand cotton embroidery floss
- Matching cotton thread
- Embroidery scissors
- Pressing cloth

Working with double-faced fabrics requires some specific seaming and finishing techniques.

In this lesson, we will demonstrate how to prepare and sew a double-faced seam in wool fabric. You can use this technique to create beautiful reversible garments.

Step 1
Prepare two pieces of double-faced wool fabric, each 4" (10cm) in the width grain by 5" (12.5cm) in the length grain. We have chosen a two-tone fabric for demo purposes.

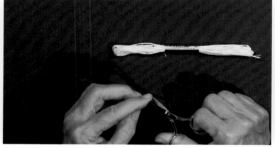

Step 2
There is a fair amount of basting (tacking) in this lesson, so we use 100 percent cotton embroidery thread. This is heavier than regular cotton thread and easier to use for basting. You will also need a pair of very sharp, pointed-edge embroidery scissors.

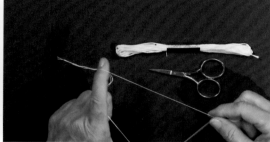

Step 3
Cut an 18" (46cm) length of cotton embroidery thread and separate a single strand. We will use only one strand for basting.

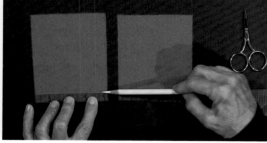

Step 4
Place your thimble on the middle finger of your sewing hand, then thread and knot the size 8 betweens needle with the single strand of thread.

Step 5A
Mark your seam allowance using a white pencil and ruler. Mark a ½" (1.3cm) seam allowance on the width edge of one of your fabric pieces.

Step 5B
Now draw another line ½" (1.3cm) away from the first, 1" (2.5cm) away from the edge.

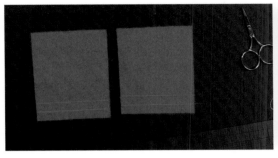

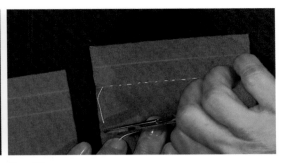

Step 5C
Repeat this process on the second piece of wool fabric. Note that we are marking the fabric on the same side, and not on the dark side of the fabric. The benefit of this type of seam is that the garment can be reversible and that there is no need for interfacing.

Step 6A
You will now sew a row of short basting stitches along the 1" (2.5cm) chalk line on one of your pieces. This will hold the fabric together once you have separated the fabric layers to create the seam. Begin and end your row of stitches with a backstitch.

Step 6B
Remember the rule: "The shorter the needle, the shorter the stitches." For this project your basting stitches should be no longer than ¼" (6mm). When you reach the end, clip the thread but leave a small thread tail, 1½" (3.8cm) long.

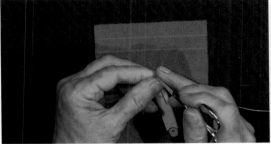

Step 7A
Repeat the process for the second fabric piece. Here, the instructor is demonstrating how to use a needle threader to thread her needle. She places the wire loop of the threader into the eye of the needle.

Step 7B
Then she uses the tip of her embroidery scissors to open the wire loop so that the thread can pass through.

Step 7C
The thread is then passed through the loop.

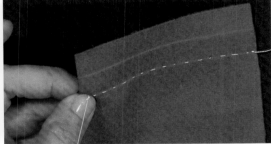

Step 8A
The instructor's method of creating a knot begins with wrapping the thread around the needle twice. She slides the thread along the needle and down along the thread with her fingernail to form the knot.

Step 8B
Now baste the second piece of fabric as you did the first, at 1" (2.5cm) away from the edge on the white pencil line. Trim the end thread.

Step 1
Gently separate the seam allowance layers of the fabric, beginning at a corner of one of your pieces.

Step 2A
Using the tip of your embroidery scissors, snip into the threads holding the two fabric layers together. Be careful not to stretch the fabric as you do this, or accidently snip into the fabric.

Step 2B
You will be snipping the threads up to the basting stitch line, but not beyond that 1" (2.5cm) point.

Step 2C
Continue to separate the layers gently with your fingers as you work. Do not pull them apart, though, or you will stretch the fabric out of shape.

Step 2D
Continue this process until you have snipped all of the threads and have separated the 1" (2.5cm) seam allowance across the entire width of the first fabric piece.

Step 3A
Now repeat this process on your second fabric piece. Again, snip until you reach the 1" (2.5cm) row of basting stitches.

Step 3B
Once you have finished snipping the threads and separating the layers on both pieces, open the two layers of the seam allowance, as shown.

Step 4A
Next, remove the loose threads on the seam allowance that held the two layers of fabric together. To do this, cut small pieces of adhesive tape and press them, sticky side down, along the 1" (2.5cm) seam allowance. Pull the tape up to remove the threads.

Step 4B
Repeat this process until you have removed all of the threads from both sides of the seam allowance, using a new piece of tape once each piece has become covered with thread. You could also use packing tape to remove the threads.

Step 4C
Trim the excess threads with your embroidery scissors. Now repeat these steps on your other fabric piece.

Step 4D
Remove as many threads as you can; this will help remove any excess bulk at the seam line. Do not worry, though, if a few threads remain.

Module 3:
Preparing the Seam

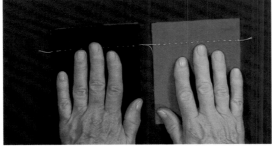

Step 1A
If you are using a two-tone double-faced wool fabric, decide which side of the fabric you want to be on the outside of the garment. We chose the royal blue side for this lesson.

Step 1B
Match the right sides of the fabric seam allowance.

Step 1C
Pin the layers together in preparation for sewing them together at the sewing machine.

Step 2
Sew the ½" (1.3cm) seam using cotton thread at 10–12 stitches per inch (spi; stitch length 2.1–2.5mm).

Step 3
Open the seam and press it lightly, using steam.

Step 4A
Now mark the seam allowance layers, ¼" (6mm) away from the seam on both sides, using your tailor's chalk and ruler.

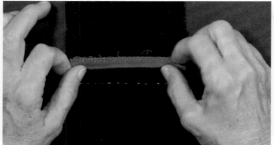

Step 4B
Removing excess seam allowance will reduce the amount of bulk at the seam. Trim away the excess fabric from the seam allowance layers along the chalk lines.

Step 5A
Fold the under layer's seam allowance under by ½" (1.3cm) and align it with the seam line.

Step 5B
Parallel-pin the folded seam allowance in place, ⅛" (3mm) away from the seam.

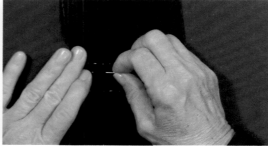

Step 5C
Now repeat this process. This time, fold the other side of the under layer's seam allowance so that it meets in the center of the seam.

Step 5D
Pin the seam allowance in place so that the folded edge is kissing the folded edge of the other side.

Module 4:
Sewing the Seam

Step 1A
In preparation for sewing the underside of the seam, place your thimble on the middle finger of your sewing hand. Then thread a single strand of cotton thread onto a size 8 sharps needle before knotting it.

Step 1B
Pass your thread across the surface of some beeswax, or the conditioning product Thread Heaven. This will coat the thread so that your stitches will glide through the fabric as you sew.

Step 1C
We are using 100 percent cotton white thread for demo purposes, but of course for an actual garment you would use a matching color cotton thread.

Step 2A

Join the folded edges with a connecting blind stitch. Start by inserting the needle in between the *bottom* fold layer closest to you, ⅛" (3mm) away from the edge. Then pull the thread up to the surface.

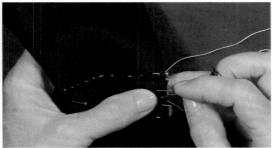

Step 2B

Take the next stitch by inserting the needle into the fold of the *top* fold layer. The stitch is directly across from the first stitch. It gets tunneled into the fold, is ⅛" (3mm) long, and comes out and into the fold of the bottom layer.

Step 2C

Now repeat the steps of inserting the needle on the fold of the top layer directly in line with the last stitch, and connecting in the fold of the bottom layer. The goal is to connect the two folded layers with blind stitches that are ⅛" (3mm) apart, and hidden. Remove the pins as you sew.

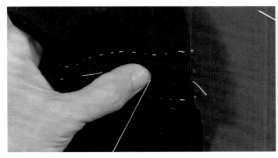

Step 2D

Note how, even though we are using white thread, the stitches are hidden from view. When blind stitching, do not pull the threads too tightly or your seam will pucker. Another tip is to stop periodically and flatten the seam with your fingers.

Step 3

When you reach the end, hide the last stitch in the fold, then clip the end thread.

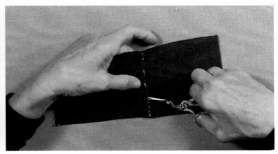

Step 4

Remove the basting threads by taking your embroidery scissors and clipping the thread at intervals on the right side of the fabric. Never pull basting threads out in one strand, as this will create holes in the fabric.

Step 5A

Once your basting threads have been removed, place a pressing cloth over the right side of the double-faced wool fabric and press, using steam.

Step 5B

Turn the wool piece over to the wrong side and press it flat, using a pressing cloth and steam. Pat the piece flat with your hands and then allow the fabric to cool before removing it from the ironing board.

Step 6

The finished double-faced seam.

Slot Seam

Tools and supplies:

- White cotton printed fabric
- Yellow cotton printed fabric
- Seam ripper and tweezers
  (or Seam-Fix seam ripper)

A slot seam is a decorative technique used on pockets, blouses, dresses, jackets, and coats. Our instructor will show you just how easy it is.

This unique seam finish will give your designs a tailored touch with an element of surprise.

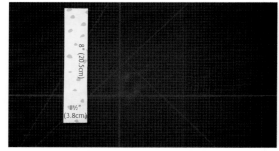

Step 1
Cut a piece of white cotton printed fabric 1½" (3.8cm) wide by 8" (20.5cm) long.

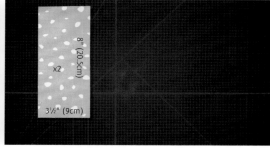

Step 2
Prepare two pieces of yellow cotton printed fabric, each 3½" (9cm) wide by 8" (20.5cm) long. We are using two different colored fabrics for demonstration purposes, but you could use the same color and a different type of fabric.

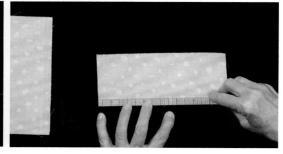

Step 3
Using tailor's chalk, mark a ½" (1.3cm) seam allowance line along the length edge of each of your 3½" (9cm) by 8" (20.5cm) fabric pieces.

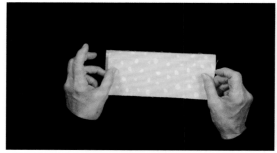

Step 4A
With right sides together, match up the seam allowance edges.

Step 4B
Pin the layers together along the ½" (1.3cm) seam allowance line.

Step 5
Sew the ½" (1.3cm) seam allowances together along the marked line with your sewing machine, using a basting stitch of 8 stitches per inch (spi; stitch length 3.2mm). Then clip the end threads.

Step 6
Press the stitched seam allowance flat on the wrong side, using steam.

Step 7
Now open the seam allowance and press it flat with steam.

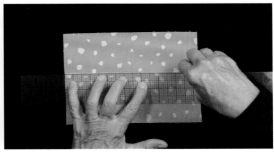

Step 8
Turn the piece to the right side and chalk a stitching line ¼" (6mm) away from the seam, on both sides of the piece.

Module 2:

Creating the Slot Seam

Step 1A
With the wrong side facing you, position your 1½" (3.8cm) by 8" (20.5cm) fabric strip along the seam allowance. Make sure that the seam is in the center of the strip and that the right side of the strip is facing the wrong side of the top piece.

Step 1B
Position the strip so that it covers the seam allowance and lines up at the ends with the larger fabric piece.

Step 2
Carefully flip the pieces over to the right side and place the layers, right side up, on your 18" (46cm) clear plastic ruler.

Step 3A
Pin the layers together, inserting the pins perpendicular to the seam.

Step 3B
Once the pieces are pinned together, turn the fabric over to check that the strip is perfectly centered.

Step 4A
Move to the sewing machine and stitch along the ¼" (6mm) chalk lines, removing the pins as you sew. Use a stitch length of 10–12 spi (2.1–2.5mm), as this will become the seam.

Step 4B
Turn the piece and repeat the stitching along the ¼" (6mm) chalk line on the other side of the seam.

Step 5A
Press the stitching flat on the right side, using steam. You would use a pressing cloth if this were an actual garment.

Step 5B
Flip the fabric piece over to the wrong side and press.

Module 3:
Final Steps

Step 1
Using your seam ripper, carefully remove the basting stitches.

Step 2
Take care not to tear your fabric as you rip the threads.

Step 3A
Position your fingers underneath the slot seam and remove the basting threads with tweezers.

Step 3B
Another option for removing the basting threads is to use a Seam-Fix seam ripper. You loosen the threads with the rounded, eraser-like end and then pick the threads out with your fingers.

Step 3C
This is how your slot seam looks when the seam is opened.

Lapped Seam

Tools and supplies:

- Double-faced wool fabric
- Matching cotton thread
- Buttonhole twist thread
- Size 8 sharps needle

A lapped seam can be used when working with fabrics or other materials that do not fray.

This is a very popular finish for garments made from double-faced wool, leather or faux leather, and suede.

Module 1:

Lesson Prep

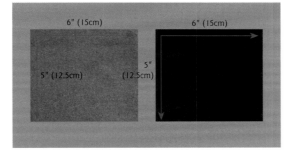

For this lesson you will need to prepare:
Two pieces of a double-faced wool fabric, each measuring 6" (15cm) in the width grain and 5" (12.5cm) in the length grain. We are using two colors to illustrate the technique.

Module 2:

Basting the Lapped Seam

Step 1
Before you start sewing, make sure that you are working with a very straight, even edge.

Step 2A
We will be lapping the left fabric piece over the right by ½" (1.3cm).

Step 2B
To help keep the seam straight, chalk a line along the length of the right-hand piece, ½" (1.3cm) in from the short edge.

Step 3

The left side of the piece will be a raw edge. Chalk a stitching line at ⅛" (3mm) away from that raw edge. If your fabric is somewhat stretchy, stabilize it with a ¼" (6mm)-wide interfacing strip, placed on the wrong side, slightly recessed from the edge.

Step 4

Place the left side over the right, lining up the raw edge with the chalked ½" (1.3cm) line of the right-hand piece. Then secure the layers with pins.

Step 5

Baste the layers together to keep them from shifting as you machine-stitch. Here we are using a size 8 sharps needle, with a knotted single thread. We are hand-stitching at approximately ⅛" (3mm) away from our chalk mark. Sew a loop and knot the end. Trim the end thread and remove the pins.

Silk embroidery thread

Heavy cotton thread

Step 6A

We have threaded the needle of the sewing machine with buttonhole twist so that the stitch is more pronounced.

Step 6B

Alternatively, you could use silk embroidery thread...

...or heavy cotton thread. In the bobbin of the machine, we used regular cotton thread.

Module 3:

Sewing the Lapped Seam

Step 1

Line up the sewing machine needle with your ⅛" (3mm) chalk line. Set your machine stitch to 8 stitches per inch (spi; stitch length 3.2mm) and start with a backtack, or backstitch.

Step 2

Continue to guide the fabric through the machine. End with a backtack.

Step 3

Clip the end threads and then remove the hand-basting stitches.

Step 4
Turn the piece to the wrong side and trim the seam allowance to within ¼" (6mm) to eliminate some of the bulk. Then press the seam flat, using steam.

Step 5
This is the finished lapped seam.

Self-evaluation

☐ Can I make a sample of every seam in the chapter?
☐ Can I identify the correct seam to use for the following?
    ☐ an unlined velvet jacket
    ☐ a full chiffon skirt
    ☐ a fitted organdy blouse
    ☐ jeans
    ☐ a wool skirt
    ☐ a cotton dress
    ☐ a reversible jacket
(answers on page 352)

5 Hem Finishes

A hem finish can be invisible and discreet, or created deliberately to make a design statement. **Hem finishes for lightweight fabrics** such as organza, voile, chiffon, and georgette require very careful sewing. We begin with a beautiful hand-rolled hem. It is quite labor intensive, so machine-made alternatives are also provided. A horsehair hem will give shape to lightweight fabrics, while a ribbon-edge hem will both finish the fabric edge and provide an extra design detail. And a wide straight-grain hem incorporates a folded-over double hem, giving a beautiful border effect.

The next section introduces you to **hem finishes suitable for medium-weight fabrics** such as cotton, linen, wool, or blends. We begin with two of the most popular finishes in this category—a hem finished with tape, and a hem that has its raw edge overlocked (or serged) before being stitched in place. A Hong Kong hem offers a more luxurious finish, binding the raw edge with a strip of organza, while a pinked and stitched hem finish is a useful option for fabrics that do not fray easily.

Hem Finishes for Lightweight Fabrics

Learning objectives

☐ Work a hand-rolled hem for a narrow finish, and utilize faster options such as the machine-foot baby hem and the tailored edge/baby hem

☐ Add structure by using horsehair in a hemline to shape and stabilize

☐ Create a design detail for a garment by working a ribbon-edge hem and a wide straight-grain hem

A seamstress adjusting a machine-foot baby hem on a chiffon dress.

In this section:

- Hand-rolled Hem
- Machine-foot Baby Hem
- Tailored Edge/Baby Hem
- Horsehair Hem
- Ribbon-edge Hem
- Wide Straight-grain Hem

Hand-rolled Hem

Tools and supplies:

- Silk chiffon
- Matching cotton thread
- Size 10 or 12 beading needle
- Silk pins

For our first lesson, we will demonstrate how to sew a beautiful hem finish on a sheer fabric.

You will learn how to handle your fabric, and how to roll the edge meticulously so that you can secure it with a slip stitch. This finish is definitely labor intensive, but has all the finesse necessary for a couture garment.

Module 1:

Lesson Prep

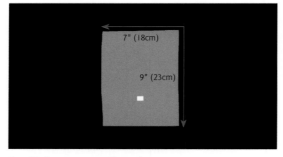

For this lesson you will need to prepare:
One piece of silk chiffon fabric, measuring 7" (18cm) wide by 9" (23cm) long. Use a sticker to indicate the wrong side of the fabric.

Step 1
Place a stitch ¼" (6mm) away from the width edge of your fabric piece.

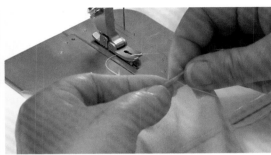

Step 2A
Using your fingers, roll the stitched edge over ⅛" (3mm), beginning at the right end.

You will be using a slip stitch to secure the hem, which will be almost invisible, and you will continue rolling the hem as you work.

Tip
When working with sheer fabric, be careful not to pull the thread too tight. This can make your seam or hem pucker.

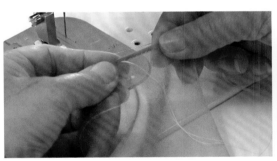

Step 2B
With your needle and knotted thread, pick up a single thread from the main body piece, then pick up another small stitch from the folded edge, on the diagonal. Come back in where you came out and grab another stitch on the main body piece.

Step 2C
Continue this process, rolling the hem as you sew. Your hem stitches should be evenly spaced, about ¼" (6mm) apart. For demonstration purposes, we are using thread in a contrasting color.

Step 3
Secure the hem to your ironing board with a pin at one end and lightly press on the wrong side. Then turn it over and press on the right side. Be careful not to press the hem flat. It looks much nicer if the hem has a slight roll to it.

Step 4
This is the finished hand-rolled hem.

Machine-foot Baby Hem

Tools and supplies:

- Silk chiffon
- Matching cotton thread
- ⅛" (3mm) hemming foot
- Silk pins

The machine-foot baby hem is a common way to hem sheers and other lightweight fabrics, using a hemming foot attached to a sewing machine.

You will learn how to manipulate the fabric through the foot, and how to press the hem correctly. This is an easy way to create a nice hem finish that would take days to complete if you sewed it by hand.

Module 1:

Lesson Prep

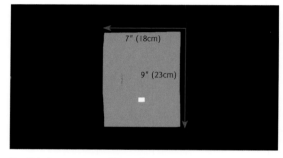

For this lesson you will need to prepare:
One piece of silk chiffon fabric, measuring 7" (18cm) wide by 9" (23cm) long. Use a sticker to indicate the wrong side of the fabric.

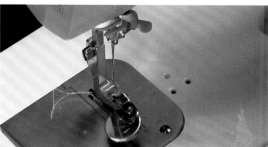

Step 1
Begin this lesson by first changing your regular foot to a
⅛" (3mm) hemming foot attachment.

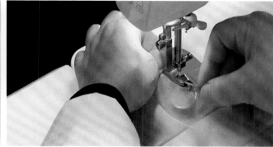

Step 2A
Fold your fabric over at the edge and position it so that it curls
around the inside knob of the hemming foot.

Step 2B
Continue to fold the fabric as you feed it through the foot to sew
the hem.

Tip
Hemming
attachments for
low- and high-
shank sewing
machines and snap-
on attachments
for home sewing
machines are
available in widths
of ⅛" (3mm), ³⁄₁₆"
(4mm), and ¼"
(6mm).

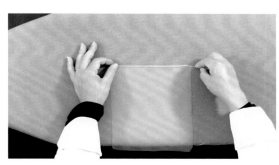

Step 3
Insert a pin through one end of the hem, securing it to your
ironing board. This will keep the hem straight as you press.

Press your hem flat on the wrong side first, holding the other
end with your fingers.

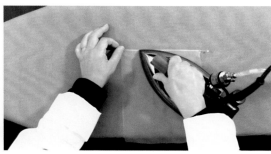

Work along until you reach the end of the hem, then turn it over
and press on the right side.

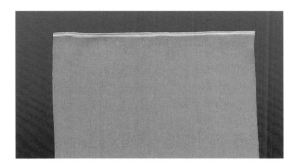

Step 4
This is the finished machine-foot baby hem.

Tailored Edge/Baby Hem

Tools and supplies:

- Silk chiffon
- Matching cotton thread
- Silk pins

A tailored edge, or baby hem, is a great choice for sewing a narrow hem on any sheer or soft, lightweight fabric.

This is similar to the previous lesson, except here there is no need to purchase a hemming foot for your machine. Once you have mastered this sampler, you will be ready to tackle that voluminous skirt hem, and finish it in no time at all.

Module 1:

Lesson Prep

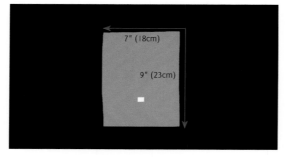

7" (18cm)

9" (23cm)

For this lesson you will need to prepare:
One piece of silk chiffon fabric measuring 7" (18cm) wide by 9" (23cm) long. Use a sticker to indicate the wrong side of the fabric.

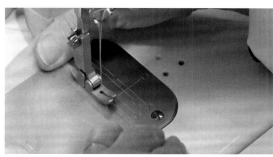

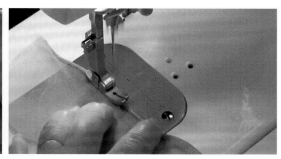

Step 1
With the wrong side facing up, turn the edge of the fabric over by ⅛" (3mm) and stitch close to the edge.

Be careful not to stretch the fabric as you sew.

Step 2
Turn the edge over by another ⅛" (3mm) and run another stitch next to the first stitch.

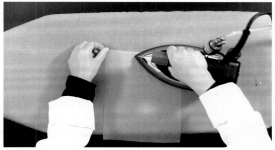

Step 3
Insert a pin through one end of the hem to secure it to your ironing board, then press your hem flat on the wrong side.

Then turn the sample over and press it on the right side.

Step 4
This is the finished tailored edge/baby hem finish.

Horsehair Hem

Tools and supplies:

- Silk chiffon
- Matching cotton thread
- Horsehair
- Silk pins

Horsehair comes in many sizes and colors, and is used to create hems on sheer fabrics when extra structure is required.

Here, we will teach you how to finish a hem with ½" (1.3cm)-wide horsehair. Once you have completed this lesson, you will be able to employ the same technique for any designs that call for extra shape and structure.

Module 1:

Lesson Prep

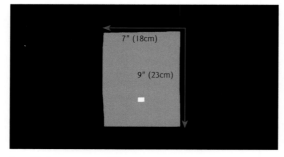

7" (18cm)

9" (23cm)

For this lesson you will need to prepare:
One piece of silk chiffon fabric measuring 7" (18cm) wide by 9" (23cm) long. Use a sticker to indicate the wrong side of the fabric.

Module 2:

Creating the Horsehair Hem

Step 1

With the right side of the fabric facing up, attach the horsehair to your fabric, stitching ⅛" (3mm) away from the width edge of the fabric. Use the ⅛" (3mm) mark on your machine plate as a guide for your stitching.

Step 2

Turn the horsehair over onto the wrong side of the fabric and carefully roll the edge flat with your fingers.

Step 3

Stitch the edge of the horsehair to the wrong side, making sure that the hem is flat and even as you sew.

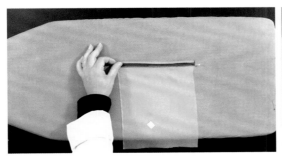

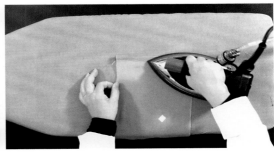

Step 4A

Insert a pin through one end of the hem to secure it to your ironing board. This will help keep the hem straight as you press it.

Now press your hem flat on the wrong side.

Then then the fabric over and press it on the right side.

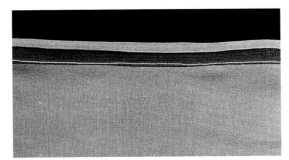

Step 4B

This is the finished horsehair hem.

Ribbon-edge Hem

Tools and supplies:

- Silk chiffon
- Matching cotton thread
- ⅜" (1cm)-wide satin ribbon

This decorative hem finish will add structure and detail to the hem of any sheer garment.

A length of ribbon is sewn to the hem before being turned to the other side, and you can choose whether to attach the ribbon to the right or wrong side of a garment for two different finished effects.

Module 1:

Lesson Prep

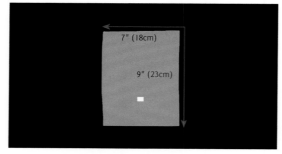

7" (18cm)

9" (23cm)

For this lesson you will need to prepare:
One piece of silk chiffon fabric measuring 7" (18cm) wide by 9" (23cm) long. Use a sticker to indicate the wrong side of the fabric.

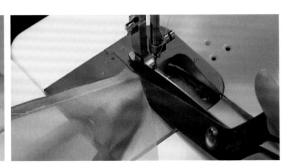

Step 1A
For the ribbon to be on the inside of the garment hem, start with
the wrong side of the fabric facing up and pin the wrong side of
the satin ribbon, slightly recessing it, to the width edge of the
fabric's right side.

Step 1B
Stitch along the bottom edge of the ribbon. Gently guide the
fabric through the machine with your right hand, removing the
pins as you sew.

Step 1C
Trim the ribbon when you get to the end.

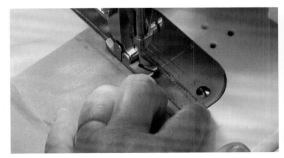

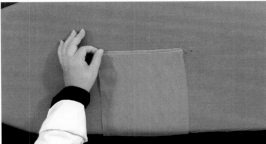

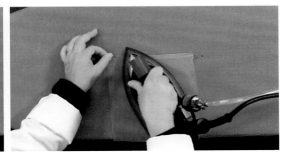

Step 2
Turn the ribbon over onto the wrong side of the fabric and
then stitch the top edge of the ribbon onto the wrong side
of the fabric.

Step 3
Before pressing, insert a pin through one end of the hem to
secure it to your ironing board.

Press your hem flat on the right side.

Now turn the sample over and press the wrong side.

Step 4
This is the finished ribbon-edge hem.

Wide Straight-grain Hem

Tools and supplies:

- Silk chiffon
- Matching cotton thread
- Size 10 or 12 beading needle
- Silk pins

A wide straight-grain hem is a finish commonly used on sheer fabrics such as chiffon, organza, and georgette.

We will teach you how to fold the fabric properly, and how to create a blind-stitch hem for a beautiful effect. Use this finish on sleeves, pockets, dresses, skirts, and pants, or wherever you have an area that is cut on the straight grain.

Module 1:

Lesson Prep

7" (18cm)

17" (43cm)

For this lesson you will need to prepare:
One piece of silk chiffon fabric measuring 7" (17cm) wide by 17" (43cm) long. Use a sticker to indicate the wrong side of the fabric.

Module 2:
Creating the Wide Straight-grain Hem

Step 1
Using your clear plastic ruler, measure up 4" (10cm) from the bottom edge of the fabric on the wrong side and insert a pin. Do the same at the other end.

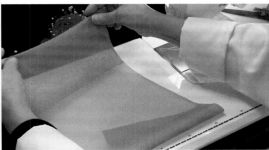

Step 2A
Fold the piece over and then fold it again.

Position the hem so that it is actually three layers thick.

Step 2B
Pin the hem in place, making sure that each layer is kept even. For this demonstration we have created a 4" (10cm)-wide hem, but you may change the width of the hem if you choose.

Step 2C
Continue to pin along the folded edge in preparation for hand-stitching the hem.

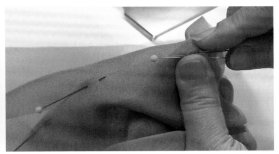

Step 3A
A blind stitch is an almost invisible hem stitch. Thread your needle and knot the end. Blind stitch your hem, removing your pins as you sew: grab a small single thread from the main body piece, then pick up another small stitch from the folded edge of the hem, on the diagonal.

Step 3B
Your hem stitches should be even, about ¼" (6mm) apart, and should be hidden in the fold.

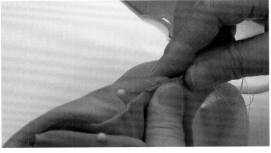

With practice, you will be able to catch several stitches at a time with your needle, as demonstrated here.

Pull your needle through, but be careful not to pull your thread too tight as this will cause your hem to pucker.

Make sure your finished hem is lying nice and flat.

Step 4
Gently press your hem on the wrong side...

...and then on the right side.

Step 5
This is the finished wide straight-grain hem.

Making the final adjustments to a hem.

Hem Finishes for Medium-weight Fabrics

Learning objectives

☐ Understand basic hems: a hem-tape hem, and an overlocked hem

☐ Work a Hong Kong hem for a high-quality item

☐ Apply a pinked and stitched hem to a non-fraying fabric

In this section:

• Hem-tape Hem
• Overlocked Hem
• Hong Kong Hem
• Pinked & Stitched Hem

Hem-tape Hem

Tools and supplies:

- Worsted wool fabric
- Size 8 sharps needle
- Matching cotton thread
- Matching hem tape

A hem finished with hem tape is the most commonly used hem finish in the fashion industry, suitable for a wide variety of garments.

Here you will learn the technique by sewing some hem tape to the edge of a wool fabric sampler, then securing it in place using a catch stitch. This is a versatile finish that will come in handy for many of your future creations.

Module 1:

Lesson Prep

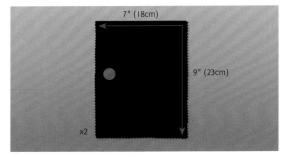

For this lesson you will need to prepare:
Two pieces of wool fabric, each measuring 7" (18cm) wide by 9" (23cm) long. Use stickers to indicate the wrong side of the fabric.

Step 1
Begin by joining the right sides of the fabric pieces together along the length edge to create a seam. Press the seam open, then place your hem tape over the hem edge, ¼" (6mm) away from the raw edge on the fabric's right side.

Sew down the inside edge of the tape.

Step 2A
Press the hem flat.

Step 2B
Measure 1½" (3.8cm) up from the hem-tape edge and mark it with chalk.

Step 2C
Turn the hem to the wrong side on this line and press.

Step 3A
You will be using a catch stitch to secure the hem in place. Begin by pinning the hem up, making sure that the seam remains aligned up the center.

Step 3B
Knot your thread, then fold back the hem tape and start stitching from the left side. Pick up one thread from the seam allowance.

Step 3C
Then cross over diagonally to the body fabric, picking up only a single thread.

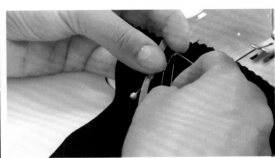

Step 3D
Repeat this at ¼" (6mm) intervals.

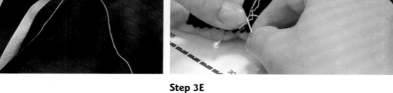

Be careful not to pull the stitches too tightly or you will cause the fabric to pucker. Do not pick up more than one thread on the body side or the pick stitches will be visible on the right side of the sampler.

Step 3E
Finish by backstitching on the wool seam allowance.

Secure the thread with a knot before trimming the thread end.

Step 4A
Press the sampler on the wrong side and then the right side, using a pressing cloth.

Step 4B
This is the finished hem-tape hem.

Overlocked Hem

Tools and supplies:

- Worsted wool fabric
- Silk organza
- Matching cotton thread
- Size 8 sharps needle
- Serger (overlocker)

An overlocked hem is created using an overlock machine, and is a fast, easy, and economical way to clean-finish the raw edge of a hem. It is commonly used in the industry, and popular with home sewers.

We will teach you how to overlock your raw edge, then how to slip stitch the hem in place by hand. This hem is a great choice for light- to medium-weight fabrics—especially those that fray easily.

Module 1:

Lesson Prep

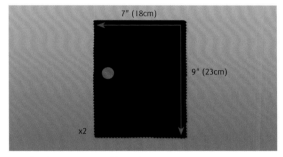

For this lesson you will need to prepare:
Two pieces of wool fabric, each measuring 7" (18cm) wide by 9" (23cm) long. Use stickers to indicate the wrong side of the fabric.

Module 2:

Creating the Overlocked Hem

Step 1
Begin by sewing the length edges of the fabric pieces, right sides together, to create a seam. Press the seam open and then overlock the raw width edge.

Step 2
Measure up 1½" (3.8cm) to establish the width (depth) of the hem. Mark this line with chalk on the right side of the fabric.

Fold the hem up along this line and press.

Step 3A
Pin the hem in place, making sure that the seam is aligned. Using a needle and thread, pick up a thread from below the overlocked edge to start your slip stitch.

You will now be using a pick stitch to secure the hem in place. Using a needle and thread, pick up a thread from below the overlocked edge.

Step 3B
Then pick up a thread from the body at a distance of ¼" (6mm) away from the first stitch.

Repeat this process along the hem, making sure that you pick up only a single thread each time. This will mean that the pick stitches will not be visible on the right side of the fabric.

Step 4A
Press the sampler on the wrong side...

...and then on the right side, using a pressing cloth.

Step 4B
This the finished overlocked hem.

Hong Kong Hem

Tools and supplies:

- Worsted wool fabric
- Silk organza
- Size 8 sharps needle
- Matching cotton thread

When you see a Hong Kong bound hem, it is always the sign of a high-quality garment. This finish can be used on wools, or any light- to medium-weight fabric.

Here, we will demonstrate the technique by sewing a bias silk organza strip to the hem edge on a wool fabric sampler. You will then learn how to complete the hem by hand, using a catch stitch.

Module 1:

Lesson Prep

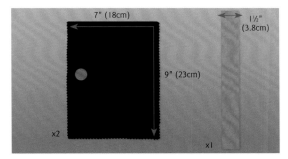

For this lesson you will need to prepare:
Two pieces of wool fabric, each measuring 7" (18cm) wide by 9" (23cm) long, and one piece of silk organza cut on the bias, 1½" (3.8cm) wide by 15" (38cm) long. Use stickers to indicate the wrong side of the fabric.

Step 1A

Join the length edges of the two wool pieces, right sides together, with a ¾" (2cm) seam allowance. Press the seam open.

Once the seam has been created and pressed open, place your bias organza piece on the right side of the fabric, along the hem edge, and stitch ¼" (6mm) away from the raw edge. Be careful not to pull the bias strip, as this will stretch it.

Step 1B

Now finger-press the bias strip up and over to the wrong side of the fabric. Then, holding it in place with a finger, "stitch in the ditch" on the right side. This involves sewing as close as possible to the existing seam.

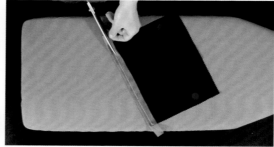

The organza strip shown wrapped around the raw edge of the wool sampler. You will now need to remove the excess organza on this side.

Step 2A

Trim the bias strip on the wrong side to ¼" (6mm) away from the seam.

Then trim the ends.

Step 2B

Measure and mark the hem width (depth) at 1½" (3.8cm), using chalk.

Step 2C

Fold the hem back along this line and lightly press it. Pin the hem in place, making sure you align the center seam.

Step 3A

Now catch-stitch your hem. Begin by knotting your thread, then roll back the organza binding and start stitching from the left side.

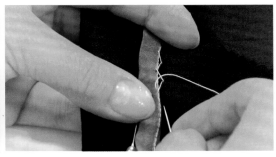

Step 3B

Pick up one thread from the organza binding and then cross over diagonally to the wool body fabric, picking up another single thread here.

Repeat this step at ¼" (6mm) intervals.

Be careful not to pull the stitches too tightly or you will cause puckering. And do not pick up more than one thread on the wool fabric or the stitches will be visible on the right side of the sampler.

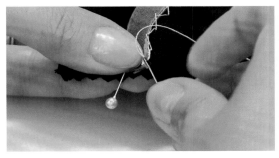

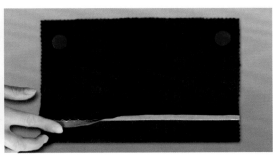

Step 3C

When you reach the end, secure your thread with a backstitch on the organza binding.

Step 4A

Finally, press your hem.

Step 4B

This is the finished Hong Kong hem.

Pinked & Stitched Hem

Tools and supplies:

- Worsted wool fabric
- Size 8 sharps needle
- Matching cotton thread
- Pinking shears

This hem is a popular choice for fabrics that do not fray easily, such as wool, wool flannel, tropical worsted wool, and gabardine.

You will learn how to create this quick and easy finish by using pinking shears and a sewing machine, before securing the hem in place by hand with a catch stitch.

Module 1:

Lesson Prep

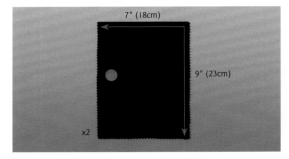

For this lesson you will need to prepare:
Two pieces of wool fabric, each measuring 7" (18cm) wide by 9" (23cm) long. Use stickers to indicate the wrong side of the fabric.

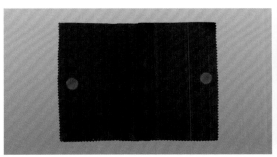

Step 1A
Start by stitching the right sides of the fabric pieces together along the length edge to create a seam. Press the seam open.

"Pink" the hem edge by trimming it with your pinking shears.

Step 1B
Measure up 1½" (3.8cm) from the pinked edge and draw a line on the right side of the fabric using chalk.

Turn the hem to the inside along this line and press.

Step 2A
Trim the corners of the seam allowance at the hem to eliminate any excess bulk.

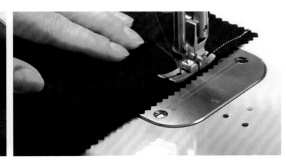

Step 2B
Then run a stitch ¼" (6mm) away from the pinked hem edge.

Step 3A
Pin the hem up in preparation for hand-stitching it.

Step 3B
Knot a single thread, then start stitching from the left side, using a catch stitch. Pick up one thread from the seam allowance on the stitch line. Then cross over diagonally to the wool, picking up a single thread here.

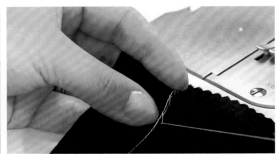

Step 3C
Repeat this at ¼" (6mm) intervals. Do not pull the stitches too tightly or it will create puckering. Do not pick up more than one thread on the wool, either, or your stitches will be visible on the outside of the sampler.

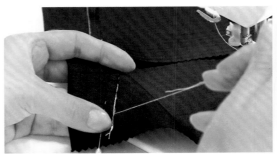

Step 3D
When you reach the end, finish by securing your thread with a tack on the seam allowance.

Your hem should now be lying nice and flat.

Step 4A
Press the hem on the wrong side.

Then turn it over and press the right side, using a pressing cloth.

Step 4B
This is the finished pinked & stitched hem.

Self-evaluation

☐ Can I make a sample of every hem in the chapter?
☐ Can I identify the correct hem to use for the following:
    ☐ a silk scarf edge
    ☐ a full chiffon skirt
    ☐ a decorative sheer skirt
    ☐ a wool skirt with finished edge
    ☐ when the least expensive hem finish is needed
(answers on page 352)

Decorative hem finish by Fendi Roma, 2016.

6 Buttons & Buttonholes

Buttons are available in all sorts of shapes, sizes, and materials. This chapter offers an **introduction to buttons and buttonholes** before you move on to practical lessons. You will learn about the two basic types of button, how they are sized, and how to attach them to a garment. We demonstrate how to plan buttonholes for vertical and horizontal placements, and show you the tools that will simplify the process.

You are now ready to learn how to sew your buttons like the professionals. We will teach you how to sew a **shank button** properly, and then introduce you to a fast and easy method for attaching a **four-hole button** to fabric using a thread shank.

The next stage is creating a **machine-made buttonhole**. You will learn two variations—a straight buttonhole and a keyhole-shaped alternative—using a buttonhole attachment on your sewing machine. We will show you how to establish the correct length, how to line the buttonhole up correctly on the fabric, and how to complete the stitching for a perfect finish.

Introduction to Buttons & Buttonholes

Learning objectives

☐ Identify the different button types, shapes, and sizes

☐ Choose the right button for your project

☐ Calculate the correct position and spacing for buttons

☐ Establish the size and type of buttonhole needed, and know the correct terminology

☐ Machine-stitch a buttonhole and cut the opening

David Dixon updates a short jacket with decorative buttons, 2016.

What is a Button?

According to the American Society for Testing & Materials (ASTM), the definition of a button is a knob, disc, or similar object that, when forced through a narrow opening or a buttonhole, fastens one part of a garment or other flexible substrate to another.

What is a Buttonhole?

A buttonhole is a slit or opening in fabric large enough to allow a button to pass through. Buttonholes are usually rectangular and finished with very close stitches. Buttonholes can be made by machine or by hand.

Button Types

Buttons are available in two basic types: holed and shank.

A holed button may have two, three, or four holes through its center, and is sewn directly onto fabric through these holes.

A shank button has a stem extending from its underside so that it sits away from the fabric for easier buttoning and unbuttoning. It is sewn to a garment through a hole at the end of the shank. (A similar result is achieved by using the thread shank technique, described opposite.)

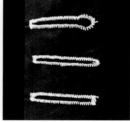

Holed buttons   Shank button

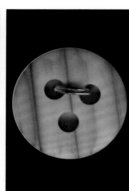

Two holes   Three holes   Four holes

Button Shapes

Buttons come in all kinds of shapes: flat, rimmed, domed, half ball, full ball, tubular, triangular, and even square. Other specific shapes are referred to by names such as French bevel, shank, fisheye, slotted well, English rim, and double dome.

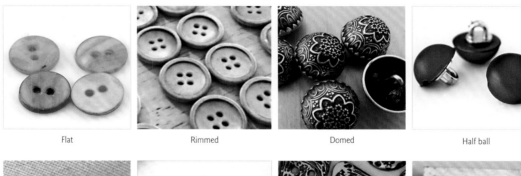

Flat | Rimmed | Domed | Half ball

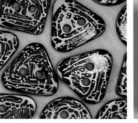

French bevel | Shank | Fisheye | Slotted well | English rim | Double dome

Full ball | Tubular | Triangular | Square

Four-hole Button Stitching

Sewing a four-hole button uses the same technique as a two- or three-hole button. However, you can choose from several stitch configurations, as shown.

What is a Thread Shank?

This is another technique for attaching shankless buttons. The button is attached at a slight distance from the fabric, held in place by a thread extension, or shank. As with a shank button, this allows for easier buttoning and unbuttoning. The height of the shank is determined by the thickness of the fabric that the button will hold in place when the garment is closed.

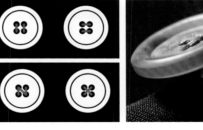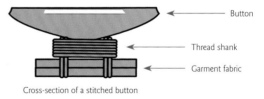

Cross-section of a stitched button

- Button
- Thread shank
- Garment fabric

Button Reinforcements

For certain fabrics, a reinforcement may be required to help secure the button to the fabric and prevent the fabric from tearing after repeated buttoning and unbuttoning. On a man's shirt, for example, you will often find a small piece of cotton or felt acting as a reinforcement on the underside of the collar button, while on leather jackets you will find a small plastic button is used as reinforcement to prevent the leather from tearing.

Cotton/felt button underside reinforcement | Underside button reinforcement

Stitching Tools

When stitching buttons onto a garment, you will need certain tools. You can choose between sewing thread or Hy-Mark thread, which is a bit stronger than regular thread. To keep the thread from tangling and fraying, and to help it glide through the material, run the thread across some beeswax or Thread Heaven first to condition it. Ironing the thread afterward will help remove some of the residue. A size 5 betweens needle is a good choice for buttons, since it is shorter than a sharps needle and therefore easier to use when creating small stitches.

Regular sewing thread (Tex 30)   Hy-Mark thread   Beeswax   Betweens needles of assorted sizes

Module 3:

Button Materials

Buttons can be made from just about anything the imagination can dream up. However, a designer must remember that clothes containing buttons will need to be either laundered or dry-cleaned, and any buttons, therefore, will need to be tested. Sometimes button color can bleed onto fabric, or buttons can crack during the dry-cleaning process or even melt when hit with a hot iron. So always test your button choice.

Some of the most common buttons are made from natural materials, including bone, glass, horn, nuts, leather, pearls, shells, wood, metal, rubber, and jet (a type of gemstone).

Buttons can also be made from synthetic materials such as melamine, nylon, polyester, and urea (synthetic resin).

Whether made from natural or synthetic materials, buttons must always be tested for wearability.

Natural Buttons

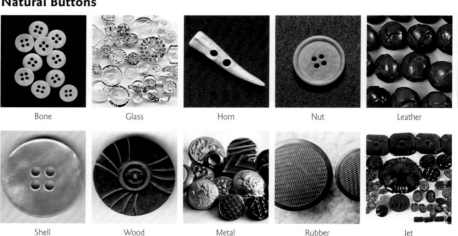

Bone   Glass   Horn   Nut   Leather   Pearl

Shell   Wood   Metal   Rubber   Jet

Synthetic Buttons

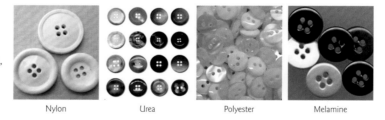

Nylon   Urea   Polyester   Melamine

Fabric Weight & Button Size

There is a direct correlation between the weight of the fabric and the weight of the button—and, therefore, the size of the button and the length of the buttonhole. The general rule is: the lighter the fabric, the smaller the button, and the heavier the fabric, the larger the button.

Interfacing

Interfacing should always be used as a support material between your fabric layers on both sides of your garment—the button-stitching side and the buttonhole side.

Button Sizes

Button sizes are determined by diameter, and are classified using a unit of measurement called a "ligne" (L), with 40 lignes equal to 1" (25mm)—a system that was first used by German button-makers in the eighteenth century.

Since there are 40 lignes in an inch, a 40L button will have a diameter of 1" (25mm). The chart gives a selection of conversions from ligne into inches and millimeters.

Measuring Devices

Buttons can be measured using a button card or a button gauge.

Button Size Chart

Diameter of Button	Ligne Size	Metric Size
¼"	12L	7mm
⁵⁄₁₆"	14L	8mm
³⁄₈"	16L	9.5mm
⁷⁄₁₆"	18L	11mm
½"	20L	13mm
⁹⁄₁₆"	22L	14mm
⅝"	24L	16mm
¾"	30L	19mm
⅞"	36L	23mm
1"	40L	25mm
1⅛"	45L	28mm
1¼"	50L	32mm
1½"	60L	38mm

(Note: Metric sizes may be rounded.)

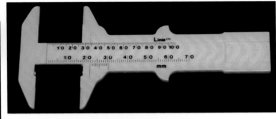

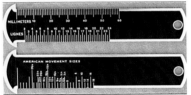

Button gauges

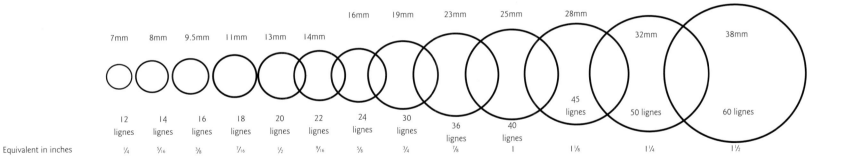

| | 16mm | 19mm | 23mm | 25mm | 28mm | 32mm | 38mm |

| 7mm | 8mm | 9.5mm | 11mm | 13mm | 14mm |

| 12 lignes | 14 lignes | 16 lignes | 18 lignes | 20 lignes | 22 lignes | 24 lignes | 30 lignes | 36 lignes | 40 lignes | 45 lignes | 50 lignes | 60 lignes |

Equivalent in inches: ¼ ⁵⁄₁₆ ⅜ ⁷⁄₁₆ ½ ⁹⁄₁₆ ⅝ ¾ ⅞ 1 1⅛ 1¼ 1½

Tip
Button extension means the amount of fabric between center front, center back, or a seam, and the center of the button.

Women's Button Placement
The front closure of women's clothing always laps RIGHT over LEFT, with the buttonholes placed on the right side of the garment and the buttons sewn on the left side of the garment.

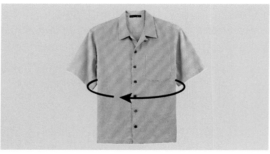

Men's Button Placement
For menswear, button placement is the opposite of women's—that is, the front of a garment closure laps LEFT over RIGHT. Buttonholes are placed on the left side of the garment and the buttons are sewn on the right side of the garment.

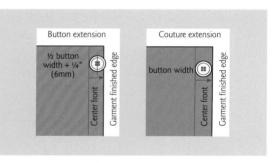

Button Extension Rules
Whether for menswear or womenswear, the rule for a button extension is: half the width of the button, plus ¼" (6mm). However, for couture and higher-priced clothing, the extension is usually the full width of the button. The same rules apply for both the button and buttonhole side of the garment extension.

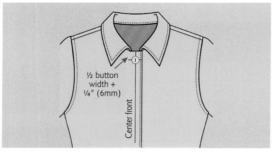

First Button Placement
The first button and buttonhole are positioned half the width of the button plus ¼" (6mm) away from the neckline.

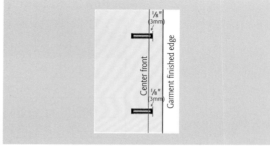

Horizontal Buttons & Buttonhole Placement
When planning the placement of your buttonholes and buttons, the rule is that you place your buttonhole mark into the extension, ⅛" (3mm) beyond the center front of the garment toward the finished edge. The buttons are stitched on the center front line.

Vertical Buttons & Buttonhole Placement
Vertical buttonholes are stitched on the center front or the center back line of the garment. The buttons are stitched on the centerline and are centered in the buttonhole.

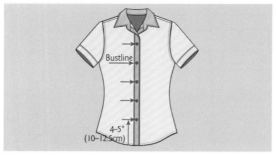

Stress Points and Last Button Placement
A tight garment must have buttons at the stress points—for example, on the bustline or at the waist of a fitted garment. The last button and buttonhole are positioned 4–5" (10–12.5cm) from the bottom of a shirt or blouse.

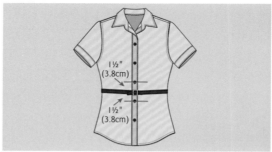

Button Placement on Belted Garments
Buttons and buttonholes on a belted garment should be placed 1½" (3.8cm) above and below the belt.

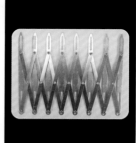 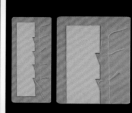

Button Placement Aids
A SimFlex Expanding Sewing Gauge (above left) is a handy tool for establishing the position of buttons and buttonholes.

Another way to mark the positions for buttons and buttonholes is with a piece of oaktag (card) that has been marked with the correct spacing (above right). It is placed on the garment so that the positions can be transferred via markings on the fabric.

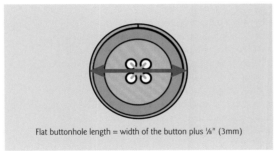

Flat buttonhole length = width of the button plus ⅛" (3mm)

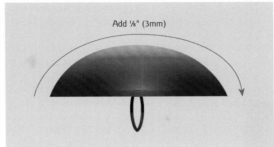

Add ⅛" (3mm)

Buttonholes for Flat Buttons
The correct buttonhole length for a flat button is the full width of the button plus ⅛" (3mm).

Buttonholes for Shank Buttons
To establish the correct buttonhole length for a shank button, measure from one end of the button cap to the other and then add ⅛" (3mm).

Machine-made Buttonholes
Machine-made buttonholes come in four different shapes—keyhole, straight, rounded, and bound—depending on the options available on your sewing machine. (Industrially produced bound buttonholes are made using specialist buttonhole-binding machinery.) Gimp or cord can be used to give your buttonholes added dimension.

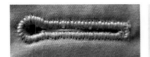

Keyhole

Straight

Rounded

Bound

Gimp/Cord

Creating Buttonholes with a Sewing Machine
There are three possible methods for creating a buttonhole using a domestic sewing machine, depending on the capabilities of your particular model: automatic buttonholes, one-step buttonholes, and four-step buttonholes.

Automatic Buttonholes
Automatic buttonholes are made on a computerized sewing machine. The length of the buttonhole can be programmed into the machine, or determined by placing a button in a special buttonhole foot that then acts as a guide. Buttonhole styles range from straight to rounded, keyhole, and eyelet.

One-step Buttonholes
One-step buttonholes are made with the turn of a dial or the use of a special foot.

Four-step Buttonholes
Four-step buttonholes are made in four separate steps, manually selecting the correct type of stitch at each stage—the narrower zigzag for the long sides, and the wider zigzag for the bar tack at either end (see next page for the sequence of steps).

Buttonhole Anatomy

A straight buttonhole consists of two components: a wide zigzag bar tack located at top and bottom, and two parallel rows of narrower zigzag stitching known as thread bars. The stitching binds the raw edges of the buttonhole.

Bar tack

Thread bar

Buttonhole Terminology

The various parts of a buttonhole are referred to using specific terminology. The buttonhole length is the overall length of the buttonhole, including the bar tacks at the end. Bar tack length refers to the amount of bar tack stitching on each end. The buttonhole opening is the length needed for the button to pass through. The cutting width is the area between the buttonhole stitches, which is cut open for the button to pass through once the buttonhole is complete. Stitch density refers to how compact and tight the threads are, whereas stitch bite describes the width of the individual stitches.

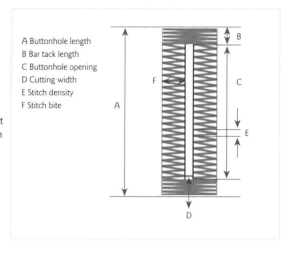

A Buttonhole length
B Bar tack length
C Buttonhole opening
D Cutting width
E Stitch density
F Stitch bite

Buttonhole Stitching Sequence

Machine-made buttonholes are sewn in a particular sequence, as illustrated below.

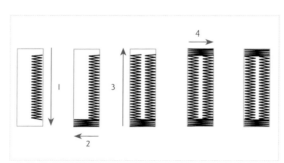

Sewing a Test Buttonhole

Before sewing the final buttonholes on a garment, sew a test buttonhole on a sample that has been prepared exactly like the final garment. The sample should be cut on the same grain as the garment, and properly interfaced.

Refer to your sewing machine's manual for the available buttonhole features, and start with a new needle and a full bobbin. Finally, make sure your stitches align exactly with the buttonhole position that you have marked, and are sewn in the correct sequence, so that the final placement is as intended.

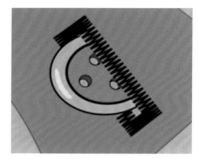

Module 8:

The Buttonhole Opening

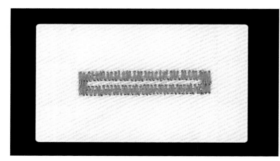

Opening a Buttonhole

Opening a buttonhole, once it has been stitched, can be done in one of four ways: with the tip of some sharp fabric shears, with a buttonhole chisel tool, with a seam ripper, or with a single-edge razor blade.

Sharp-pointed shears

Single-edge razor blade (top), chisel tool and rubber mat (bottom)

Seam ripper

Sewing Buttons: Shank & 4-hole Button

Learning objectives

☐ Place and sew on a shank button

☐ Secure a 4-hole button by positioning and sewing the button, and creating a thread shank

Tools and supplies:

- Melton (wool) cloth
- Matching polyester thread
- 40L shank button
- 40L holed button (4 holes)
- Size 12 sharps needle

Tip

Buttons with metal or plastic shanks are more durable than sew-through buttons. Shank buttons are often used on coats, which are buttoned and unbuttoned often, and other garments made from heavy fabrics.

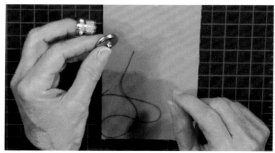

Step 1

In this lesson you will be sewing a shank button to your fabric.

Step 2

Begin by making a mark on the right side of your fabric to indicate the desired placement of the button.

Step 3

This is the shank part of the button. Your thread will pass through the hole located here.

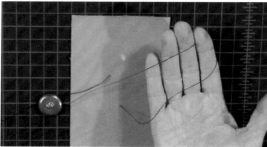

Step 4

Thread your size 12 sharps needle with no more than 12–18" (30.5–46cm) of thread.

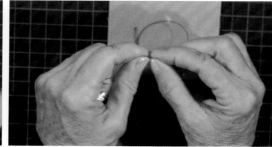

Step 5

Add a small knot at the end.

Step 6A

Now insert your needle right through the point where you want your button to sit.

Step 6B

Come back through the fabric.

Step 6C

Now take a few stitches right at that point, passing through the hole in the shank.

Step 6D

We are using a single strand of a strong polyester thread. You could also use a buttonhole twist, which is made of strong silk.

Step 6E
After one or two stitches, start to hold the button slightly away from the fabric, just to loosen the connection a little bit.

Step 6F
Continue to make your stitches.

Step 7A
When you have completed a few more stitches, come back up through the fabric to the button side. Since you have held the button loosely, you will now be able to wrap the thread around the stitches made so far, right under the shank.

Step 7B
Then take your needle through the fabric...

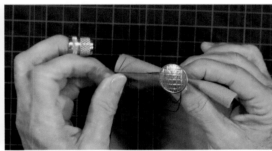

Step 7C
...and knot your thread.

Step 7D
Carefully clip the thread end.

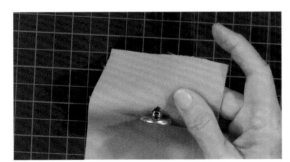

Step 7E
You have now finished sewing a shank button.

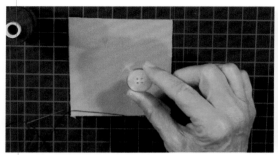

Step 1A

You will now sew a 4-hole button to fabric, using a size 12 sharps needle, and creating a thread shank.

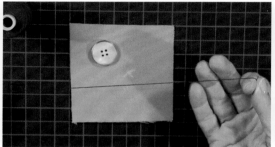

Step 1B

The thread being used here is a strong thread manufactured by Gütermann. Begin by cutting a length of thread, 12–18" (30.5–46cm).

Step 2

Then make a small knot at the end.

Step 3

Mark the right side of the fabric to indicate where your button will go.

Step 4A

Insert your needle on the right side of the fabric.

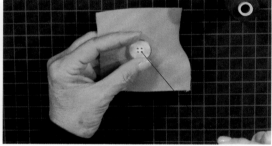

Step 4B

Then re-emerge through the fabric and up through the first hole in the button.

Step 4C

Then take your needle back down through the adjacent hole.

Step 4D

Now cross over to emerge through this hole.

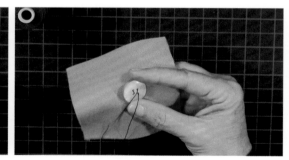

Then reinsert the needle through the fourth hole, as shown.

Oversized metallic shank buttons decorate a coat by Vawk, Fall 2015.

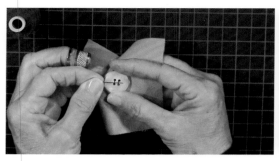

Step 4E
Now take a pin and place it right under the threads. You can also use a toothpick, but make sure it is not too thick.

Now, with the pin remaining in place under the threads, continue to stitch the button in place, passing through the four holes in the same sequence as before.

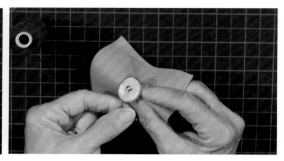

Step 5A
When the button is securely attached, remove the pin or toothpick from your threads.

Step 5B
Bring your needle through to the back of the button.

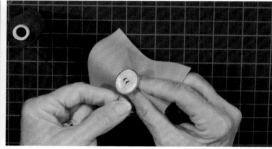

Step 5C
Then wrap the thread around the threads holding the button in place, on the underside of the button.

Step 5D
Finish by creating a knot.

Step 5E
Then pass the needle to the back of the fabric...

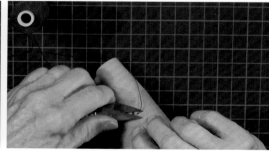

...where you will trim your thread end.

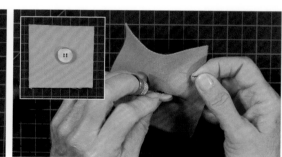

Step 5F
You have now finished sewing a 4-hole button with a thread shank.

The focal point of this jacket by Burberry Prorsum is the double row of decorative metal buttons. Autumn/Winter 2016.

Machine-made Buttonholes: Straight & Keyhole

Learning objectives

- ☐ Set up a sewing machine with an automatic buttonhole attachment and sew a straight buttonhole
- ☐ Place and sew a keyhole buttonhole using an automatic buttonhole attachment

Tools and supplies:

- Sewing machine
- Buttonhole attachment
- Wool flannel fabric
- Fusible interfacing
- Matching cotton thread
- Clippers

Tip
Your machine may offer settings whereby you can control the stitch bite (the width of each stitch) and the stitch density (how compact the stitches are). Always consider your fabric when making these decisions—too many stitches on a lightweight fabric, for example, can tear the fabric.

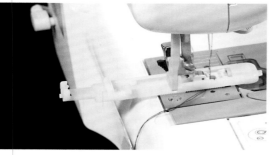

Step 1
For this lesson we have attached the automatic buttonhole attachment that came with our particular sewing machine. Always make sure that you have enough thread on the top and in the bobbin before you start.

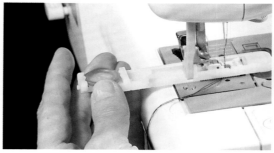

Step 2
Start by placing your button in the attachment, as demonstrated. The attachment will then create a buttonhole that is the correct length for that particular button, in this case 1" (2.5cm). Select the machine's straight buttonhole setting.

Step 3
The piece of fabric used here was prepared with fusible interfacing between the fabric layers to keep the buttonhole from stretching, and the position of the buttonhole was marked on the fabric.

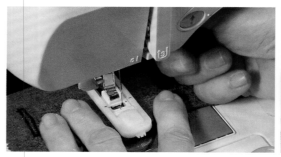

Step 4
Now position your needle so that it aligns with your buttonhole marking. Remember to always do a test buttonhole on a scrap of fabric before tackling your actual garment. We are using contrast thread for demonstration purposes.

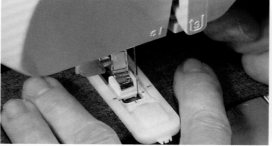

Step 5
Lower the presser foot, making sure that the buttonhole attachment is at a right angle to both the folded edge of the fabric and your centerline marking.

Step 6
Now start the machine and watch as the buttonhole is stitched automatically. Gently hold the fabric with your hands while the machine completes the process.

Step 7
The machine will stitch along one side, then the other, and will automatically stop once the buttonhole is complete.

Step 8
Once the buttonhole is finished, lift the presser foot and trim the end threads.

Step 9A
To open the buttonhole, fold the buttonhole in half and use your clippers to snip into the center of the buttonhole, as demonstrated here.

Step 9B
Now use the tip of your clippers to open the buttonhole at the corners. Clip one side, then turn the buttonhole and clip the other so that the buttonhole is fully opened. You must work with sharp-tipped clippers, scissors, or a razor blade. Take care not to cut into the buttonhole stitches.

Step 9C
You have now sewn a machine-made straight buttonhole.

Module 2:

Sewing a Keyhole Buttonhole

Tip
Garments with keyhole buttonholes are easier to unbutton than those with straight buttonholes, which is why keyhole buttonholes are often used on jackets and coats.

Step 1
Start by selecting the keyhole buttonhole setting on your machine, as well as your desired length, stitch bite, and stitch density.

Step 2
Now slip your fabric under the machine foot, with the needle aligned with the buttonhole marking, and lower the presser foot, just as you did for the straight buttonhole. Start the machine to begin the process.

Step 3
Gently guide the fabric as the machine creates the buttonhole automatically. The rounded portion of the buttonhole must be closest to the centerline.

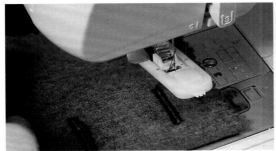

Step 4
Once the machine has completed the buttonhole, lift the presser foot and remove the fabric from the machine.

Step 5A
Trim the end threads on both sides of the keyhole buttonhole.

Step 5B
You have now sewn a machine-made keyhole buttonhole.

7 Knit Fabrics

Woven and knit fabrics behave very differently, so we begin this chapter with an **introduction to knit fabrics**. You will learn how they are structured, and discover the difference between a weft knit and a warp knit. Next, we introduce **knit fabric principles**, exploring in detail the key factors to consider when choosing the correct knit for your design: stretch, recovery, weight, and shrinkage. Find out about the different directions of stretch and stretch ratios.

Using the appropriate machine technique for seams and hems will ensure professional-looking knit garments every time. **Knit seam finishes** include overlocked and taped seams, safety-stitched seams, and chainstitched seams—all made using a serger (overlocker). **Knit hem finishes** can be made using overlocking, coverstitching, and chainstitch.

Choosing the best finish for a **knit neckline** is crucial for a polished result. We look at two options—an overlocked and chainstitched neckline, and a neckline that is overlocked and then completed with a machined coverstitch.

Zalando's casual jersey hoodie is accessorized with a cinch belt. September 2016.

Introduction to Knit Fabrics

Learning objectives

- ☐ Distinguish between woven and knit fabric structures, recognize different types of knit construction, and use the correct terminology

- ☐ Classify and describe the various weft knits—jersey/ single knits, purl knit, ribbed knits, and specialty knits such as interlock, ponte di Roma, and double knits

- ☐ Warp knits: recognize the difference between tricot and Raschel fabrics

- ☐ Gain an overview of common knit fibers and blends

Module 1:

Woven Fabric Structure

Plain woven fabric is created by interlacing two sets of yarns. Here we have a piece of #1 muslin (lightweight calico). The length, or warp, grain runs in a vertical direction, while the cross, or weft, grain runs in a horizontal direction.

With woven fabric, there is no stretch in the warp. There is a small amount of stretch in the weft (or the crosswise grain), but the greatest amount of stretch is along the bias, as demonstrated here.

The instructor also demonstrates on a small swatch how a single warp yarn on a woven fabric can be gently pulled out, leaving an empty space, mimicking a "run" in a pair of stockings.

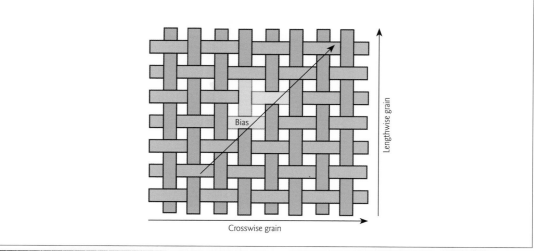

Woven fabric stretches a little on the cross grain   Woven fabric stretches mostly on the bias   A single warp yarn removed

A knit fabric is created by interlooping yarns using needles to form loops. As a new loop is pulled through an older loop, a basic stitch is made. The lengthwise row of stitches on a knit fabric is called a wale, and the crosswise row of stitches is called a course.

The basic stitch created when a new loop is pulled through an older loop is called a plain stitch, or a knit stitch. The reverse side of a knit stitch is called a purl stitch.

Patterns for knit garments are very different to patterns for woven garments. Woven garments include wearing ease—that is, the extra fabric needed to move in a garment—and additional design ease. Knit garments have very little ease, or no ease at all, which is sometimes referred to as "negative" ease.

A knit fabric may be constructed in a horizontal orientation, referred to as a weft knit (also known as a filling knit). Or it can be constructed in a vertical orientation, known as a warp knit.

The stretch of a knit fabric comes from the construction of the fabric and the type of fiber used for the yarn. Knit stitches allow the fabric to stretch in the crosswise grain, and sometimes in the lengthwise grain.

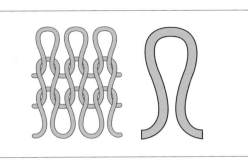

Interlooping yarns create knit fabric

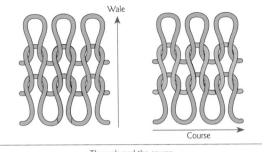

The wale and the course

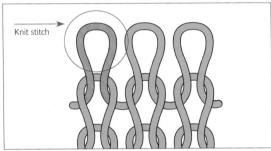

Forming the basic knit stitch

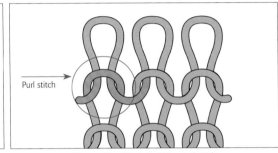

Reverse side of the knit stitch = purl stitch

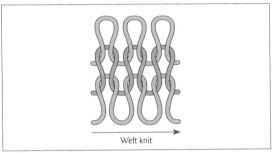

Horizontal knit fabrics = weft knit or filling knit

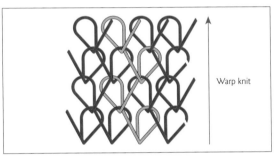

Vertical knit fabrics = warp knit

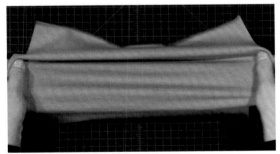

Knit fabric

The most familiar method for producing knit fabrics is by hand, using knitting needles. This produces a weft knit fabric.

Knit fabrics can also be produced by machine. The first type is a circular knitting machine, which produces a tube of weft knit fabric. Pantyhose (tights) are knitted on a circular machine.

The second type of machine is a flat-bed knitting machine. This produces flat yardage of knit fabric, which may be a weft or warp knit fabric.

Hand knitting

Circular knitting machine

Flat-bed knitting machines

Module 3:

Weft Knits

Weft Knits

Weft knits may be produced by hand or machine and are classified into three basic types, all of which make use of the simple knit and purl stitch:
1. Jersey knits/single knits
2. Ribbed knits
3. Purl knits

Jersey or Single Knits

Jersey knit fabrics have a "technical front" (displaying simple knit stitches) and a corresponding "technical back" (displaying purl stitches). This means that the face of the fabric is smooth, while the back is textured.

Jersey knits are produced on flat or circular knitting machines, with one set of needles in one needle bed. Jersey machines are also called plain knit or single knit machines. All needles pull the stitch in one direction.

The key characteristic of a jersey knit is its unbalanced structure (with knit stitch on the front and purl on the back), which gives the edges a tendency to curl. When one yarn breaks, it causes the unraveling of adjoining stitches in the wale known as a "run."

When knit fabrics are plied up on the cutting table, they should always be plied in the same direction so that the fabric will run from the hem of the garment up, and not from the neck down.

Tip
When knit fabric is laid on the table to be cut, each layer is called a ply. When multiple layers or plies are laid out, they are referred to as "plied up."

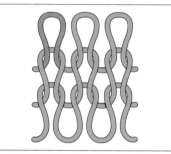
Jersey knit/single knit technical front

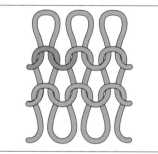
Jersey knit technical back

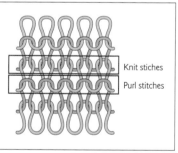
Knit stiches
Purl stitches
Purl knit

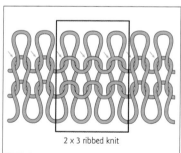
2 x 3 ribbed knit
Ribbed knit

Ribbed Knits

Rib-knit fabrics alternate wales of knit and purl stitches on both sides of the fabric. Each wale has all knit stitches or all purl stitches. Ribbed knits lie flat and do not curl up.

A 2 x 2 ribbed knit features two wales of knit stitches and two wales of purl stitches. A 2 x 3 ribbed knit has two wales of knit stitches and three wales of purl stitches

Ribbed knits are produced on flat or circular knitting machines with two sets of needles at right angles to each other and two needle beds.

Purl Knits

Purl-knit fabrics have a horizontal orientation of stitches. Alternate courses of knit and purl stitches result in a reversible fabric.

Purl knits are produced on a purl-knit machine, which can be flat or circular, and is sometimes called a links-links machine. This has two sets of needle beds and one set of double-headed latch needles. This is the most versatile type of knitting machine, able to produce plain, rib, and purl-knit fabrics.

Purl knits lie flat, do not curl, and have more stretch in the lengthwise direction. Their construction produces a thicker fabric, which is a better insulator than jersey fabric, so they are commonly used for sweaters and outerwear.

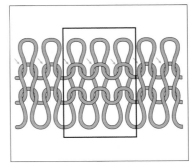

2 x 3 rib-knit fabric

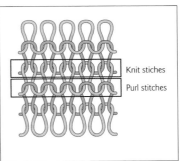

Knit stiches
Purl stitches

Purl-knit fabric

Specialty Knit Fabrics

Specialty weft knits are also available, including interlock (which is also called double knit or double jersey) and a double-knit variation called ponte di Roma.

Interlock

This rib-knit variation is made on an interlock machine, which produces columns of wales sitting directly behind each other. To identify interlock, spread the fabric crosswise: if the knit stitches sit one behind the other, the fabric is an interlock; if wales of knit stitches alternate with purl stitches, the fabric is a regular ribbed knit.

Interlock is a smooth, stable fabric that tends not to stretch out of shape. It is a better insulator and more expensive than a regular weft knit. It is also a good surface for printing by screen or heat transfer.

Ponte di Roma

This specialty ribbed knit is produced on a rib machine or an interlock machine. Close stitches result in good stability, good shape retention, and a fabric that is thicker and heavier than jersey.

Double knits

Simple types of double knit are similar on both sides, while complex double knits can look different on the face and back, and sometimes feature a patterned or design effect.

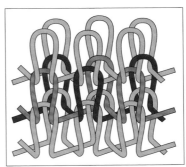

Interlock fabric

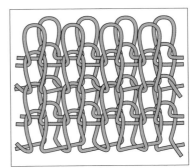

Ponte di Roma

Module 4:
Warp Knits

Warp Knits

Warp knits are only produced on a flat-bed machine. The yarns of a warp knit traverse from side to side in a vertical orientation to create the fabric. The two main types of warp knits are tricot and Raschel fabric.

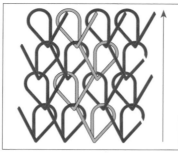

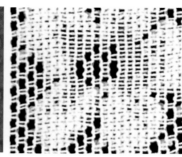

Warp knit   Tricot fabric (face)   Tricot fabric (back)   Raschel fabric

Tricot Fabric

Tricot fabrics are lighter in weight and more commonly produced than Raschel knits. On the reverse side of a tricot knit, the yarns create a "Z" pattern. Tricot knits are mostly used in lingerie and loungewear. They are also used as a lightweight fusible interfacing in the apparel industry.

Raschel Fabric

This warp knit is similar to tricot but requires a Raschel knitting machine. Raschel fabrics range from lacelike material and power net fabrics for foundation garments and swimwear, through to heavy blankets. A Raschel machine can also produce three-dimensional fabrics, such as the waffle-surfaced fabric used for thermal underwear.

Module 5:
Knit Fibers

Knit Fibers

Knit fabrics come in a variety of fibers, such as:
- Wool
- Acetate
- Cotton
- Rayon
- Spandex
- Cashmere
- Bamboo
- Polyester

The most common knit fabric is a blend of fibers such as cotton/polyester. Knits may also be made of a single fiber, such as wool, silk, or even linen.

Knit fabrics may be blends of:
- Cotton/spandex
- Modal/spandex
- Nylon/spandex
- Rayon/spandex

In European countries, spandex is known as elastane, and rayon is known as viscose. Lycra is a brand name of spandex.

On a garment label, blends are often shown with a forward slash "/" between the fibers. The label may also indicate the percentage of each fiber in the yarn.

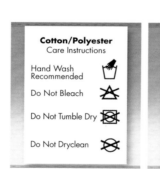

Knit Fabric Principles

Learning objectives

☐ Know the key characteristics of knit fabrics: stretch, recovery, weight, and shrinkage

☐ Establish if a knit has one-, two-, three-, or four-way stretch, and use the finger stretch recovery test

☐ Use stretch categories and the stretch percentage chart, and establish the stretch ratio on a sample of flat fabric

☐ Calculate and check the stretch on a dress form, to help you choose the correct sloper (block)

Tools and supplies:

- Dress form (tailor's dummy)
- Adhesive ¼" (6mm) style tape
- Safety pin
- Fine spandex (elastene) ribbed knit
- Ponte di Roma
- Matte jersey
- Single-knit jersey
- Single-knit spandex (elastene) jersey
- Ribbed knit
- Fabric Weight Chart
- Stretch Percentage Chart
- Stretch Calculations on the Dress Form Chart

When purchasing or designing with knit fabrics, there are four key characteristics that you need to take into account:

1. Stretch
2. Recovery
3. Weight
4. Shrinkage

Stretch

Knits can be stretched vertically, horizontally, or in both directions, depending on their knit structure and fiber content. The degree to which they stretch also varies. Both of these aspects will be discussed in detail in Modules 2 and 3.

Recovery

In addition to the direction in which a knit fabric stretches, and to what degree, you also need to consider whether or not it has good recovery. In other words, when stretched in both directions, does the fabric return to its original state? Or does it remain "stretched out" and, therefore, increased in size?

Here the instructor is poking a knit fabric with her finger to check the recovery. We all have seen knit pants (trousers) where the knees remain stretched out after only being worn a few times. In the textile industry, this unrecovered stretch is known as "growth."

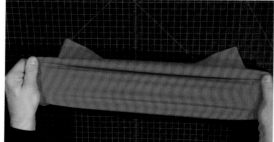
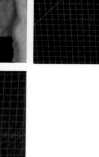

Testing for recovery

Weight

As with woven fabrics, weight should always be considered when designing different types of knit garments. For example, a knit T-shirt would require a much lighter-weight fabric than, say, a pair of pants or a jacket.

5oz or 170 grams

T-shirt jersey

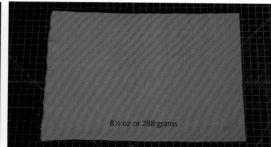

8½ oz or 288 grams

Ponte knit

The weight of knit fabrics can be expressed as the number of ounces per square yard, or the number of grams per square meter. For example, a jersey that is suitable for a T-shirt may weigh 5oz (142g), while a ponte knit that is perfect for a pair of pants may weigh 8½oz (241g).

The chart below shows the weight of our samples, ranging from extra light through to extra heavy. You may notice a discrepancy in the description of a fabric versus the weight classification. For example, our navy rib knit is described as "lightweight" yet it falls in the heavy category on the chart, and our royal blue rib knit is described as "heavyweight" and falls into the "extra heavy" classification. A more familiar example is the classification and description of T-shirts. T-shirts may be described as lightweight (weighing 4⅓oz/123g), heavyweight (weighing 6⅛oz/174g), and standard (at 5½oz/156g).

Fabric Weight Chart

Fabric Weight	Oz/Sq Yard	Grams/Sq Meter	Weight of our Samples
Top Weight = below 8oz (227g)			
Extra Light	2–4oz	68–136g	
Light	4–6oz	136–204g	5⅖oz/153g (gray) single knit jersey
Bottom Weight = 8oz (227g) or above			
Medium	6–8oz	204–272g	7⅘oz/221g (violet) jersey
Medium Heavy	8–10oz	272–339g	8¼oz/234g (orange) Ponte knit
Heavy	10–12oz	339–407g	10¼oz/291g (navy) lightweight rib knit
			10⅖oz/295g (cranberry wine) double knit
Extra Heavy	12–14oz	407–475g	13¹/₁₀oz/371g (royal blue) heavyweight rib knit
			13½oz (burnt wine) fine rib knit

Shrinkage

Shrinking of knit fabrics may occur for several reasons:
- If the knit fabric was not finished properly at the mill, it will shrink when the garment is pressed during the final stage of production.
- When the fabric reaches the factory for cutting and sewing, it may relax once it is spread and plied up on the table prior to cutting. Cut-and-sew factories should always spread a fabric out and allow it to relax overnight before cutting the garment parts.
- When a fabric is knitted and then rolled onto tubes, the stitches can distort and stretch out of shape. If a fabric is cut and stitched while in this distorted state, the final garment will shrink when the fabric relaxes.
- Another type of shrinkage can occur in the repeated laundering of a finished garment. The use of preshrunk fabric, or altering a pattern to compensate for the eventual shrinkage, may address this issue.

One-, two-, and four-way stretch

The direction of stretch in a knit fabric can vary, but there are three main categories: one-, two-, and four-way stretch.

Knit fabrics that are described as having *one-way stretch* are those that stretch only in the cross direction and not in the length. This is due to the structure of the knit stitches.

Many knits have the ability to stretch in both directions, but the term *two-way stretch* is mostly used to definine a knit fabric that can stretch 50 percent or more in the crosswise direction, and 50 to 70 percent in the lengthwise direction.

Four-way stretch is found in fabrics knitted with yarns containing a high percentage of spandex (elastene), resulting in extreme stretch of 100 percent or more in both directions.

One-way Stretch

This 100 percent wool single-knit jersey stretches in the cross (from selvage to selvage), but not in the length. This would therefore be categorized as a one-way stretch knit.

In addition, the instructor is determining how good the recovery of the jersey is by poking a finger into it. This particular fabric is shown to recover well.

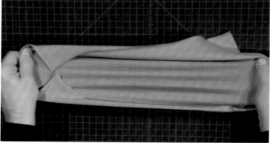

Stretch in the cross

No stretch in the length

The finger test

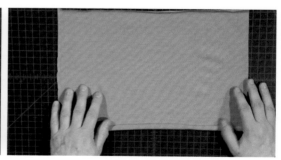

The fabric has recovered well

Two-way Stretch

Now we will take a look at a two-way stretch knit. The fabric sample shown here is a single-knit jersey blend of rayon, bamboo, and spandex. In addition to testing the stretch factor of this fabric, the instructor will test its recovery by measuring the swatch before and after stretching. Before stretching, our swatch measures 14" (35.5cm) wide by 9" (23cm) long.

The instructor now stretches the fabric in the cross and in the length, confirming that it has a true two-way stretch—50 percent crosswise stretch, and between 50 and 70 percent lengthwise stretch.

The swatch is then laid flat on the table again and smoothed out. After stretching, this jersey still measures 14" (35.5cm) wide by 9" (23cm) long, which means that it would be a good choice for a tight-fitting, close-to-the-body silhouette.

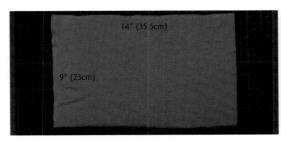

The initial swatch: 14" (35.5cm) across and 9" (23cm) in the length

The swatch is stretched both crosswise and lengthwise

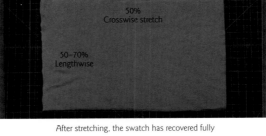

After stretching, the swatch has recovered fully

Four-way Stretch

To demonstrate the amount of stretch that a fabric with four-way stretch has in the cross and length directions, we have chosen a rayon/spandex single-knit jersey that contains 8 percent spandex.

As the instructor pulls in both the length and the width direction, she demonstrates the extreme amount of stretch possible in both directions. Remember, to qualify as having four-way stretch, a fabric must have at least 100 percent stretch in both the cross and the length.

Next, the instructor carries out the finger stretch-recovery test to demonstrate that, due to the high percentage of spandex in this fabric, it has excellent stretch recovery and would be an ideal choice for activewear, shapewear, or swimwear, where optimal stretch is required. The fabric recovers nicely as the instructor places it back on the table within the same grid marks on the mat.

Rayon/spandex single-knit fabric swatch

Pulling in the width direction

Pulling in the length direction

The finger test

The sample demonstrates good stretch recovery

Stretch-ratio Categories

Stretch ratio is the degree of stretch of a particular knit, determined both by its knit structure and the type of fiber used to make it. There are six categories of stretch percentage that you will need to be familiar with when planning a knit design:

Stable knit
Moderate-stretch knit
Two-way stretch knit
Super-stretch knit
Ribbed knit
Four-way stretch knit

The stretch percentage for super-stretch and ribbed knits is the same.

Before creating any knit pattern, you should always test your knit fabrics for stretch, as demonstrated in the exercises that follow. If a knit fabric stretches less than 18 percent, a pattern for a woven garment should be used.

An easy method for determining the stretch of a fabric is by using the Knit Rule made by Fairgate. However, for our demonstration we will use a tape measure. Our stretch ratios will be based on a 5" (12.5cm) measurement, as with the Fairgate Knit Rule.

A Fairgate Knit Rule provides an easy way of determining stretch. Measure a 5" (12.5cm) section of fabric and then record the degree to which the sample will stretch

Knit Fabrics

Stretch Percentage Chart

Each of the six categories of knit is determined by its stretch percentage range, as summarized in the chart below, based on a 5" (12.5cm) stretch ratio.

Fabric Type	Percentage of Stretch in Crosswise Direction	5" (12.5cm) Stretches to...
Stable one-way stretch knit	Stretches 18%* to 25%	5⅞" (14.5cm) to 6¼" (16cm)
Moderate stretch knit	Stretches 25% to 50%	6¼" (16cm) to 7½" (19cm)
Two-way stretch knit	Stretches 50% or more in the crosswise and 50% to 75% in the lengthwise direction	7½" (19cm) to 10" (25.5cm)
Super-stretch knit	Stretches 75% to 100% in the crosswise	Up to 10" (25.5cm) or more
Ribbed knit	Stretches up to 100%	Up to 10" (25.5cm) or more
Four-way stretch knit (Lycra)	Stretches 100% in both directions. Addition of Lycra contributes to stretch	10" (25.5cm) or more

*If a fabric stretches less than 18%, a pattern for a woven garment should be used

$$\text{Percentage of Stretch} = \frac{\text{New Length} - \text{Original Length}}{\text{Original Length}} \times 100$$

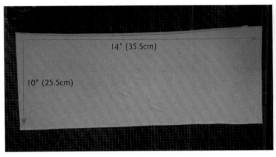

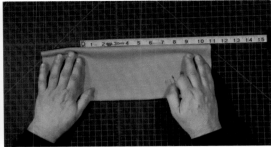

Stable knit: stretches 18 to 25%

First we will demonstrate the degree of stretch in a stable knit. Our sample is a 100 percent wool single-knit jersey with one-way stretch, measuring 14" (35.5cm) wide by 10" (25.5cm) long.

Fold the fabric over in a crosswise direction, then line up the folded edge of the fabric with your tape measure, with about 3" (7.5cm) of fabric extending out beyond the start of the tape measure.

Use a safety pin to pin the two layers together at the "0" point on the tape measure. Place another pin at the 5" (12.5cm) mark.

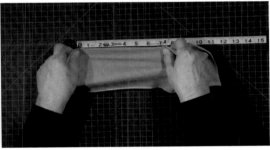

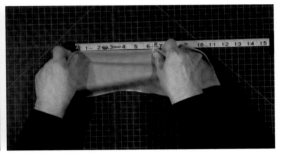

With both hands firmly gripping the fabric at the pins, pull the fabric to the right while holding it in place at the "0" point.

As you pull the fabric, you will feel it start to stiffen as the knit stitches are pulled to their maximum extent. Reduce some of the pressure so that the fabric is less strained. If folds appear, the fabric has been stretched too far.

Since this fabric stretched to a maximum of 6¼" (15.9cm), it has a stretch factor of approximately 25 percent. Referring to the chart opposite, that places this wool jersey in the stable knit category.

To calculate the percentage of stretch, we used the formula on page 226:
1. New Length minus Original Length
   6¼" minus 5" (15.9cm minus 12.7cm) = 1¼" (3.2cm)
2. Divide the answer by the Original Length
   1¼" divided by 5" (3.2cm divided by 12.7cm) = 0.25
3. Multiply the new answer by 100 for the percentage
   0.25 x 100 = 25%

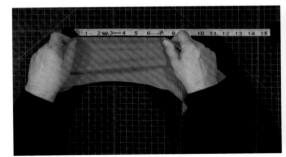

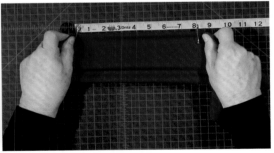

Moderate knit: stretches 25 to 50%

We are now testing a swatch of cotton/spandex ponte di Roma, 14" (35.5cm) wide by 10" (25.5cm) long. Here the swatch grows to almost 7" (18cm), which puts it into the moderate-stretch category. Even though this fabric stretches in both directions, it does not stretch to more than 50 percent in the cross, and therefore would not be considered a two-way stretch knit.

Two-way stretch knit: stretches 50% and over

To demonstrate an example of a two-way stretch knit, we are testing a fine ribbed knit made of viscose and 5 percent spandex. Repeating the process of pinning and then stretching the fabric, we can see that it stretches to approximately 8" (20.5cm) in the cross—a stretch factor that places it in the category of a two-way stretch knit.

Super-stretch knit: stretches 100%
This swatch is a modal/spandex single-knit jersey containing 8 percent spandex. After pinning and stretching, this stretches to around 10" (25.5cm)—a 100 percent stretch factor, which puts this fabric in the category of super-stretch knits.

Ribbed knit: stretches to 100%+
Next we will demonstrate the stretch factor of a 2 x 2 100 percent tubular wool rib, measuring 11" (28cm) wide. The sample portion grows to beyond the 11" (28cm) mark—more than 100 percent—placing it in the ribbed-knit category.

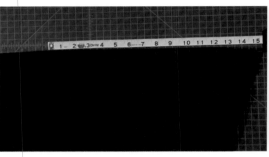

Matte jersey
To get an idea of the stretch factor and category of another popular knit fabric, here we will demonstrate the stretch factor of a 100 percent rayon matte jersey.

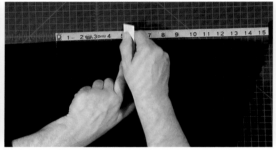

Use a piece of chalk to mark and measure the fabric. Here we are placing a mark at point "0" and then measuring over 5" (12.7cm) and making another mark.

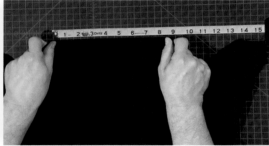

Repeating the process of holding and pulling the fabric, we find that this matte jersey grows to 8" (20.5cm), or 60 percent, which puts it into the two-way stretch-knit category.

Step 1A

To evaluate the stretch of a particular knit so that you can decide which knit sloper (block) to use, you can test your fabric on a dress form. This will also enable you to see first hand how your fabric will perform on the body. We will demonstrate how to test five different knit categories on the bustline of a dress form.

Step 1B

Before we can test these fabrics we must first apply style tape to the dress form—from bust point to bust point, all the way round the form. Make sure that your style tape is parallel to the floor. Anchor pins every few inches to act as guides; you will then be able to feel the bustline, or bust level, through the fabric.

Step 2A

We have also style taped the center back. The tape begins at the neck...

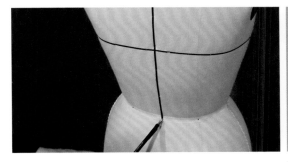

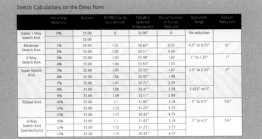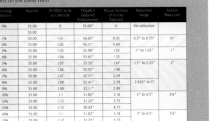

Stretch Calculations on the Dress Form

	Percentage Reduction	Bustline	DIVIDED to % as a decimal	=EQUALS Reduced Measurement	Actual Number of Inches Reduced	Returnon Range	Sample Reduction
Stable 1-Way Stretch Knit	0%	35.00	0	35.00"	0	No reduction	
		35.00					
Moderate Stretch Knit	1%	35.00	1.01	34.65"	0.35	0.5" to 0.75"	½"
	2%	35.00	1.02	34.31"	0.69		
2-Way Stretch Knit	3%	35.00	1.03	33.98"	1.02	1" to 1.25"	1"
	4%	35.00	1.04	33.65"	1.35		
Super Stretch Knit	5%	35.00	1.05	33.33"	1.67	1.5" to 2.25"	2"
	6%	35.00	1.06	33.02"	1.98		
	7%	35.00	1.07	32.71"	2.29		
	8%	35.00	1.08	32.41"	2.59	2.625" to 3"	
	9%	35.00	1.09	32.11"	2.89		
Ribbed Knit	10%	35.00	1.1	31.82"	3.18	3" to 4.5"	3½"
	12%	35.00	1.12	31.25"	3.75		
	15%	35.00	1.15	30.43"	4.75		
4-Way Stretch Knit Spandex/Lycra	10%	35.00	1.1	31.82"	3.18	3" to 4.5"	3½"
	12%	35.00	1.12	31.25"	3.75		
	15%	35.00	1.15	20.43"	4.57		

Tip

A sloper is a basic foundation block, without seam allowances, from which various design stylizations are created. Slopers can be developed through the pattern-making process using body measurements, or by draping them on a dress form.

...and ends at the waist.

Step 2B

To follow along with this project, you can refer to the measurements provided in the Stretch Calculations on the Dress Form chart on page 230. This chart illustrates calculations based on a 35" (89cm) bust measurement.

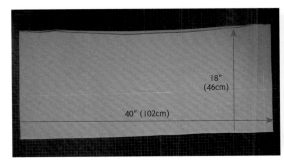

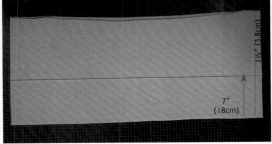

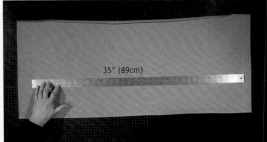

Step 3A

First we will be testing a stable knit—a 100 percent wool single-knit jersey—first. Our sample piece measures 40" (102cm) in the cross direction by 18" (46cm) in the length direction.

Step 3B

Chalk mark the fabric 1½" (3.8cm) in from the right-side length edge. This will represent center back. Also chalk mark the bust level, 7" (18cm) up from the bottom edge, across the width of the fabric.

Step 3C

Using a 36" (91cm) metal ruler, measure over on the bust level from the 1½" (3.8cm) mark, the distance of your bust width measurement, and place a chalk mark. In this case the bust circumference is 35" (89cm).

Stretch Calculations on the Dress Form

	Percentage Reduction	Bustline	Divided by % as a decimal	Equals Reduced Measurement	Actual Number of Inches Reduced	Reduction Range	Sample Reduction
Stable one-way stretch knit	0%	35.00"	0	35.00"	0	No reduction	
		35.00"					
Moderate stretch knit	1%	35.00"	1.01	34.65"	0.35	0.5" to 0.75"	½"
	2%	35.00"	1.02	34.31"	0.69		
Two-way stretch knit	3%	35.00"	1.03	33.98"	1.02	1" to 1.25"	1"
	4%	35.00"	1.04	33.65"	1.35		
Super-stretch knit	5%	35.00"	1.05	33.33"	1.67	1.5" to 2.25"	2"
	6%	35.00"	1.06	33.02"	1.98		
	7%	35.00"	1.07	32.71"	2.29		
	8%	35.00"	1.08	32.41"	2.59	2.625" to 3"	
	9%	35.00"	1.09	32.11"	2.89		
Ribbed knit	10%	35.00"	1.1	31.82"	3.18	3" to 4.5"	3½"
	12%	35.00"	1.12	31.25"	3.75		
	15%	35.00"	1.15	30.43"	4.57		
Four-way stretch knit (spandex)	10%	35.00"	1.1	31.82"	3.18	3" to 4.5"	3½"
	12%	35.00"	1.12	31.25"	3.75		
	15%	35.00"	1.15	30.43"	4.57		

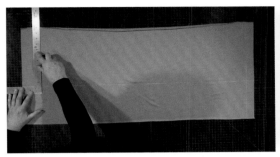

Step 4
Resting the L square on the bust circumference mark, square a line off the bust level, the length of the fabric, first on one side and then on the other. This line will represent the stable knit marking.

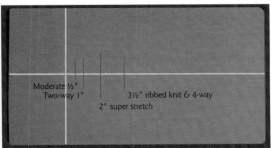

Moderate ½"
Two-way 1"
2" super stretch
3½" ribbed knit & 4-way

Step 5
Next, chalk four additional knit-category marks on the bust level, all measured from the *stable knit* vertical line: one at ½" (1.3cm) away, representing a *moderate stretch knit*; one at 1" (2.5cm) away, representing a *two-way stretch knit*; another at 2" (5cm), representing a *super-stretch knit*; and the last at 3½" (9cm) representing a *ribbed knit* and a *four-way stretch knit*.

Tip
You may wonder why the fabric has been marked at such small increments for each category. After testing many fabrics, the instructor determined a working range of reductions to apply to each category that would create a good fit, and prevent broken stitches, pulled seams, and fabric distortion. The *Stretch Calculations on the Dress Form* illustrates mathematically how these amounts were determined.

Step 6A
Align the bust level of the fabric with the dress form's bust style tape and along the center back. Pin the fabric to the form at the shoulder, the center-back/bust-level intersection, and above the bust level along center back.

Anchor pins along the center back, working down to the waist.

Step 6B
Carefully wrap the fabric around the form, keeping the chalked bustline parallel to the style-taped bustline of the dress form.

Bring the fabric to the center front...

Step 6C
...and across the apex, continuing to match the bustline of the fabric with that of the dress form.

Step 6D
Now match the center-back/bustline intersection of the fabric to the stable knit mark on the fabric.

Step 6E

Once these are matched, insert a pin to hold the fabric in place at this point.

Insert additional holding pins at the top of the fabric to keep it from curling over.

Check with your fingers to make sure that the bustline mark on the fabric is level with the style tape bustline, feeling for the pins underneath.

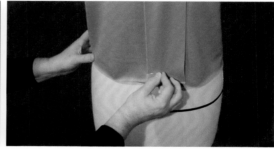

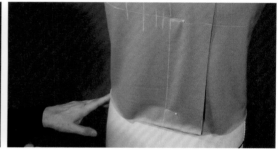

Step 6F

Continue to check, feeling for the pins on the bustline style tape at the back, the sides, and the front, making sure that the fabric's bust level is level with the dress form's bust level all the way round, and that there are no stress points on the fabric along the bust.

Step 6G

Pin the waist at center back, aligning the chalk lines with the center back of the dress form.

Step 6H

There is no fitting ease or design ease with this fabric and it fits the body exactly around the bust at 35" (89cm), which is also the dress form's bust circumference.

Step 7A

Since the fabric hangs nicely and has no stress or stretch, you could therefore choose a stable knit sloper if you were to use this fabric for your garment design.

Next, test the fabric to the next chalk line—the moderate stretch knit marking.

Unpin the fabric along the center back in preparation for repeating the testing process.

This time, align the moderate stretch knit mark with the center-back/bustline intersection.

Pin the waist at the center-back chalk mark.

Step 7B
Now test the moderate stretch knit by turning the form to the front and, while making sure that the bustlines are level, evaluate if there are any stress lines between the right and left apex points.

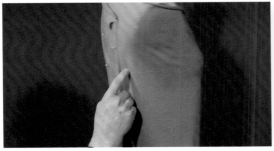

Step 7C
Since there still no noticeable stress lines at the moderate stretch knit marking, this sloper could be used, especially if your design called for a slightly tighter fit than what you would get from using a stable knit sloper.

Step 8A
Next, see what happens to this jersey when you repeat the steps and test the fabric to the two-way stretch mark.

Step 8B
Once you have unpinned the fabric from the center back, align the two-way stretch mark to the dress form's center-back/bustline intersection. Note how the instructor has to tug on the fabric to get it to align.

Pin the fabric in place at this point.

Step 8C
As she aligns the bustline of the fabric with the bustline of the dress form, the instructor finds that there is a fair amount of pulling going on between the apex points, thereby demonstrating that this would not be an acceptable choice of knit sloper for her design.

Choosing a knit sloper that is too tight for the stretch of a particular fabric will result in a poorly fitting garment with cracking and splitting seams.

Step 9A

Although we already have demonstrated that a two-way stretch sloper would not be a good choice for this fabric, the instructor demonstrates the fabric pinned to the super-stretch knit mark.

Step 9B

The result demonstrates that a super-stretch knit sloper would absolutely not work.

Step 10

You can repeat these steps to determine the stretch factor for any stretch fabric when planning your slopers and patterns.

Knit Fabrics

Knit Seam Finishes

Learning objectives

☐ Create basic overlocked seams for lightweight to medium-weight knits: the three-thread overlocked seam, the safety stitch seam, and the chainstitch seam

☐ Find out how to tape a shoulder seam

☐ Explore the basic sewing machine seam, the zigzag seam

Tools and supplies:

- Wool single-knit jersey
- Ponte di Roma spandex (elastane) knit
- Matching cotton thread
- Cotton twill tape, ¼" (6mm) wide

- Overlocker (serger)
- Sewing machine

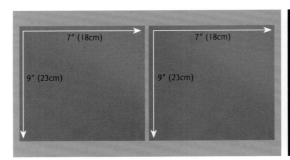

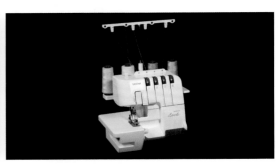

Step 1A

For this lesson you will need to prepare two pieces of wool single-knit jersey measuring 7" (18cm) in the width grain and 9" (23cm) in the length grain. This seam finish can also be used on other types of lightweight to medium-weight knits.

Step 1B

Mark an "X" with tailor's chalk on the wrong side of each jersey piece, then pair them up with the right sides of the fabric facing each other.

Step 2A

We will be demonstrating this lesson using a Brother 3034D Lock overlocker set to "overlock," with two threaded needles.

Step 2B

Raise the overlock machine foot and feed the top length edges of the paired jersey pieces under it. Then lower the foot.

Step 3

Now sew along the edge. Avoid stretching the fabric, and always check the bottom edges of the piece as you sew to be sure that they are still matching. The small knife attached to the overlocker will have a tendency to trim the edge—some trimming is fine, but try not to trim too much or you will alter the seam width.

Step 4A

A handy seamstress tip when ending the seam is to have a small scrap of knit fabric ready. When you reach the end, raise the foot, place the fabric scrap under the foot, lower the foot, and then sew off and onto the end of the scrap. This helps to keep the end threads from breaking.

Step 4B

Now clip the end threads between the scrap and your sewn fabric pieces.

Step 4C

You have now finished sewing an overlocked knit seam. This seam is used in activewear, sportswear, and swimwear, where a thin seam allowance is desired.

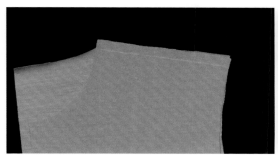

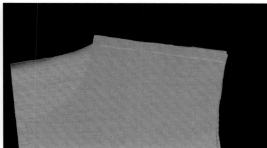

Step 1

For this lesson you will need to prepare a mock front and back shoulder out of wool single-knit knit jersey and mark the wrong sides with an "X." Then place the right sides together.

Step 2

Chalk the shoulder seam at ½" (1.3cm) away from the raw edge.

Step 3

Center the ¼" (6mm)-wide twill tape over the width of the shoulder seam and clip the end with your fabric shears.

Step 4

Pin the fabric layers and the twill tape together along the shoulder seam.

Step 5A

Sew the tape to the shoulder using your regular sewing machine at approximately 10 stitches per inch (spi; 2.5mm stitch length), starting with a backtack. Remove the pins as you stitch.

Step 5B

Be sure to control the twill tape with your fingers so that the fabric does not stretch beyond the twill tape at the end of the stitching. Sew a backtack and trim the end threads.

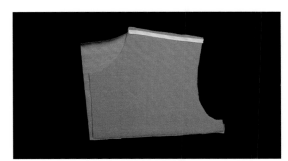

Step 6

You have now finished taping and sewing a knit shoulder seam. This method will stabilize the seam and keep it from stretching.

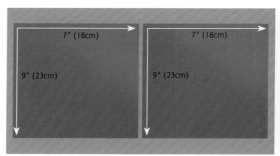

Step 1A
For this lesson you will need to prepare two pieces of wool jersey measuring 7" (18cm) in the width grain and 9" (23cm) in the length grain. This seam finish is appropriate for all lightweight and medium-weight knit fabrics.

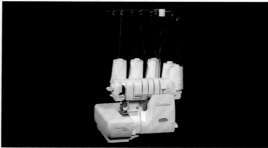

Step 2A
We will be demonstrating this lesson using a Baby Lock Evolution overlocker set to "safety stitch." This stitch consists of a chainstitch seam and an overlocked edge finish.

Step 2B
Lift the presser foot and feed the length grain of your paired knit pieces, right sides together, under the foot.

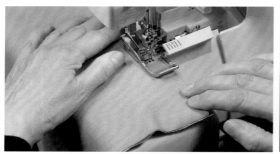

Step 3A
Using the machine foot as a guide, begin sewing. Check the bottom edges of the piece as you sew to be sure that they still match and that the pieces have not stretched while sewing. The knife of the overlocker will trim the edge—some trimming is fine, but do not trim too much or you will alter the seam width.

Step 3B
Run off a few stitches once you reach the end, then carefully clip the end threads.

Step 4A
Note the type of stitch that is created on one side of the piece.

Step 4B
Then flip the piece over to see the chainstitch seam that has been created on the other side.

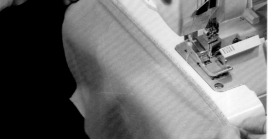

Step 4C
The threads in this type of knit seam, when stretched, will not crack, making it an excellent choice of finish for activewear.

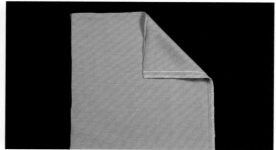

Step 4D
You have now finished sewing a safety stitch seam.

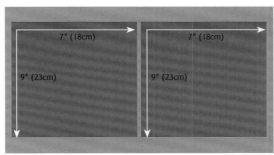

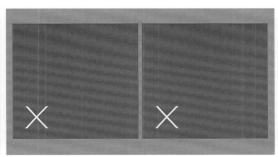

Step 1A

For this lesson you will need to prepare two pieces of wool ponte di Roma measuring 7" (18cm) in the width grain and 9" (23cm) in the length grain. This seam finish works for all lightweight and medium-weight knit fabrics.

Place an "X" in chalk on each piece to designate the wrong side of the fabric.

Step 1B

Chalk a ½" (1.3cm) seam allowance from the length edge on the wrong side of one of the pieces.

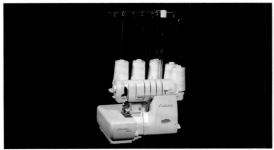

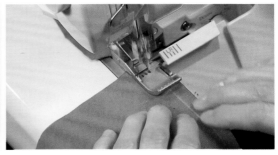

Step 2

We will be demonstrating this lesson using a Baby Lock Evolution overlocker set to "chainstitch."

Step 3A

Begin with the right sides of your fabric pieces facing each other and with the right length edge aligned with the right side of the machine foot. Note that our small fabric scrap, which we will use to start the stitch, is already under the machine foot.

Step 3B

Make the first few stitches on the fabric scrap and then continue to feed your fabric pieces under the foot as you stitch along your chalked stitching line.

Step 3C

Always check the bottom edges of the piece as you sew to be sure that they are still matching and that the pieces have not stretched while sewing. As mentioned previously, the small knife attached to the machine will have a tendency to trim the edge. However, while some trimming is fine, try not to trim too much or you will alter the seam width.

Step 3D

As you reach the end of the seam, grab another small piece of scrap knit fabric and run the stitch off and onto the scrap.

Step 4

Then clip the end threads.

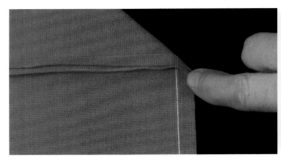

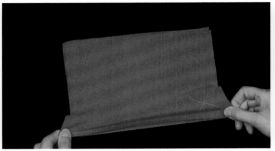

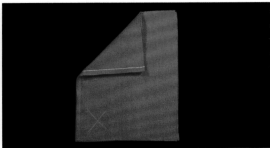

Step 5A
Note that the top machine stitches look like regular lockstitch machine stitches, while the lower machine stitch is like a chainstitch.

Step 5B
When you stretch the seam you will find that the stitches will not break or crack.

Step 5C
You have now finished sewing a chainstitch seam. This seam is most often used on double knits and rayon matte jerseys where the edges do not curl.

Module 5:

Zigzag Seam

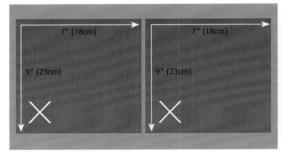

Step 1A
For this lesson you will need to prepare two pieces of wool ponte di Roma measuring 7" (18cm) in the width grain and 9" (23cm) in the length grain. Chalk an "X" on both pieces to designate the wrong side of the fabric.

Step 1B
We will be demonstrating this lesson on a Brother Pacesetter 3700 sewing machine. We set the width of the zigzag stitch to ⅛" (3mm), and the stitch length to approximately 12 stitches per inch (spi; 2.1mm stitch length).

Step 2A
With the right sides of the fabric pieces together, feed the length edge of your fabric pieces under the machine foot at 1" (2.5cm) away from the edge.

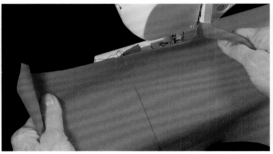

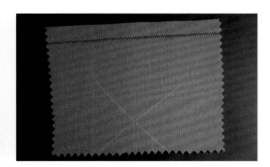

Sew from the top to the bottom.

Step 2B
Turn your pieces to the right side to see the finished seam stitch. Then clip the end threads.

Step 3
Trim your seam allowance to ⅜" (1cm). You have now finished sewing a zigzag seam, which will work for all light- to medium-weight knit fabrics.

Knit Hem
Finishes

Learning objectives

☐ Make a hem with an overlock machine, both the overlocked hem with catch stitch and the chainstitch hem

☐ Use a coverstitch machine to create a two-needle coverstitch hem and a three-needle coverstitch hem

Tools and supplies:

- Single-knit jersey
- Ponte di Roma spandex (elastane) knit
- Matching cotton thread
- Overlocker (serger)
- Coverstitch machine

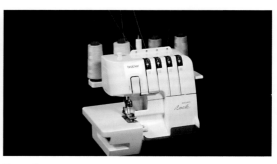

Step 1A

For this lesson you will need to prepare a piece of wool ponte di Roma measuring 10" (25.5cm) in the width grain and 8" (20.5cm) in the length grain. You could also use a double knit or other medium-weight knit fabric.

Step 1B

On the wrong side of the fabric piece, measure up 1½" (3.8cm) from the width edge and mark your hem fold with tailor's chalk.

Step 2A

We will be demonstrating this lesson using a Brother 3034D Lock overlocker set to "overlock," with two threaded needles.

Step 2B

Raise the foot of the overlock machine and feed the wrong-side width edge of the fabric under it. Then lower the foot.

Step 3

Sew along the width edge of the piece. Note that the small knife attached to the overlock machine will have a tendency to trim the edge if you sew too close. Some trimming is fine, but try not to trim too much or you will alter the hem width.

Step 4A

When you reach the end of the fabric piece, run off an extra few stitches.

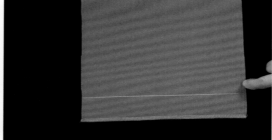

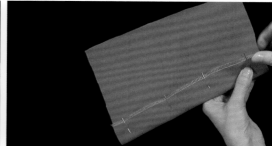

Step 4B

Now raise the machine foot and clip the end threads close to the fabric.

Step 5A

Turn up the hem along your chalked hem foldline.

Step 5B

Pin the hem in place, with your pins set at right angles to the hem.

Step 6A

Thread a hand-sewing needle with a single strand of knotted thread, then insert the needle below the overlocked edge on the underside of the hem. Pull the thread to the top.

Step 6B

Now, with the needle pointing away from you, pick up a single yarn from the body fabric with the point of your needle.

Step 6C

Insert the needle back into the hem at the first stitch to lock the first stitch in place. Then pull the thread through to the top.

Step 7

The second stitch is spaced ½" (1.3cm) away from the first. With the needle pointing away from you, repeat the process of picking up a single yarn from the body fabric with the point of your needle. Then pull the thread through to the top.

Step 8

Now place a third stitch ½" (1.3cm) away from the previous one—again, with the needle pointing away from you and the stitch positioned below the hem overlocked stitch. Each stitch should be about 1/16" (2mm) long and sewn as loose as possible so that the stitches will not crack when the fabric is stretched.

Step 9

Continue to sew the hem by repeating these steps, removing the pins as you progress. Remember to keep your stitches loose since they will need to stretch when the fabric stretches, otherwise the thread will break.

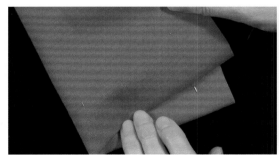

Step 10

Turn the fabric piece over to the right side to check that none of your stitches are visible.

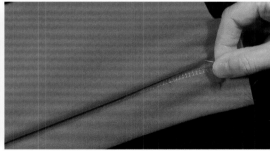

Step 11

Test the thread tension by stretching the fabric to be sure that your stitches do not break.

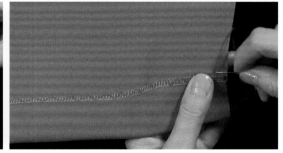

Step 12

When you reach the end, you will sew a double lockstitch. To do this, sew one stitch on the body fabric and a corresponding stitch on the hem and form a loop. Pass your needle through the loop to lock the stitch into place. Repeat this process to create a second lockstitch, then clip the end thread.

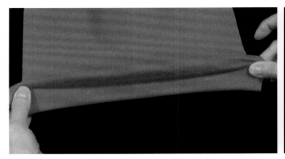

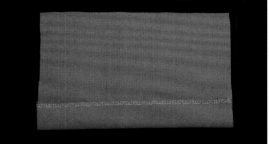

Step 13A
Turn the fabric over to the right side to check once more that, when the hem is stretched, your stitches do not crack or break.

Step 13B
You have now finished sewing an overlocked hem edge with a catch stitch hem.

Module 2:

Two-needle
Coverstitch Hem

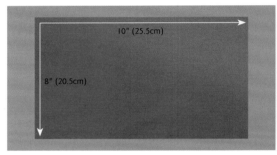

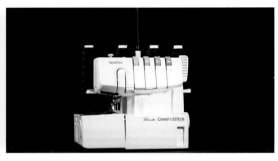

Step 1
For this lesson you will need to prepare a piece of wool jersey measuring 10" (25.5cm) in the width grain and 8" (20.5cm) in the length grain. This hem finish is appropriate for all lightweight and medium-weight knit fabrics.

Step 2
On the wrong side of the fabric piece, mark an "X" with tailor's chalk. Measure up 1½" (3.8cm) from the width edge and mark your hem fold.

Step 3
We will be demonstrating this lesson using a Brother 2340CV Pacesetter Coverstitch machine, with two threaded needles.

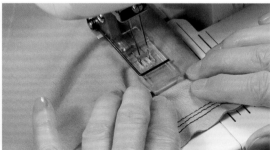

Step 4A
Fold the hem up along the foldline, with the wrong side of the fabric piece face up. Using the left side of the machine foot as your guide, position your hem edge under the foot. Make your first few stitches on a fabric scrap before progressing on to the wool jersey piece. This will avoid any broken threads.

Step 4B
Gently guide the fabric through the machine. Be careful not to pull the fabric as you sew.

Step 5
When you reach the end, have another small fabric scrap ready to sew onto to prevent the threads from breaking.

Step 6
Then clip the end threads.

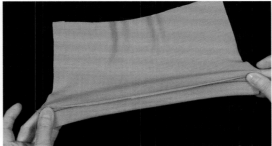

Step 7A
Note how the threads do not break when the hem is stretched, which is important for activewear and swimwear garments.

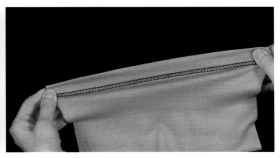

Step 7B
Turn the piece over to the right side to see the coverstitching. Note how, when the fabric is stretched, the stitch also stretches.

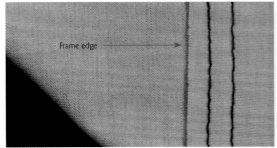

Frame edge →

Step 8A
You may wish to trim the remaining hem allowance to within ⅛" (3mm) of the edge.

Step 8B
You have now finished sewing a two-needle coverstitch hem.

Module 3:

Three-needle
Coverstitch Hem

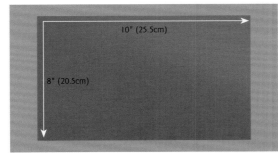

10" (25.5cm)

8" (20.5cm)

Step 1
For this lesson you will need to prepare a piece of wool jersey measuring 10" (25.5cm) in the width grain and 8" (20.5cm) in the length grain.

Step 2
On the wrong side of the fabric mark an "X" with tailor's chalk. Then, measure up 1½" (3.8cm) from the width edge and mark your hem fold.

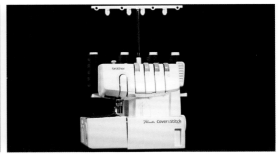

Step 3
We will be demonstrating this lesson using a Brother 2340CV Pacesetter Coverstitch machine, with three threaded needles.

Step 4A

Fold the hem up along the foldline, with the wrong side of the fabric piece face up. Using the left side of the machine foot as your guide, position your hem edge under the foot. Make your first few stitches on a fabric scrap before progressing on to the hem itself.

Step 4B

Gently guide the fabric through the machine. Be careful not to pull the fabric as you sew. Note that there is a ¼" (6mm) seam allowance along the edge of the hem.

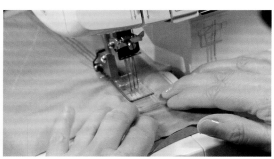

Step 4C

When you reach the end, have another fabric scrap ready that you can sew onto so that the threads will not break.

Step 4D

Then clip the end threads.

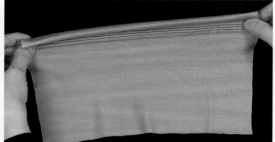

Step 5A

Note how the fabric hem can be stretched without the threads breaking, just as for the two-needle coverstitch.

Step 5B

Turn the fabric over to see the coverstitching. You will notice that the three-needle coverstitch is denser than the two-needle coverstitch, but still has the same amount of stretch.

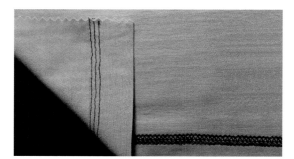

Step 6

You may wish to trim the remaining hem allowance to within ⅛" (3mm) of the edge. You have now finished sewing a three-needle coverstitch hem.

Module 4:

Chainstitch Hem

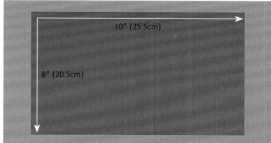

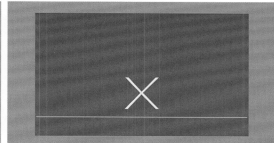

Step 1
For this lesson you will need to prepare a piece of wool ponte di Roma measuring 10" (25.5cm) in the width grain and 8" (20.5cm) in the length grain. This hem finish is appropriate for all knit weights.

Step 2
Use tailor's chalk to mark an "X" on the wrong side of the fabric and a hem fold marking 1" (2.5cm) up from the width edge.

Step 3
We will be demonstrating this lesson using a Baby Lock Evolution overlocker set to "chainstitch."

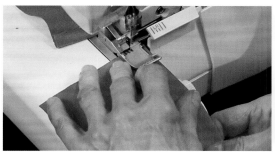

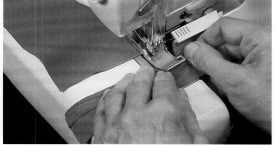

Step 4
Make the first few stitches on a fabric scrap. Then feed your 1" (2.5cm) folded fabric hem, right side up, under the machine foot and continue sewing. Align the hem fold with the right side of the machine foot edge; this will act as your guide as you sew.

Step 5A
Once you reach the end of the hem, have another small fabric scrap ready to place under the machine foot. Run your stitching over onto this scrap to avoid breaking the thread.

Step 5B
Then trim the end threads.

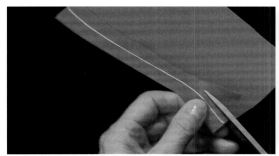

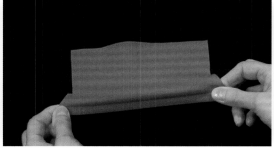

Step 6A
Turn the piece over to the wrong side and trim the excess hem allowance to within ¼" (6mm) of the chainstitching.

Step 6B
Turn the fabric to the right side and test how it stretches.

Step 6C
Then turn the piece over. Note how the chainstitch stretches without breaking when the fabric is stretched.

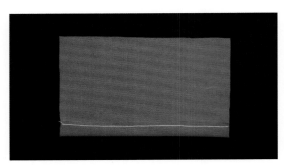

Step 6D
You have now finished sewing a chainstitched hem.

Isabel Marant combines a crew-neck knit sweatshirt with a shirt-sleeve cuff. Spring/Summer 2017.

Knit Necklines

Learning objectives

☐ Construct an overlocked and chainstitched neckline for a knit garment

☐ Make a banded neckline with two-needle coverstitch, including sewing the band in place with chainstitching, and coverstitching to finish

Tools and supplies:

- Cotton/spandex (elastane) knit jersey
- Matching cotton thread
- Cotton twill tape, ¼" (6mm) wide
- Overlocker (serger)
- Coverstitch machine
- Sewing machine

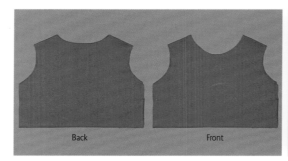

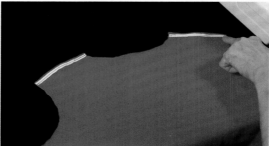

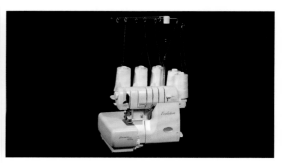

Step I
For this lesson you will need to prepare a mock T-shirt, front and back, out of a cotton/spandex jersey.

Step 2
In preparation for sewing the neckline, sew your front and back shoulder seams together using twill tape, as demonstrated in the Taped Shoulder Seam module on page 237.

Step 3A
We will be demonstrating this lesson using a Brother 3034D Lock overlocker with three threads for the overlocked edge...

Knit Fabrics

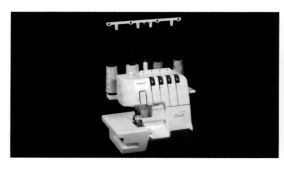

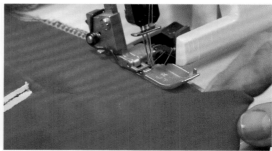

...and a Baby Lock Evolution machine for sewing the chainstitched neckline.

Step 3B
You will first overlock the neckline's edge by feeding the right side of the neckline's raw edge underneath the machine presser foot. Use the foot's right-side edge as your sewing guide. Begin by making your first few stitches on a fabric scrap, before progressing on to the neckline itself.

Step 3C
Begin sewing just before the shoulder seam and continue to sew around the neckline.

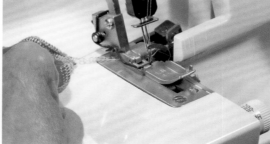

Step 3D
Gently guide the fabric as you sew. Take care not to stretch the neckline or sew too close to the edge, otherwise the machine knife will cut too much fabric from the edge, which will change the shape of the neckline.

Step 4A
Run off a few extra stitches when you reach the end.

Step 4B
This is what the neckline should look like when you have finished overlocking the edge.

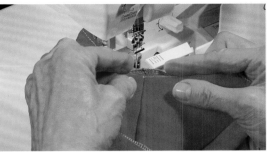

Step 5A
Now chalk a ½" (1.3cm) seam allowance around the neckline and then fold the neck seam allowance under along this line.

Step 5B
We will now move to the Baby Lock Evolution machine, which has been set to "chainstitch." Raise the presser foot, position the folded neckline face up under the foot, and then lower the foot.

Step 5C
Gently guide the folded neckline through the machine, taking care not to stretch the neckline as you sew. Use the right-side edge of the presser foot as your guide, positioned in line with the folded edge of the fabric.

Step 5D
Continue to turn the seam allowance under as you stitch the neckline, and make sure that the stitching catches the edge on the wrong side.

Step 5E
Before you reach the end, clip the threads to separate the small scrap that you used when starting the stitch.

Step 5F
When you reach the end, sew a few extra stitches. Lift the presser foot, gently pull the threads while turning the machine wheel, and then clip the end threads.

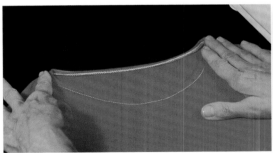

Step 5G
Lay the piece on the table. Note that the top stitch is a straight stitch, while the wrong side is a chainstitch. You could also choose to reverse this and feature the chainstitch on the face of the garment instead.

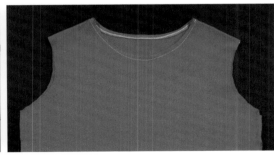

Step 5H
You have now finished overlocking and chainstitching a knit neckline finish.

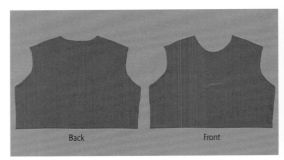

Step 1A
For this lesson you will need to prepare a mock T-shirt, front and back, out of cotton/spandex jersey.

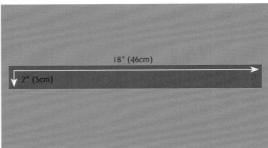

Step 1B
You also need to cut a knit neckband measuring 2" (5cm) wide, cut in the length direction of the fabric, by 18" (46cm) long, cut in the width direction of the fabric.

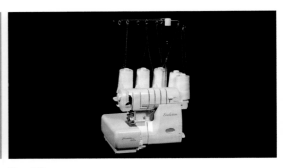

Step 2A
We will be demonstrating this lesson using a Baby Lock Evolution overlocker...

252

Knit Fabrics

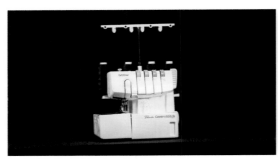

Step 2B
...and a Brother Pacesetter 2340CV Coverstitch machine.

Step 3A
Fold your neckband fabric strip in half widthwise and then pin it together along the long edge, to prevent the edges from curling, in preparation for setting it into the neckline.

Step 3B
You also need to sew your front and back shoulder seams together using twill tape, as demonstrated in the Taped Shoulder Seam module on page 237.

Step 4A
Begin by matching up the neckline at the shoulder seam.

Step 4B
Lay the neckline flat on the table and position it so that you can find the center front and center back of the T-shirt. Use tailor's chalk to mark the neckline at both center front and center back.

Step 5A
Now fold the neckband in half lengthwise and mark the center front with chalk, as demonstrated.

Step 5B
Then turn the neckband over and mark the center front on the other side.

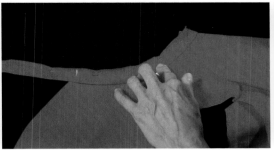

Step 6A
The next step is to "walk" the neckband into the neckline, starting at center front.

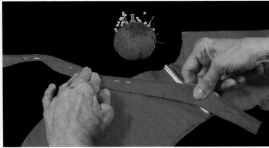

Step 6B
However, for the neckband to lie flat you must slightly stretch it as you walk it along the neckline, as demonstrated.

Step 6C
Try not to stretch the band too much or your neckline will start to pucker.

Step 6D
When you reach the shoulder seam, mark it with chalk.

Step 6E
Continue to walk the neckband into the back neckline. When you reach the center back, place another chalk mark.

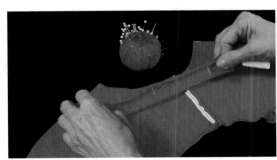

Step 7A
Now fold the neckband in half and transfer the shoulder and center-back markings to the other side of the band.

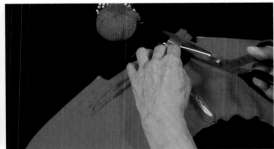

Step 7B
Add ¼" (6mm) seam allowance to the center-back seam, and trim away the excess fabric.

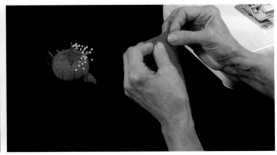

Step 8A
Remove the pins, open the neckband, and match the center-back seam with right sides together.

Step 8B
Now join the center-back seam with a chainstitch and then clip the end threads.

Step 9A
Transfer the center-front neck marking to the right side.

Step 9B
And transfer the center-back marking to the right side.

Step 9C
Turn the T-shirt to the wrong side and, with the center-back seam opened, align the center back of the neckband with the center back of the neckline.

Raise the chainstitch presser foot and place the center-back neckline under the foot. Then lower the presser foot.

Step 9D
Now match up the center front of the neckband with the center front of the T-shirt.

Then pin them together.

Step 9E
Note the length of the neckband from center front to center back, compared to length of the T-shirt's neckline. That difference is the amount of stretch that you will need to incorporate when sewing.

Step 9F
Match the seams next and hold them together with a pin.

Step 10A

You will now sew the neckband into the neckline, stretching the band to fit as you work. Because jersey has a tendency to curl, you will need to hold the edges down with your free hand as you sew.

Step 10B

Remove the shoulder pin, push the shoulder seam toward the back, and continue to sew the neckline, continuing the process of matching the edges and stretching the neckband as you sew.

Step 10C

Match the neckband at the shoulder on the other side and secure it with a pin. Make sure that the seam allowance is going toward the back.

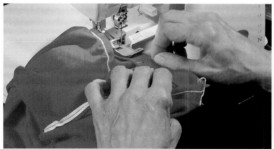

Step 10D

Then continue to stretch and sew the neckband into the T-shirt's neckline. Be sure to remove the pins at center front and at the shoulder as you go. Note how the instructor is using her fingers to keep the neckband's edges flat as she sews.

Step 10E

When you reach the end, run a few extra stitches, then remove the work from the machine and clip the end threads.

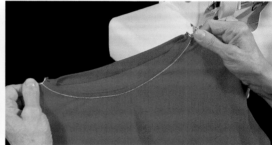

Step 10F

This is what the sewn band looks like after it is sewn, and before the coverstitch process.

Step 10G

Turn the T-shirt to the right side to check the neckband. Once the coverstitch is completed and the neckband is pressed, the neckline will lie flat and not pucker.

Step 11A

Here we are switching to the Brother Pacesetter 2340CV Coverstitch machine set for a two-needle coverstitch. Run off a few stiches on a fabric scrap, then raise the presser foot to place the neckband under the foot at center back. Position the neck seam so that it is in the center of the two needles.

Step 11B

To avoid bulk at the neck, open the ¼" (6mm) neckline seam allowance as you sew the coverstitch.

Step 12A
Now, with the seam allowance opened and the neck seam centered between the two needles, sew the coverstitch. You may want to press the seam allowance before you sew to make the sewing easier.

Step 12B
You will notice that the middle opening on the machine foot will be your guide when positioned in line with the neck seam.

Step 12C
Continue to sew the coverstitch.

Step 12D
Sew a few extra stitches when you reach the end. Then raise the presser foot and remove your work from the machine.

Step 12E
Trim the end threads.

Step 12F
Another option is to have your coverstitch showing on the face of the garment instead. Press the neckline with your iron.

You have now finished sewing a banded neckline with a two-needle coverstitch.

Self-evaluation

☐ Can I tell the difference between a weft knit and a warp knit?
☐ Can I identify a jersey from a double knit?
☐ Can I tell if a knit fabric has one-, two-, or four-way stretch?
☐ Am I able to choose which knit seam and hem finish are right for my knit fabric?

A classic T-shirt with rib-band neckline from Nicole Miller, Spring 2016.

8 Binding

A bias binding is used to trim necklines and armholes and is particularly useful for sleeveless tops and dresses. First you will sew a **single-fold bias binding with an edgestitch**, then employ the same technique using a **crack stitch**, a clean finish with no stitching on the binding itself.

French piping offers a clean finish to raw edges on sheer and lightweight fabrics. We show you how to sew French piping onto a neckline. A **binding with a slip stitch** can also be applied to raw fabric edges. You will learn the technique by attaching a single-fold binding to the neckline and armhole of a blouse, finishing by hand using an almost invisible slip stitch.

Spaghetti straps are commonly used for evening dresses and other garments that require a delicate finish and minimal coverage. You will create a bias strip, sew it into a tube, and use a loop turner to turn it to the right side. Professional pressing techniques will perfect the finished straps.

Exquisite bias binding trims armholes and neckline. Narces, Spring/Summer 2016.

Single-fold Bias Binding with an Edgestitch

Learning objectives

☐ Prepare fabric and bias binding by marking and pressing the seam allowances

☐ Apply the correct method to pin and sew basic binding in place

Tools and supplies:

- #2 muslin (lightweight calico)
- Matching cotton thread
- Red pencil

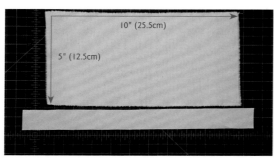

Step 1A

For this lesson you will need to prepare two pieces of #2 muslin. One piece will measure 10" (25.5cm) in the width grain, by 5" (12.5cm) in the length grain. This represents the body piece.

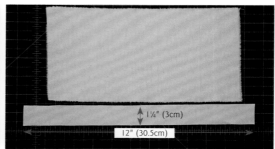

Step 1B

The second muslin piece will be a bias strip measuring 1¼" (3cm) wide by 12" (30.5cm) long. This is your binding.

Step 2A

Place the bias strip on your ironing board. Measure and turn up a ¼" (6mm) seam allowance along the length edge of the strip, using your clear plastic ruler. You could also mark the ¼" (6mm) seam allowance with your pencil.

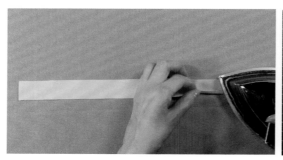

Step 2B

Now use your iron to press the ¼" (6mm) seam allowance flat, using a bit of steam. Be careful not to stretch the fabric; because it has been cut on the bias, it will be more prone to stretching.

Step 3A

Mark a ¼" (6mm) seam allowance line in pencil, along the width, on the right side of your muslin body piece.

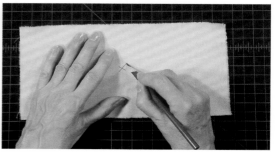

Step 3B

Turn the piece over and place an "X" in the middle of the body piece, using a red pencil. This will denote the wrong side of the fabric.

Do the same for the bias strip, placing an "X" on the wrong side, as shown.

Step 1
Line up the right side of the bias strip with the wrong side of the body piece, placing the raw edges together along the width edge.

Step 2A
Position the layers under your presser foot with the body piece on top, right side up. Then sew along the penciled stitching line. Your machine should be set to between 10 and 12 stitches per inch (spi; stitch length of 2.1 to 2.5mm). Never sew with the bias strip on the top—this will cause the strip to stretch.

Step 2B
When you reach the end, trim away some of the excess binding fabric, as well as the end threads.

Step 3A
Now turn the binding under so that the binding fold is 1/16" (2mm) below the stitching line. Then pin it in place.

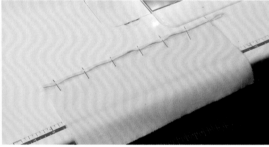

Step 3B
You must only pin into the seam allowance. If you pin into the outside of the bias binding you will create an unnecessary bump and you could also cause the binding to twist.

Step 4A
Now you are ready to sew the edgestitch. Position your needle 1/16" (2mm) away from the folded edge of the binding and stitch from one end of the body piece to the other. Remove the pins as you sew.

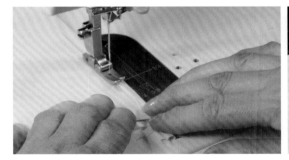

Step 4B
The idea here is to have your edgestitch showing on the outside of the garment, and positioned 1/16" (2mm) away from the folded edge of the binding. By stitching 1/16" (2mm) below the stitching line of the binding, you can reduce any excess bulk.

Step 4C
When you reach the end, trim the excess binding and the end threads.

Tip
If you are an experienced sewer, you may want to forego pinning the binding.

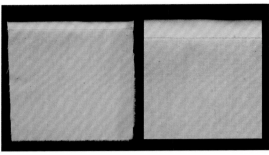

Tip
The same technique can also be used to create a clean finish on a garment's hem.

Step 5
You have now finished sewing a single-fold bias binding with an edgestitch.

A bias binding frames the neck and armholes of this ballgown by Carolina Herrera, Fall 2015.

Single-fold Bias Binding with a Crack Stitch

Learning objectives

☐ Prepare fabric and bias binding

☐ Add binding without visible stitching, including sewing with crack stitch (also known as stitch in the ditch)

Tools and supplies:

- #2 muslin (lightweight calico)
- Matching cotton thread
- Ditch quilting machine foot
- Red pencil

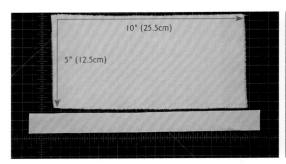

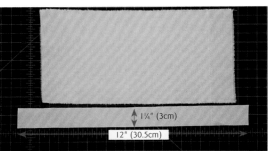

Step 1A

For this lesson you will need to prepare two pieces of #2 muslin. One piece will measure 10" (25.5cm) in the width grain, by 5" (12.5cm) in the length grain. This represents the body piece.

Step 1B

The second muslin piece will be a bias strip measuring 1¼" (3cm) wide by 12" (30.5cm) long. This is your binding.

Step 2A

Place the bias strip on your ironing board. Measure and turn up a ¼" (6mm) seam allowance along the length edge of the strip, using your clear plastic ruler. You could also mark the ¼" (6mm) seam allowance with your pencil.

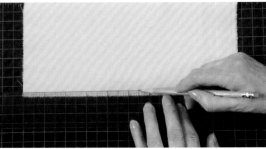

Step 2B

Now use your iron to press the ¼" (6mm) seam allowance flat, using a bit of steam. Be careful not to stretch the fabric; as before, since it has been cut on the bias it will be more prone to stretching.

Step 3A

Mark a ¼" (6mm) seam allowance line in pencil along the width, on the wrong side of your muslin body piece.

Step 3B

Place an "X" in the middle of the body piece with a red pencil to denote the wrong side. Do the same for the bias strip, placing an "X" on the folded side edge of the strip, as shown.

Step 1

Line up the right side of the bias strip with the right side of the body piece, placing the raw edges together along the width edge.

Step 2A

Place the layers under the machine presser foot with the body piece on top, wrong side up. Then stitch along the penciled stitching line. Your machine should be set to between 10 and 12 stitches per inch (spi; stitch length of 2.1 to 2.5mm). Never sew with the bias strip on the top—the strip will stretch.

Step 2B

When you reach the end, trim away some of the excess binding fabric and the end threads.

Step 3A

Now finger-press the seam, with the seam allowance going upward, in the direction of the binding. Never press this flat with an iron or it will stretch.

Step 3B

The next step will be to fold the binding over the seam allowance, then machine-stitch it in place. Your crack stitch will sit very close to the existing seam (just below it)—hence the name, "stitch in the ditch." The stitches will sit in the ditch of the previous seam, so will be barely visible from the right side.

Step 4

First pin the binding in place at one end, positioning the folded edge ⅛" (3mm) below the stitching line. Trim the excess fabric at the end of the binding, then remove the pin.

Step 5A

Now proceed with folding the bias binding over the seam allowance all the way along, keeping the binding fold approximately ⅛" (3mm) below the seam line.

Step 5B

Turn the piece to the right side and parallel-pin the binding to the muslin body piece underneath the seam or "in the ditch."

Step 5C

Because #2 muslin is semitransparent, you will be able to see the shadow of the binding fold and its position from the right side, which will make the pinning easier.

265

Single-fold Bias Binding with a Crack Stitch

Step 6
Once you have pinned the binding to the body piece, turn the piece to the wrong side to check that your pins are positioned correctly, just under the seam line. Check their position from end to end.

Step 7A
To make stitching in the ditch easier, we will sew the crack stitch using a ditch quilting foot, which has a guide on the bottom.

Step 7B
Remove the regular presser foot from your sewing machine and replace it with the ditch quilting foot.

Step 7C
Place the right side of the muslin piece under the ditch quilting foot and position it so that the guide is resting along the edge of the binding seam.

Step 7D
Begin sewing and guide the fabric through the machine, removing the pins as you sew.

Step 7E
When you reach the end, clip the end threads.

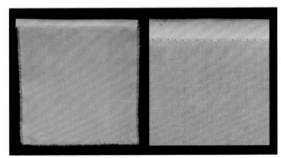

Step 7F
You have now finished sewing a single-fold bias binding with a crack stitch (close-up image on the right).

The neckline and armholes of this dress are framed with narrow French piping. Maison Marquise, 2015.

French Piping

Learning objectives

☐ Prepare bias binding and garment, including marking and cutting bias binding, taping shoulder seams, staystitching the neckline

☐ Add French piping using a sewing machine

☐ Apply French piping with hand stitching, including sewing with blind stitch and steaming the piping

Tools and supplies:

- Silk organza
- Matching cotton thread
- Size 10 sharps needle

- Silk pins
- Thimble

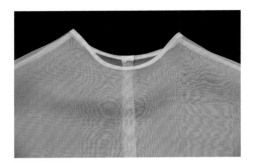

Step 1
To create a French piping finish like the one on this neckline, you need to begin by cutting out a bias strip for the piping.

Step 2A
To start, we have marked a series of bias strips on a piece of paper that is the same size as the fabric piece. Each strip is 1½" (3.8cm) in width.

Step 2B
The fabric is sandwiched between two pieces of paper (including the pre-marked paper) and then pinned together. This will make it easier to cut.

Step 3
Once you have cut your bias strip, separate it from the rest of the fabric. It will be easier and look better if there is no join in the piping, so select a strip that is long enough for the area that you are piping.

Step 4
Make sure you have prepared the shoulder seams on your bodice before you move to the next stage. Here we used French seams because organza is a sheer fabric.

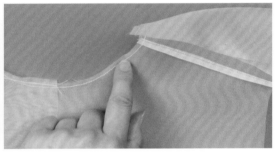

Step 5
You should also staystitch around the edge of the neck, taking care not to stretch the neckline in the bias area. The stitches used here are quite small—about 12 stitches per inch (spi; stitch length of 2.1mm).

Module 2:

Preparing the French Piping

Tip
Organza can be rather springy, so if you are new to sewing you will find it easier if you now baste (tack) the strip.

Step 1
Remove the paper from your bias strip and fold the strip in half along its length, aligning the edges. Then pin the edges together, all the way along the strip. Silk pins are best on a delicate fabric like this.

Step 2A
Here, we are adding basting stitches ¼" (6mm) from the edge, so that they will not be in the way of our machine stitching later. The red thread being used here is just for demonstration purposes.

Step 2B
Use a stitch length of about ¼" (6mm).

Step 3

Next, turn your center-back seam allowances in and pin them down. Ours are ½" (1.3cm).

Step 4A

Turn your garment so that the right side of the fabric is facing you, then pin the edge of the bias strip to the edge of the neckline. Leave about ¾" (2cm) excess at the end—you will be turning this in when you hand-stitch it later.

Step 4B

As you pin the bias strip to the garment, you need to "tug" the strip slightly; if the strip is fitted too loosely it will look baggy.

Step 4C

Keep pinning, tugging the bias strip very slightly as you progress. Be careful not to tug the neckline itself, though—just the strip.

Step 4D

The pinning is now complete. We will trim off the edges later.

Module 3:

Machine-stitching the French Piping

Step 1

You will now sew the strip to the neckline with a ¼" (6mm) seam allowance. Line up your fabric edge with the ¼" (6mm) guide on your sewing machine. Go forward a few stitches and then reverse. Then continue stitching, removing your pins as you go.

Step 2

When you get to the shoulder seams, because they are French seams, make sure they have been pressed toward the back.

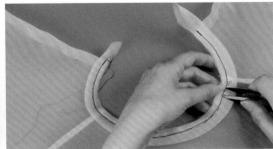

Step 3

When the bias strip has been sewn on, you can remove your basting stitches.

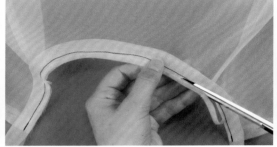

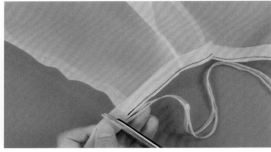

Step 4
Now trim the first end of your bias strip, leaving ½" (1.3cm) in place.

Step 5
Then trim your seam allowance down to half its width. Make sure you trim evenly because this is transparent fabric, so the edge will show through. (This finish is only good for sheer, fine fabrics. It is not suitable for heavy fabrics.)

Step 6
Trim the other end of the bias strip, again leaving ½" (1.3cm) overhanging.

Module 4:

Hand-stitching the French Piping

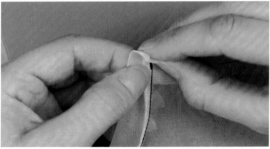

Step 1
Working on the wrong side of the fabric, at the end of the bias strip, begin by folding the seam allowance up toward the strip. Then, holding this in place, fold your ½" (1.3cm) raw end over the top of it, toward the body of the garment.

Step 2A
However, when you make the folds, it is easy to end up with raggedy edges like these.

Step 2B
Our tip is to hold the folded end in place with one hand, while using your other thumb to tuck in the raw corner edge. It is a little fiddly—you almost need three hands!—but with practice you will be able to perform this quickly and easily.

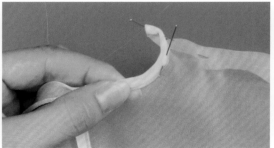

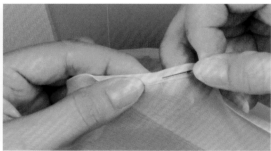

Step 3
Once the corner has been tucked in, fold it over and pin it in place. As you can see here, the ragged edge is no longer sticking out at the bottom.

Step 4A
Continue folding the seam allowance up, and the bias strip over it, pinning it down as you go. As you can see here, we are pinning our bias strip so that it sits just slightly over the stitching (which was sewn in black for demonstration purposes).

Step 4B
Make sure you keep your pins close together, because the fabric is very springy and you need to hold it firmly in place.

Step 4C

When you reach the other end, fold and pin it in the same way as for the first end.

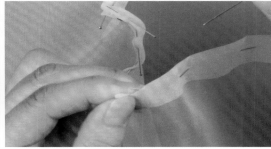

Step 5A

You are now going to stitch the strip down using a blind stitch. Thread your size 10 sharps needle with a single thread and make a knot at the end. Remove your first pin, but make sure you hold the binding securely between your fingers.

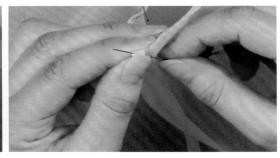

Step 5B

Bring your needle up inside the binding and through one of the folds so that you can hide the knot.

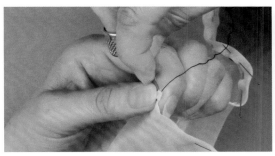

Step 5C

Tuck the knot in, then catch the other side of the binding with your needle.

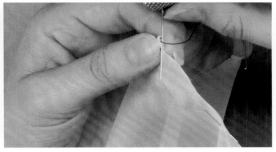

Step 5D

You are simply taking a piece from one side of the binding and then the other, to attach them together at that end.

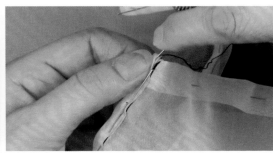

Step 6A

You will now stitch the binding down. It is helpful to hold the binding so that you can see the machine stitch sitting inside it, to make sure that your stitches will be hidden underneath. Start by taking a small pinch of fabric.

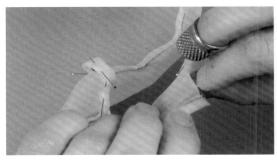

Step 6B

Always make sure that your needle is not going through to the other side.

Step 6C

Having pinched a small amount, then take your needle through the fold of the binding. It should then emerge from the binding right on the fold.

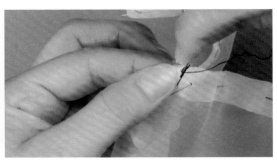

Step 6D

The idea is to tuck your stitch almost behind the binding, taking a small pinch of the fabric, and then bring your needle up into the binding, through the fold, and then out.

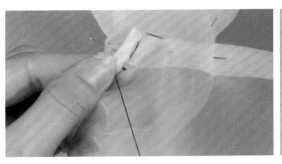

Step 6E

When you take a stitch of fabric, you are just taking this from the seam allowance that we folded inside earlier, and not passing all the way through the fabric (which would leave visible stitches on the outside). If the pins start getting in the way, just take them out.

Step 7

Finish off the far end in the same way as the first end.

Step 8A

Now take your binding and secure one end of it to your ironing board with a pin. Pull the neckline tightly so that it is taut, then pin the other end in place.

Step 8B

Now steam the binding, making sure the iron is not touching the fabric or flattening it—you want the binding to form a nice roll rather than a flat finish. Go back and forth with your steam a few times, then leave the fabric to dry on the board before removing it.

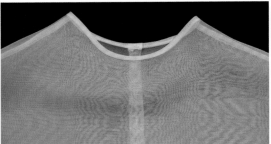

Step 8C

You have now finished sewing your French piping.

Tip

The same technique can be applied to sleeves, hems, pockets, and any edge that requires a polished finish.

Single-fold Neck/ Armhole Binding with a Slip Stitch

Learning objectives

- ☐ Prepare garment and binding
- ☐ Apply binding to a neckline, including stabilizing the bias areas on the garment, marking and matching centerline points, machine sewing the binding in place
- ☐ Apply binding to an armhole, including stabilizing bias areas and cutting away the seam allowance, sewing the side seams, matching key points, machine sewing the binding in place
- ☐ Slip stitch binding in place on the wrong side to finish

Contrast binding frames neck and armholes. Teresita Orillac. Spring/Summer 2016.

Tools and supplies:

- #2 muslin (lightweight calico)
- Muslin blouse
- Matching cotton thread
- Size 8 sharps needle
- Red pencil
- Flex curve
- Silk pins

274

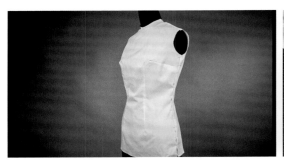

Step 1A

For this lesson we have prepared a sleeveless and collarless muslin blouse. Note that the side seams have only been pinned in place for now.

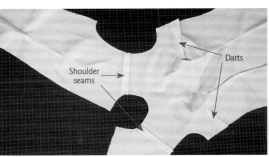

Step 1B

We have machine-stitched the darts closed and have sewn the left and right shoulder seams together.

Step 2A

Place the blouse, wrong side up, on the table. Since the binding will be folded over the raw edge of the armhole to create the finished edge, we will mark a ½" (1.3cm) stitching line on the seam allowance in red pencil so we can cut it away later.

Step 2B

Mark the stitching line all the way around, using a series of dashes.

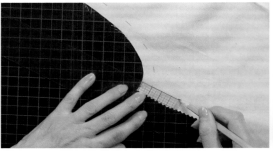

Step 3A

Now mark a ½" (1.3cm) stitching line down one side seam of the blouse with a regular pencil, for about 2" (5cm). This is for marking purposes only, and for measuring the length of your bias strip.

Step 3B

Do the same at other side seam.

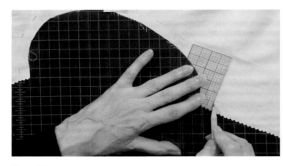

Step 4A

The next step is to mark the new armhole stitching line with your pencil, ¼" (6mm) away from the red stitching line.

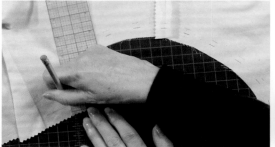

Step 4B

Continue all the way round the armhole, using dashes as before.

Step 5A

Now repeat these steps on the neckline. Mark the ½" (1.3cm) stitching line of the neckline in red pencil, in preparation for cutting the seam allowance away. Remember to always work with a sharpened pencil tip.

Step 5B
Continue all the way round the neckline, from center back to center back.

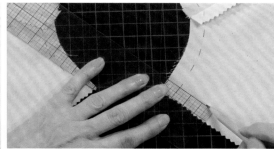

Step 6
Next, mark the ½" (1.3cm) stitching line for 2" (5cm) along the center back of the blouse on both sides.

Step 7
Then mark the new neckline stitching line with your regular pencil—again, ¼" (6mm) away from the red stitching line, as for the armhole.

Step 8
Now "walk" your tape measure along the new penciled stitching line of the neckline, as demonstrated, to determine the neck circumference.

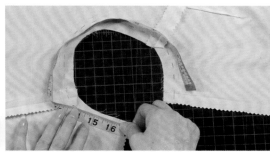

Measure from center-back pencil line to center-back pencil line. Record your neck circumference measurement.

Step 9
Now find the circumference of your armhole, again walking your tape measure along the new pencil stitching line. Be sure you begin and end at the side-seam pencil lines. You could also use a ruler or a flex curve. Record your armhole measurement.

Tip
Always test your bias strips—every fabric has a different stretch factor.

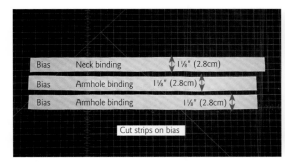

Step 10
Cut three muslin bias strips, each 1⅛" (2.8cm) wide. Cut one strip the length of your neck circumference, and the other two the length of your armhole circumference. You will not add seam allowances to these since, depending on the fabric type, bias strips tend to stretch when sewn into a seam. For this lesson we will stretch the strips ½" (1.3cm) to fit the area.

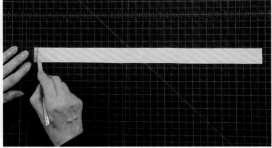

Step 11
With your pencil and ruler, mark a ¼" (6mm) stitching line on the seam allowance of the neckline bias strip—first on one end and then on the other.

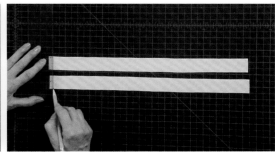

Step 12A
Now, with the two armhole bias strips positioned side by side on the table, mark a ¼" (6mm) stitching line on each of them with your pencil and ruler, first at one end...

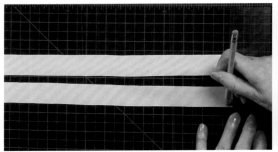

Step 12B
...and then the other.

Step 13A
Now place the strips on your ironing board. Measure and fold over ¼" (6mm) along one length edge of each strip, as demonstrated.

Step 13B
Iron the fold. Take care not to stretch the strips as you iron, since fabric cut on the bias loves to stretch. Add steam as you press.

Module 2:

Applying the Bias Binding to the Neckline

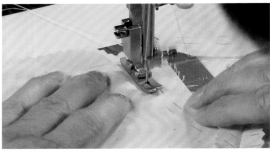

Step 1
Now you will move to the sewing machine and run a holding stitch ¹⁄₁₆" (2mm) above the penciled stitching line of the neckline. This is to prevent the bias areas from stretching. Your machine stitch should be set at 10 to 12 stitches per inch (spi; stitch length 2.1–2.5mm). Be sure to open the shoulder seam allowances as you sew.

Step 2
Now trim away the neckline along the red pencil marking using your fabric shears, as shown.

Step 3A
You will now locate the center front neck of the blouse by lining up the left and right shoulder seams.

Hold the shoulder seams together to determine the position of the center front, as shown.

Step 3B
Place a pin at the center front neckline, mark it with a pencil, then remove the pin.

Step 4
Now locate the center of your neck bias strip by matching up the ends and folding the strip in half lengthwise. Pin the center, mark it with a pencil on the raw edge side of the strip, then remove the pin.

Step 5A

Match up the center mark on the bias neck strip with the mark on the blouse's center front and pin the layers together.

Step 5B

The next step is to fold back the ½" (1.3cm) seam allowance at center back and match it up with the center-back pencil line of the bias neck strip. Then pin those layers together.

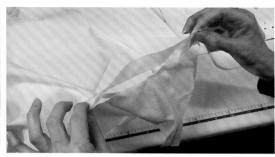

Step 5C

Remember that our bias strip was planned slightly smaller than the actual neckline and will therefore need to be pulled a bit to fit into the blouse's neck. The bias strip will lie flat on the neckline once it is sewn.

Step 5D

Pin the bias strip into the neckline, as demonstrated, with your pins at a right angle to the stitching line.

Step 5E

Now, repeat this process on the other side of the neckline, pinning the bias neck strip to the center back of the blouse, stretching the strip to fit into the neckline. The most stretch should be at the curviest part of the neckline.

You are now ready to move to the sewing machine.

Step 6

With the blouse face up and the bias strip beneath, sew along the penciled line. (If the bias is on top, it will stretch.) Note how the center-back seam allowance of the bias strip extends beyond the blouse center back. Remove the pins as you sew, and make sure the shoulder seam allowance is open and flat.

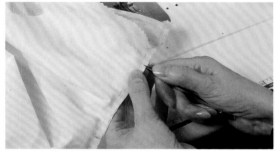

Step 7

Using your clippers, clip into the neck seam allowance at ½" (1.3cm) intervals. Be careful not to clip into your machine stitches. Clipping the neckline will release the fabric so that the binding will be able to lie flat when turned and stitched.

Step 8

Once the bias neck strip has been stitched to the neckline, finger-press the neck seam allowance so that the seam is going up, in the direction of the folded edge of the bias strip.

Step 9A
The next step is to fold the seam allowance under at one end of the bias strip before then folding the strip over to encase the seam allowance along the neckline.

Step 9B
Use the tip of a pin to help guide the binding into place, then secure it to the neckline with a pin. We will not be trimming the seam allowance as you might do on other seams, since the 1/4" (6mm) seam allowance will create a kind of "filler," making the binding more dimensional.

Step 9C
Since there are several layers to pin, and the folded edge of the bias strip must align with the stitching line of the neckline, using silk pins will make this job easier.

Step 9D
Turn the piece to the right side to check that your bias strip is not twisting as you pin.

Step 9E
Pinning only into the seam allowance and not into the body of the blouse will avoid creating a "bump" on the binding.

Step 9F
Turn the neckline to the front at intervals, to check that the binding width is consistent.

Step 9G
When you reach the end, turn the center-back seam allowance under and pin the binding to the neckline, as before. (If this were an actual garment, your zipper would already be in place in the back seam, so you would need to trim away any excess seam allowance to eliminate bulk.)

Step 1A

Just as you did for the neckline, prepare the armhole by sewing a holding stitch along the new penciled stitching line, to prevent the armhole from stretching. As certain areas of the armhole are on the bias, running a holding stitch around it is critical.

Step 1B

Remember to open the shoulder seam allowance as you sew the holding stitch, and make sure that your machine stitch is set to 10 to 12 stitches per inch (spi; stitch length 2.1–2.5mm). Sewing with a longer stitch will create shirring, which is not what you want here.

Step 2

Trim away the seam allowance with your fabric shears, cutting along the red stitching line.

Step 3A

The next step is to pin the side seams of the blouse together and sew the seam closed with your sewing machine. Remove the pins as you sew.

Step 3B

Open the seam allowance along the side seam and, since this blouse is semifitted, clip into the waist to release the fabric.

Step 4A

Stitch the side seam of the armhole binding and open the seam allowance, as demonstrated.

Step 4B

Match up the side seam of the binding with the side seam of the blouse. Pin the layers together on the blouse portion of the armhole and at a right angle to the seam.

Step 4C

Match the center mark on the binding with the shoulder seam of the blouse, then pin the layers together. Remember that when we sew the binding to the blouse, the binding will be on the bottom and therefore the pinning should be done on the blouse side, which will be on top as it passes through the machine.

Step 4D

Note the difference between the armhole and the binding, and the amount by which the binding will need to stretch to fit around the armhole.

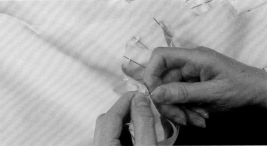

Step 4E

Working on one side first, between side seam and shoulder seam, establish the halfway point on the armhole, then pin this point to the halfway point on the binding on that side. Now pin one quarter-segment, stretching the binding to fit, then the other. This will ensure the stretch is distributed evenly.

Step 4F

Once you have finished pinning the first half of the armhole, repeat the same steps on the other side, again pinning the layers together in the middle before completing the two quarter-segments either side of it.

Step 4G

Once you have distributed the ease and pinned the binding to the armhole, you are ready to sew the binding.

Step 5A

Place the underarm seam of the blouse under the machine presser foot with the armhole side face up.

Step 5B

Stitch along the penciled stitching line, from side seam to side seam. Remove the pins as you stitch and make sure that the shoulder seam is open and flat. Backtack when you reach the side seam and then clip the end threads.

Step 6A

Just as you did on the neckline, clip into the seam allowance at ½" (1.3cm) intervals, with either your clippers or scissors. Remember that we will not be trimming the seam allowance as you might do on other types of seams, since the ¼" (6mm) seam allowance will create a nicer, more rounded binding.

Step 6B

Finger-press the seam allowance upward, toward the raw edge of the binding.

Step 7

Pin the armhole binding to the blouse, using the same technique as you used for pinning the neck binding to the neck.

Step 1

In preparation for slip stitching your neckline, thread your needle with a double strand of thread, several inches longer than the neckline's circumference. Form a knot on one end of a strand.

Step 2A

Since our instructor is right-handed, she has positioned the neckline so that she can sew from right to left, with the neckline facing her. To hide the knot, slip the needle in between the blouse and the center-back seam allowance, then come up at the top of the folded end of the binding.

Step 2B

To close the center back seam of the binding, take a series of small slip stitches, alternating between the upper and under folded edges, at approximately $1/16$" (2mm) apart.

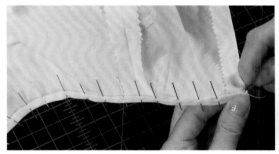

Step 2C

Remove the first pin, pick up a stitch in the seam allowance at the neck stitching line, and insert the needle at a diagonal, $1/16$" (2mm) away, and into the folded edge of the binding. Then pull the thread through to the top.

Step 2D

Take the next stitch at the neck stitching line, next to your previous stitch. Repeat the process of coming up at a diagonal, at $1/16$" (2mm) intervals, into the folded edge of the binding, and then pulling the thread through to the top. Remove the pins as you sew.

Step 2E

A slip stitch (also known as a blind stitch) is used when you want to hide your stitches. By sewing into the fold and into the seam allowance, your stitches will be almost invisible. You will be able to cover your neckline machine stitching, and hide your stitches in the fold of the binding.

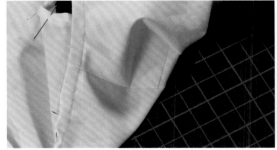

Step 2F

Remember that your neckline stitches are made into the seam allowance only, not all the way through to the front of the garment. Turn your blouse to the right side every now and then to check that your stitches are hidden.

Step 2G

When you reach the end, repeat the process of closing the center back seam of the binding by taking a series of $1/16$" (2mm) slip stitches, alternating them between the upper and under folded edges.

Step 2H

Finish by passing the needle into the binding layers to hide the end thread.

Step 2I
Then sew a backstitch on the neck stitching line with a loop and knot. Repeat the loop-and-knot step to reinforce the stitch, then trim the end thread.

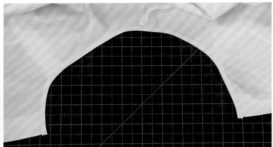

Step 2J
This is how the neckline should look on the right side after slip stitching the binding to the blouse.

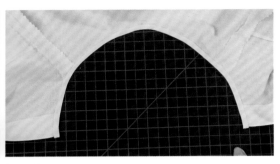

Step 2K
And this is how the neck binding looks on the wrong side of the blouse.

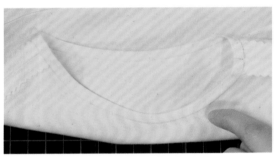

Step 3A
To slip stitch the bias binding to the armhole of the blouse, simply repeat the steps that you used for the neckline.

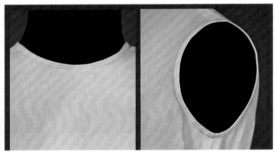

Step 3B
You have now finished sewing a neck and armhole bias binding with a slip stitch.

Self-evaluation

☐ Can I make a sample of every binding finish in the chapter?
☐ Can I identify the correct binding finish for my fabric choice?
☐ Have I sewn my spaghetti strap seam allowances evenly to create perfectly cylindrical straps?

A single spaghetti strap adds drama to this asymmetric dress from Philippines Fashion Week, 2015.

Spaghetti Straps

Learning objectives

☐ Determine the strap length, cut a bias strip, and sew a tube

☐ Finish the straps using a loop turner

Tools and supplies:

- #2 muslin (lightweight calico)
- Matching cotton thread
- Loop turner

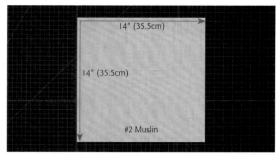

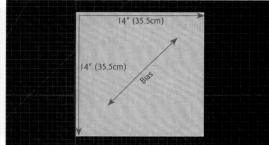

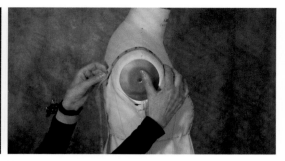

Step 1
For this lesson you will need to block and press a piece of #2 muslin measuring 14" (35.5cm) square. Blocking is the process of manipulating the fabric so that the length and cross grains are at right angles to each other.

Draw a diagonal with a pencil to indicate the bias.

Step 2
Now use your tape measure to determine how long each spaghetti strap needs to be by measuring from the seam of the front neck point, over the shoulder, to the back neck point on your dress.

Step 3
Place your muslin block on the table. Measure over 1¼" (3cm) from the diagonal line, then use your clear plastic ruler to draw a line parallel to it, from one corner to the other. This will be your bias strip. (A wider block was used for demonstration purposes.)

Step 4
With your fabric shears, cut both sides of the strip. Be careful not to stretch the grain as you cut.

Step 5A
Fold the bias strip in half lengthwise, right sides together, and pin it along the edge from one end of the strip to the other. Remember, this is bias and will stretch if you do not take care when handling the strip, so it is a good idea to pin it flat on the table.

Step 5B
Use your clippers to snip off the point of the bias strip, cutting it at a right angle.

Step 6A
Sew down the bias strip ³⁄₁₆" (5mm) away from the folded edge. Remove the pins as you progress, and try not to stretch the strip as you sew.

Step 6B
Use your clippers to snip the threads and the end of the bias strip.

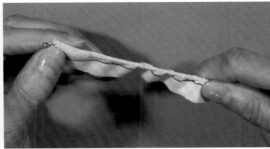

Step 1

Take your loop turner and tunnel it through the bias strip opening. Push the excess fabric down onto the loop turner until you have reached the end.

Step 2

At the end of the strip, push the loop turner's hook into the top layer of the strip to catch it. Feeling through the muslin, close the clasp of the hook to secure the tip.

Step 3

You will now turn the bias tube inside out. Push the fabric up and onto the shaft of the loop turner, as you simultaneously pull the turner down with your other hand.

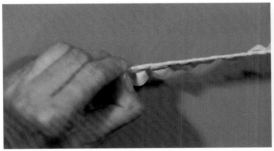

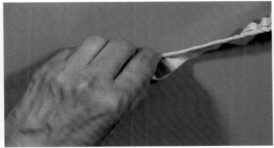

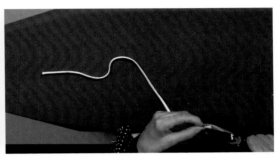

Step 4

Use your fingernail to guide the fabric so that it will release and move. It is sometimes helpful to guide the fabric with a pin, if you do not have long enough fingernails. Just be careful not to damage the fabric.

Step 5

Turning the bias strip on the loop turner will be a slow process, especially if using muslin. A silk or silk blend is easier to turn.

Step 6

Once you have finished turning, the result will be a nice, thin spaghetti strap. Remove the spaghetti strap from the loop turner and trim the end with your scissors.

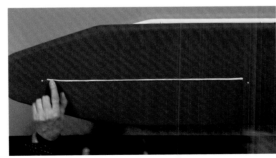

Step 7

Pin one end of the spaghetti strap to the ironing board, create a straight line with the strap, and, with a little bit of tension on the strap, pin the other end of the strap to the ironing board.

Step 8

Let your iron hover over the strap and then steam the length of the strap. When the strap is cool, cut it to fit your garment.

Step 9

You finished spaghetti strap is now ready to be attached to your dress.

9 Pockets

You will begin by sewing a classic **single-welt pocket**, which is commonly used on tailored garments. We will show you how to measure and mark the pocket opening, assemble the welt, sew it to the pocket, and insert the pocketing fabric into the welt. You will finish with some topstitching to create a beautiful end result.

A **double-welt pocket** is commonly used on pants (trousers), skirts, jackets, and coats. This technique includes interfacing on the pocket opening and each of the pocket parts. You will learn how to sew the welts, turn and reinforce the welt slit, and insert the pocketing. Again, the pocket is topstitched to finish.

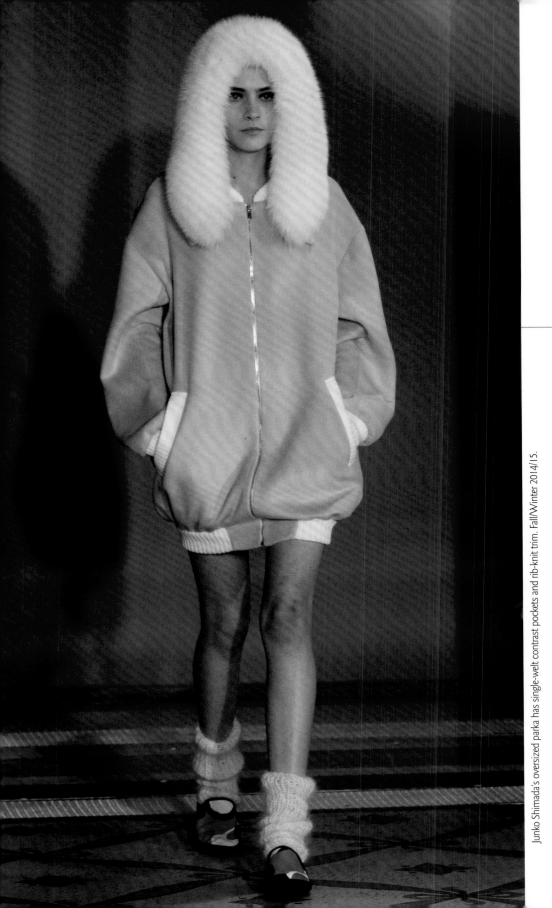

Junko Shimada's oversized parka has single-welt contrast pockets and rib-knit trim. Fall/Winter 2014/15.

Single-welt Pocket

Learning objectives

☐ Measure and mark a pocket opening, and add interfacing

☐ Sew a welt, add a pocket bag, and edgestitch to finish

Tools and supplies:

- #2 muslin (lightweight calico)
- Fusible woven interfacing
- Pocketing
- Matching cotton thread

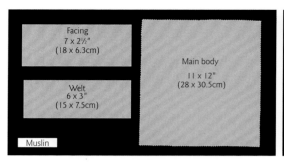

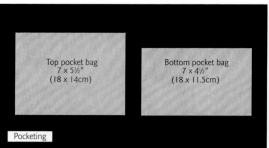

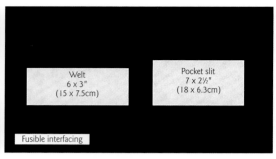

Step 1

For this lesson you will need to prepare three pieces of muslin: a main body piece measuring 11" (28cm) by 12" (30.5cm), a welt piece measuring 6" (15cm) by 3" (7.5cm), and a facing piece measuring 7" (18cm) by 2½" (6.3cm).

Step 2

Out of pocketing material you will need to cut: a top pocket bag measuring 7" (18cm) by 5½" (14cm), and a bottom pocket bag measuring 7" (18cm) by 4½" (11.5cm).

Step 3

You will also need a piece of fusible interfacing for the pocket slit, measuring 7" (18cm) by 2½" (6.3cm), and a welt piece measuring 6" (15cm) by 3" (7.5cm).

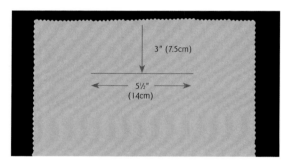

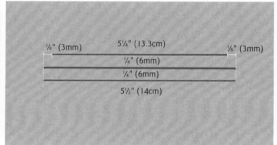

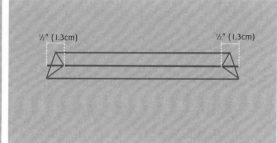

Step 4

Draw a line for the pocket slit 3" (7.5cm) down and 5½" (14cm) wide, centered on your main body piece and on the right side of the fabric.

Step 5

Mark two lines parallel to the slit, one ¼" (6mm) above it and one ¼" (6mm) below. This represents the seam allowance. The top line angles in by ⅛" (3mm) on each side and measures 5¼" (13.3cm) across, while the bottom measures 5½" (14cm).

Step 6

Now draw a triangle at each end, ½" (1.3cm) away from the end.

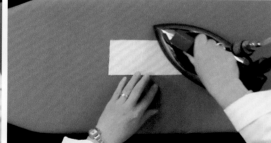

Step 7A

Turn your main body piece over to the wrong side and apply the fusible interfacing piece, sticky side down, over the center of the pocket slit.

Step 7B

Press it in place.

Step 8

Place the interfacing on the wrong side of the welt and press.

Step 1
The next step is sewing the welt. Begin by folding the welt lengthwise, right sides together. Stitch with a ¼" (6mm) seam allowance down one short side. Then sew the other side.

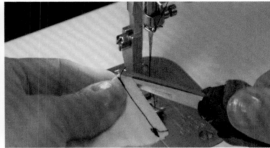

Step 2A
Trim the corners on the lower edge.

Step 2B
Then turn the corners right side out, making sure they are pointed. Use your clippers to push, but be careful not to puncture the fabric.

Step 3
Now press your welt flat.

Step 4
Position the raw edge of your welt on the center slit guideline, then sew it ¼" (6mm) away, along the bottom slit guideline. You may find it helpful to run a staystitch along the edge of the welt before attaching, for stability. Be sure to backstitch at both ends.

Step 5
Now center the facing, right side down, with the top slit guideline and the raw edge aligned with the center slit guideline. Mark the starting point with a pencil.

Then mark the end point.

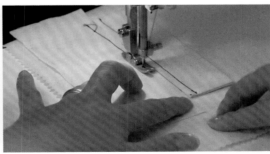

Stitch ¼" (6mm) away from the raw edge.

Be sure not to stitch beyond the end point.

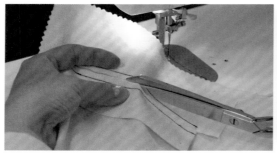

Step 6A
Starting in the middle, cut the pocket opening along the center slit guideline until you reach the tip of the triangle.

Step 6B
Clip into the triangle at an angle. Cut to the corner stitch but not any further.

Repeat this step on the other side.

Step 7
Flip the welt up and finger-press it.

Then turn the facing to the inside.

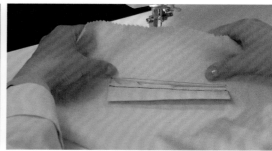

Now finger-press the facing.

The facing needs to be pressed in a downward position.

Step 8A
Flip the welt down and then fold back your fabric to reveal the facing on the wrong side. Carefully position the triangle on top of the facing.

Keeping the welt away from the stitching line, tack the triangle to the seam allowance of the facing.

Step 8B
Be sure to pull the triangle out so that you have a nice squared corner on the right side. Now do the same for the triangle on the other side.

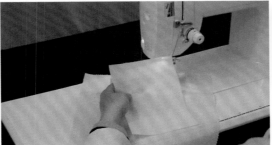

Step 9
You will now attach the top pocket bag to the bottom slit guideline.

Stitch ¼" (6mm) away from the edge, on the guideline stitch.

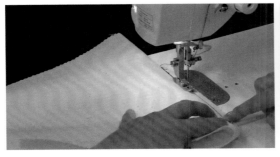

Insert the layers under the presser foot and stitch all the way along.

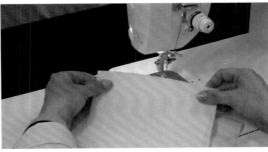

Step 10
Next, attach the bottom pocket bag to the pocket facing.

Stitch ½" (1.3cm) away from the edge.

Tip
When stitching the pocket, remember:
• Never stitch beyond the pocket markings.
• Take care when clipping into the corner stitch at the triangle.

The wrong side of your pocket should now look like this.

Step 11
Press the pocket opening under the welt on the right side.

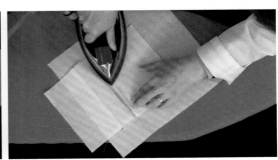

Step 12A
Turn the sampler over to the wrong side and press the top pocket bag seam allowance.

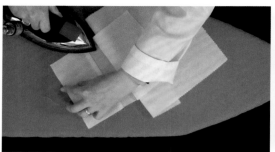
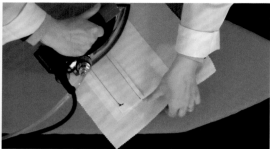

Step 12B
Then do the same for the bottom pocket bag, pulling the bag down as you press.

Step 13
Finish by pressing the complete pocket bag on the wrong side...

...and on the right side.

Step 14
You will now join the pocket bag pieces together.

Stitch around the outer edge with a ½" (1.3cm) seam allowance.

Step 15
The last step is to edgestitch the ends of the welt.

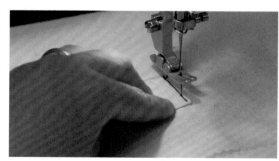
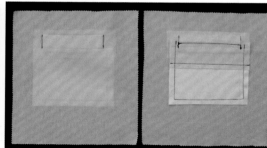

Be sure to backstitch the beginning and end of the welt.

Step 16
You have now finished your single-welt pocket.

Tong Ka Lam created this embellished jacket with a set of double-welt pockets. Fall/Winter 2015.

Double-welt Pocket

Learning objectives

☐ Measure and mark a pocket opening, add interfacing, and mark the seam allowance on the welt pieces

☐ Sew the welts: cut the opening, fold the welts to the right side, add the pocket bag, and edgestitch to finish

Tools and supplies:

- #2 muslin (lightweight calico)
- Fusible woven interfacing
- Pocketing
- Matching cotton thread

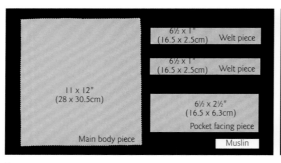

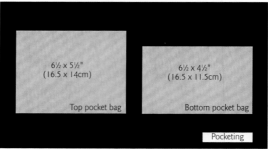

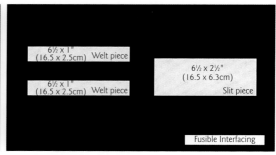

Step 1

For this lesson you will need to prepare four muslin pieces: a main body piece, 11" (28cm) by 12" (30.5cm); two welt pieces, 6½" (16.5cm) by 1" (2.5cm); and a pocket facing piece, 6½" (16.5cm) by 2½" (6.3cm).

Step 2

Out of pocketing material you will need to prepare: a top pocket bag, 6½" (16.5cm) by 5½" (14cm), and a bottom pocket bag, 6½" (16.5cm) by 4½" (11.5cm).

Out of fusible interfacing you will need: two welt pieces, 6½" (16.5cm) by 1" (2.5cm), and a slit piece, 6½" (16.5cm) by 2½" (6.3cm).

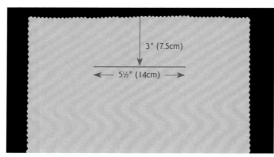

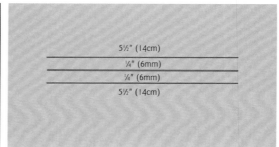

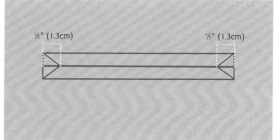

Step 3

Now draw a line for the pocket slit, 3" (7.5cm) down and 5½" (14cm) wide, centered on your main body piece and on the right side of the fabric.

Step 4

Mark two lines parallel to the slit, one ¼" (6mm) above it and one ¼" (6mm) below. This represents the seam allowance.

Step 5

Draw a triangle on each end ½" (1.3cm) away from the corner.

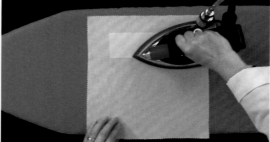

Step 6A

Turn your main body piece over to the wrong side and apply the fusible interfacing piece, sticky side down, over the center of the pocket slit. Press it in place.

Step 6B

Now place the interfacing on the wrong side of both welts and press.

Step 6C
Then fold the welts in half lengthwise and press.

Step 7A
On the welts, mark a ½" (1.3cm) seam allowance at both short ends. For demonstration purposes we are using pencil. If this were fashion fabric, you would use chalk.

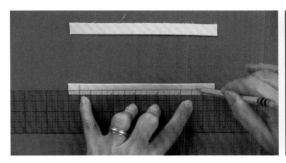

Step 7B
Then mark a seam allowance ¼" (6mm) from the folded lengthwise edge of each welt.

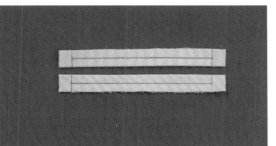

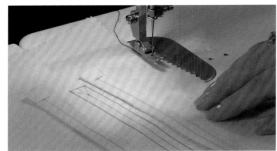

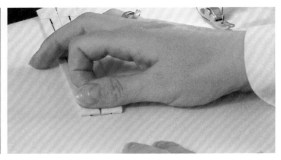

Step 1

The first step in sewing the double-welt pocket is to line up the stitching line of each welt with the stitching line of the main body piece, with the raw edges of the welts nearest the pocket slit guideline.

Step 2A

Place the corner of the first welt exactly over the corner of the slit. Be sure to backstitch at the start and the end of the stitching line, but be careful not to stitch beyond your corner markings.

Step 2B

Then do the same with the second welt. Turn back the seam allowance once you have finished, to check that the stitching lines at both top and bottom are even.

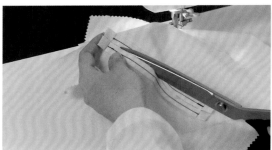

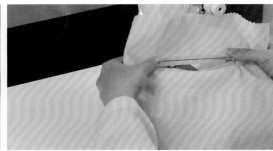

Step 3

Use the point of your scissors to clip along the center of the slit line. Cut along that line until you get to the triangle point.

Cut into both sides of the triangle to the corners. It is important to clip accurately so that your corners will be even. Repeat this step on the other side.

Step 4

Now turn the welt seam allowance under toward the wrong side.

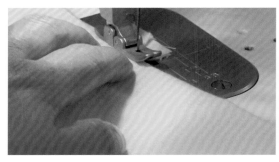

Next, position the triangle's seam allowance over the welt seam allowance.

Machine-tack the triangle in place.

Then repeat this step on the other side.

This is what your sampler now looks like from the right side.

Step 5A

Now sew the pocket facing to the bottom pocket bag with a ½" (1.3cm) seam allowance.

Step 5B

Then press the seam allowance down, toward the pocket bag.

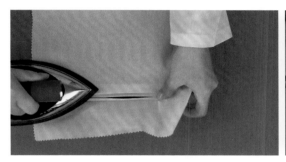

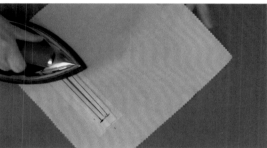

Step 6

Press the welt opening on the right side. We are using muslin here, so have not used a pressing cloth, but you should always use one when pressing on the right side of fashion fabric.

Now press on the wrong side.

Step 7A

Next, you will attach the bottom pocket bag and facing to the top welt guideline.

Line up the pocket facing piece with the seam allowance of the top welt.

Then stitch across, using a ¼" (6mm) seam allowance.

Next, you will position the top pocket bag with the seam allowance of the lower slit guideline.

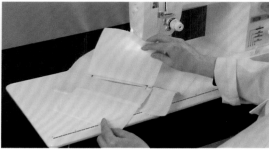

Step 7B
Align the top pocket bag with the lower welt seam allowance at ¼" (6mm) and then stitch across.

Your bags should now look like this.

Step 8A
To create an edgestitch around the welt, start by positioning your top pocket facing piece in an upward direction, and your bottom pocket bag in a downward direction.

Step 8B
On the right side of the sampler, edgestitch the pocket, starting from the middle of the lower welt, working all the way round.

Stop at the middle of the pocket opening on the other side.

Step 8C
Now turn the sampler over.

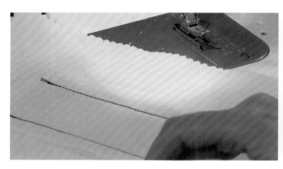

Flip the top pocket bag downward.

You can now continue edgestitching around the top welt.

Stitch all the way round to where you began.

  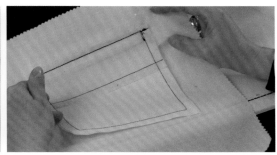

Step 9A
To close the pocket bag, you will need to join the upper and lower pocket bags. Begin at the top, using a ½" (1.3cm) seam allowance.

Continue stitching along the bottom...

...and back up the other side to close the bag.

Tip
The double-welt pocket is also known as a besom or jetted pocket.

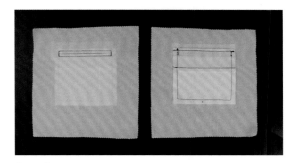

Step 9B
You have now finished your double-welt pocket.

Self-evaluation

☐ Can I make a sample of each pocket in the chapter?
☐ Did I apply my interfacings before stitching my pockets?
☐ Did I clip my pocket corners accurately while stitching?

10 Zippers

The most commonly used zipper in the industry is a **centered zipper**, which is easy to sew in place using a right-side zipper foot. A **lapped zipper** is sewn in using both a left-side and a right-side zipper foot. Next we show you a fast, easy, and foolproof method for inserting a **invisible zipper** that will be almost undetectable on the outside. We walk you through the steps required to attach a **lapped zipper with facing**, building on the lapped zipper lesson.

An **exposed separating zipper** is a popular closure on coats and jackets. You will learn an easy way to ensure your topstitching lines are perfectly even and straight, using a magnetic gauge attachment on your sewing machine.

A **fly front zipper** is commonly used on jeans, pants (trousers), and skirts, so is a key skill. New techniques here include sewing the zipper to the fly facing, and then attaching the fly shield. Finally you will hand-sew an **embellished zipper** to add a decorative touch. Ours incorporates mini pearls into the prick stitches that also hold the zipper in place.

Centered Zipper

Learning objectives

☐ Prepare to set the zipper by marking the seam allowance and zipper length

☐ Set up the sewing machine with a right-side zipper foot

☐ Position and pin the zipper correctly; sew the zipper in place

A lapped zipper front closes a dress by Vanessa Seward. Spring/Summer 2017.

Tools and supplies:

- Medium-weight cotton fabric
- Matching cotton thread
- 7" (18cm) all-purpose zipper
- Right-side zipper foot
- Pinking shears
- Sewing gauge

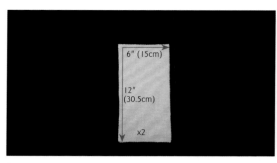

Step 1

For this lesson you will need to prepare two pieces of fabric, measuring 6" (15cm) in the width grain, and 12" (30.5cm) in the length grain. The edges here have been pinked to prevent the fabric from unraveling.

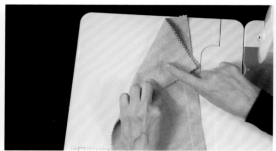

Step 2

Identify the right side of the fabric. Then, using your tailor's chalk, mark an "X" on the wrong sides of both fabric pieces.

Step 3

Also on the wrong sides of the fabric pieces, measure and draw a line for the ¾" (2cm) seam allowance—from the left length edge on one piece, and from the right length edge on the other. These are the stitching guidelines for the zipper placement.

Step 4

You will also have to sew part of the seam before you set in the zipper. An easy way to do this is to lay the zipper on the wrong side of the fabric pieces, with the top edges matching and the zipper tape aligned with the ¾" (2cm) seam stitching line. At the zipper bottom stop, and on the stitch line, pin through both layers of fabric.

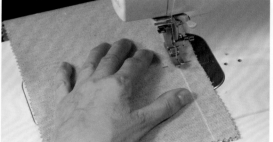

Step 5

Insert your machine needle at the pin on the stitching line. Then remove the pin, lower your presser foot, and begin sewing the seam, making sure to backstitch at the start.

Step 6

Continue sewing the seam to the lower edge and then backstitch. Clip the end threads, and then remove your work from the sewing machine.

Step 1A

In this lesson, you will be using a right-side zipper foot to attach the centered zipper.

Step 1B

Use the screwdriver that came with your machine to loosen the side bolt and remove the regular presser foot.

Step 1C

Now attach the zipper foot, tightening the bolt again with your screwdriver. The screw holding the foot needs to be tight enough to prevent the foot from slipping off while you are sewing.

Tip

Silk organza is a good choice for a pressing cloth. It is sheer, so we can see what we are pressing. The iron will also glide nicely over it, and silk organza withstands heat and steam well.

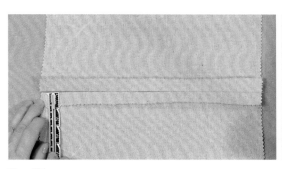

Step 2A

Use your seam gauge to check that the seam allowance is ¾" (2cm) all the way along the sewn seam and the upper edge of the zipper opening.

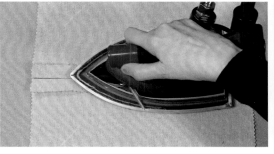

Step 2B

Press the seam and seam allowances open, with the wrong side of the fabric facing up.

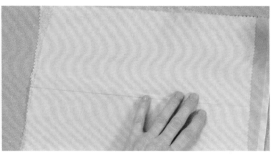

Step 2C

Turn the piece right side up, and place a pressing cloth on top to protect it. Here, we are using a silk organza pressing cloth.

Step 2D

Give the piece a final press in preparation for setting the centered zipper.

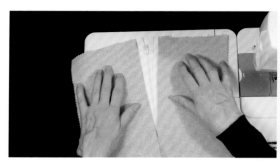

Step 1A
Begin by placing the zipper in the zipper opening and under the fabric, with both zipper and fabric face up.

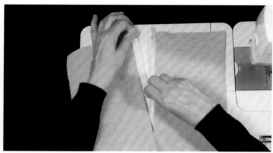

Step 1B
Now unzip the zipper, in preparation for pinning.

Step 1C
Beginning on the left side, place the zipper with the top edges matching and the zipper coil slightly in from the pressed edge of the zipper opening.

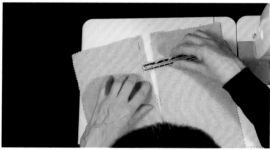

Step 2A
Pin the zipper ¼" (6mm) away from the folded, pressed edge of the fabric, from the top edge down to the zipper pull.

Step 2B
Now close the zipper to finish pinning.

Step 2C
Continue to measure and pin, until you reach the zipper bottom stop.

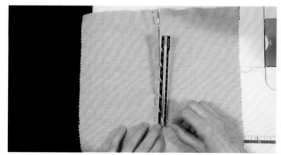

Step 2D
Now measure down ¼" (6mm) from the zipper bottom stop, and insert a pin horizontally. This pin indicates where to sew across the bottom of the zipper from the left side to the right.

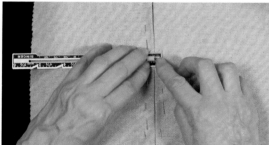

Step 2E
Now measure and pin the zipper on the right side, stopping halfway up.

Step 2F
Then open the zipper halfway down and finish pinning, making sure that the zipper coil is centered.

Step 3A

Now start stitching at the top, on the left side. Position your machine needle so that it lines up with the pin stitch guideline. Lower the zipper foot and open the zipper a few inches down from the top.

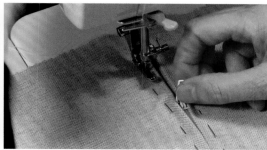

Step 3B

Begin sewing down the left side, backstitching at the start and removing the pins as you sew. Stop sewing when you reach the zipper pull. Leave your needle in the fabric, raise the foot so you can close the zipper, then lower the foot back into position.

Step 3C

Continue sewing down the left side, stopping when you reach the horizontal pin at the bottom. However, leave your needle in the fabric.

Step 3D

Now raise the foot and pivot the fabric. Remove the pin and lower the foot, so that you can sew across the bottom to the right side.

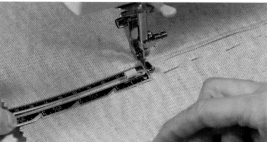

Step 3E

Measure on both sides of the seam from the foot to the lower edge of the fabric, to make sure that the measurement is the same. The stitch line should be squared at the bottom.

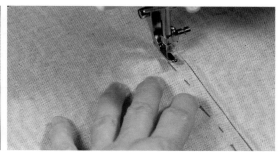

Step 3F

Stop at the pin guideline on the right side, leaving your needle in the fabric, raise the foot, then pivot the fabric again.

Step 3G

Then, before you continue sewing up the right side, measure to make sure the stitch line on the right side will also be ¼" (6mm) away from the center, as it is on the left side. Adjust it if necessary.

Step 3H

Continue sewing up the right side of the zipper, removing the pins as you sew. Stop a few inches before the top edge. Leaving your needle in the fabric, raise the foot, and open your zipper to just below the foot.

Step 3I

Finish sewing the right side, backstitching at the end.

Step 3J
Clip the end threads, and then remove your work from the sewing machine.

Step 3K
You have now finished inserting a centered zipper.

Types of Zipper

There are three main types of zipper: coil, stamped plastic, and stamped metal. Coil zippers, the most popular, are used on all types of garments. They are lightweight, flexible, and have teeth made of coiled nylon or polyester. Stamped plastic zippers have plastic teeth, are molded onto the zipper tape, and are mostly used on sportswear and activewear. Stamped metal zippers have metal teeth, pulls, and stoppers, and are most often used on jackets and coats. All three types of zipper are available as a dress/skirt type zipper or a separating zipper, with a choice of teeth width and zipper length. Another option is an invisible zipper, with its coil on the back.

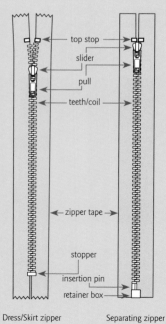

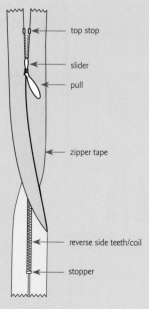

Dress/Skirt zipper   Separating zipper   Invisible zipper

Lapped Zipper

Learning objectives

☐ Prepare the opening by marking the seam allowance and zipper length

☐ Sew the seam below the opening, establish the lap, and press the seam

☐ Position and pin the right side of the zipper, position the lap, and use a right-side zipper foot to sew the lap in place

Tools and supplies:

- Wool flannel fabric
- Matching cotton thread
- 7" (18cm) all-purpose zipper
- Left-side and right-side zipper feet
- Pinking shears
- Sewing gauge

Module 1:

Lesson Prep

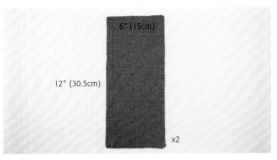

Step 1

For this lesson you will need to prepare two pieces of fabric, measuring 6" (15cm) in the width grain, and 12" (30.5cm) in the length grain. The edges here have been pinked to prevent the fabric from unraveling.

Step 2

Identify the right side of the fabric. Then, using your tailor's chalk, mark an "X" on the wrong sides of both fabric pieces.

Step 3

Also on the wrong sides of the fabric pieces, measure and draw a line for a ¾" (2cm) seam allowance—from the left length edge on one piece, and from the right length edge on the other. These are the stitching guidelines for the zipper placement.

Module 2:

Preparing to Set the Zipper

Step 1

You will need to sew part of the seam before you set the zipper. An easy way to do this is to lay the zipper on the wrong side of the fabric pieces, with the top edges matching and the zipper tape aligned with the ¾" (2cm) stitch line. At the zipper bottom stop, on the stitch line, pin through both layers of fabric.

Step 2A

Insert your machine needle at the pin on the stitch line. Then remove the pin, lower the presser foot, and begin sewing the seam, making sure to backstitch at the start.

Step 2B

Continue sewing the seam to the lower edge and then backstitch. Clip the end threads, and then remove your work from the sewing machine.

Step 3A

Lay your partially sewn fabric pieces flat on the table, wrong side facing up, with the sewn seam on your right. Using your plastic ruler, measure out ⅛" (3mm) from the stitch line and draw another line. This is your guideline for the right side extension of the zipper.

Step 3B

Now fold and press back that half of the seam allowance on the ⅛" (3mm) guideline.

Step 3C

Next, open the fabric pieces and lay them flat on the ironing board, wrong sides facing up. Locate the ¾" (2cm) seam allowance guideline on the left half of the seam allowance.

Step 3D
Press back the ¾" (2cm) seam allowance on that guideline for the lap half of the zipper.

Step 3E
Then turn your fabric pieces face up, and give a final press to the sewn seam only. Remember to use a pressing cloth to avoid iron marks or unwanted shine on the face of the wool.

Module 3:

Setting the Zipper—
Right Side

Step 1
Now you are ready to sew your lapped zipper.

Step 2A
Place the zipper under the fabric, both face up, with the top edges matching, and open the zipper halfway.

Step 2B
You will begin on the right side with the ⅛" (3mm) extension. Place the folded, pressed edge of the fabric against the back edge of the zipper coil, so that the zipper coil is exposed to the left of the fabric.

Step 3A
Begin pinning on the right top edge, making sure to keep the zipper coil exposed. Continue until you reach the zipper pull.

When you reach the zipper pull, close the zipper.

Step 3B
Then continue pinning to the zipper bottom stop, making sure that there is a ⅛" (3mm) fabric extension at the bottom.

Step 4A
You will be using the left-side zipper foot to sew the right half of the zipper.

Step 4B
Remove your general-purpose zipper foot from the sewing machine, and replace it with the left-side zipper foot. Make sure you tighten the foot securely with your screwdriver.

Step 5A
Begin sewing at the top, positioning your machine needle so that you are stitching very close to the folded, pressed edge of the fabric. Be sure to backstitch at the start.

Step 5B
Leaving your needle in the fabric, raise the foot, and open the zipper for several inches. Then lower the foot and continue stitching very close to the folded, pressed edge of the fabric, stopping at the zipper pull.

Step 5C
Again, leaving your needle in the fabric, raise the foot, and this time close the zipper, lower the foot, and continue stitching very close to the folded, pressed edge of the fabric, removing the pins as you sew.

Step 5D
Stitch to the end of the zipper tape and backstitch.

Step 5E
Clip the end threads, and then remove your work from the sewing machine.

Phillip Lim accentuates the front of a jumpsuit by exposing the metal teeth of a centered zipper. September 2016.

Module 4:

Setting the Zipper—
Lap Side

Step 1A

Lay your work face up on the table, in preparation for pinning the left, or lap, side of the zipper.

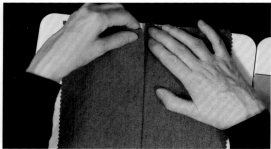

Step 1B

Lap the left side over the right side. The lap side should cover the stitching on the right side, while the folded, pressed edge forms a straight line up to the top edge.

Step 1C

Next, place holding pins along the edge of the lap side, catching the fabric layer only, pinning from the top to the bottom of the zipper opening.

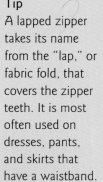

Tip
A lapped zipper takes its name from the "lap," or fabric fold, that covers the zipper teeth. It is most often used on dresses, pants, and skirts that have a waistband.

Step 1D

Turn up the lower edge of your work to the wrong side, and locate the zipper bottom stop.

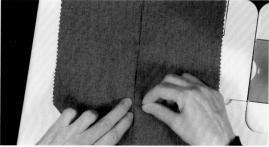

Step 1E

Then turn it face up again, and insert a pin at the seam, going across the lap side, about 1/8" (3mm) below the zipper bottom stop. This pin indicates where to sew across the bottom of the lap side.

Step 1F

Next, you will be measuring ½" (1.3cm) from the folded, pressed edge to the lap side, for a stitching guideline.

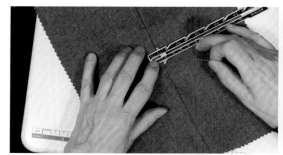

Step 1G

Continue measuring and pinning vertically, indicating the stitch guideline down the lap side of the zipper.

Stop when you reach the pin across the bottom.

Step 1H

Once you have pinned the lap side, you can remove the pins from the folded, pressed edge of the fabric.

Tip
When replacing a zipper foot, make sure you tighten the new foot securely with your screwdriver.

Step 2A
You will be using a right-side zipper foot to sew the lap side of the zipper.

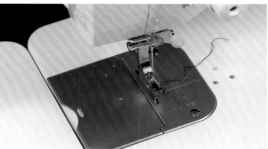

Step 2B
Remove your left-side zipper foot from the sewing machine and replace it with the right-side zipper foot.

Step 3A
Begin sewing at the top, positioning your machine needle so that it lines up with the pin stitch guideline. Start the stitch with a backstitch.

Step 3B
Leaving the needle in the fabric, raise the foot, and open the zipper a little. Then lower the foot and continue stitching, following the pin stitch guideline, removing the pins as you sew. Stop at the zipper pull.

Step 3C
Again, leaving your needle in the fabric, raise the foot, and this time close the zipper, then lower the foot so you can continue sewing, removing the pins as you sew.

Step 3D
Sew down to the pin across the bottom and stop.

Step 3E
Leaving your needle in the fabric, raise the foot and pivot the fabric so you can sew across the bottom lap side.

Step 3F
Lower the foot, sew across the bottom, stopping at the seam, and then sew a backstitch.

Step 3G
Clip the end threads, and then remove your work from the sewing machine.

Step 3H
You have now finished sewing the lap side of the zipper.

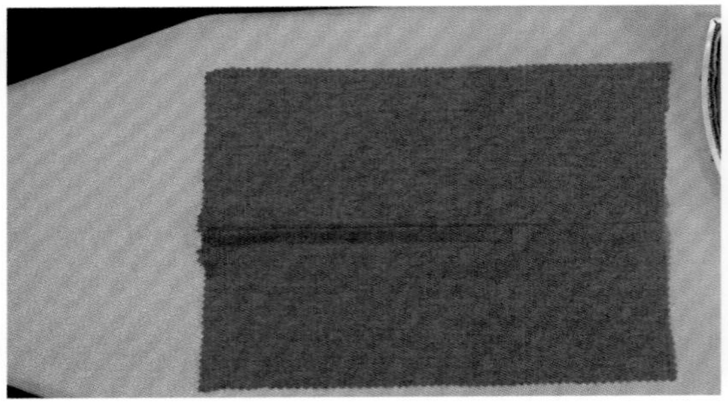

Step 4A
Lay your finished work face up on the ironing board.

Step 4B
Using a pressing cloth, give the zipper a final press.

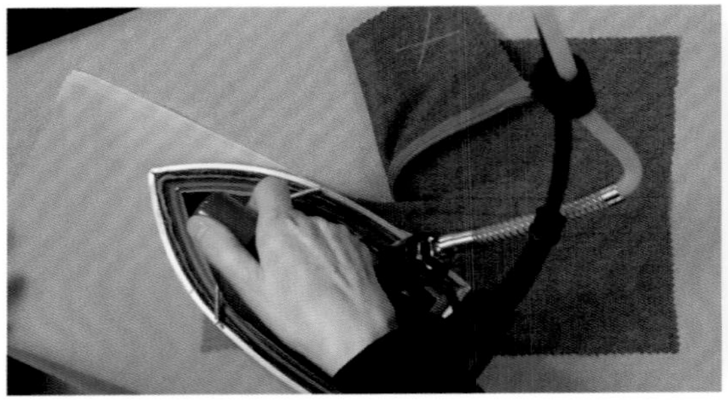

Step 4C
You may have to open the zipper partway to press the top edges. Again, remember to place the pressing cloth on top of the fabric before pressing.

Step 5
You have now finished sewing a lapped zipper.

An invisible zipper is the perfect choice for this bridal dress.

Invisible Zipper

Learning objectives

☐ Prepare to set the zipper by marking the seam allowance, pinning the left side of the zipper in place, and fixing an invisible zipper foot on the sewing machine

☐ Sew the zipper in place, deal with the zipper stop, and sew the seam below the zipper

Tools and supplies:

- Medium-weight cotton fabric
- Matching cotton thread
- 7" (18cm) invisible zipper
- Invisible zipper foot
- Right-side zipper foot
- Pinking shears
- Sewing gauge

Module 1:

Lesson Prep

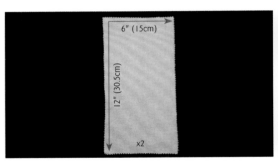

Step 1
For this lesson you will need to prepare two pieces of fabric, measuring 6" (15cm) in the width grain, and 12" (30.5cm) in the length grain of the fabric. The edges here have been pinked to prevent the fabric from unraveling.

Step 2
Identify the right side of the fabric. Then, using your tailor's chalk, mark an "X" on the wrong sides of both fabric pieces.

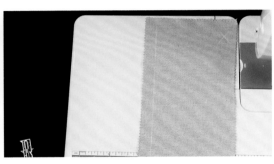

Step 3
Also on the wrong sides of the fabric pieces, measure and draw a line for a ¾" (2cm) seam allowance—from the left length edge on one piece, and from the right length edge on the other. These are the stitching guidelines for the zipper placement.

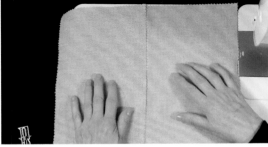

Step 4
Turn the fabric pieces face up, with the ¾" (2cm) seam-allowance edges facing each other.

Module 2:

Setting the Zipper—
Left Side

Step 1
Begin by unzipping the invisible zipper.

Step 2
Now flip the zipper over to the wrong side so that the left half of the zipper is facing the right fabric piece, right sides facing each other.

Step 3
Lay the left half of the zipper face down on the right fabric piece. Make sure the top edges of the zipper and the fabric meet, and that the edge of the zipper tape is facing left, toward the pinked edge of the fabric piece.

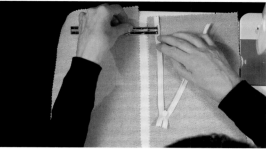

Step 4

In addition to the guidelines you have drawn on the wrong side of the fabric pieces, you can also use a sewing gauge to measure the ¾" (2cm) seam allowance for your zipper placement. Measure from the zipper coil to the pinked edge of the fabric.

Step 5

Pin the left half of the zipper to the fabric. Insert the pins parallel to the zipper coil, so that they are easy to remove as you sew.

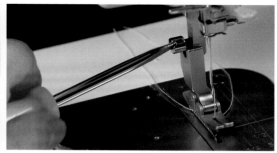

Step 6A

Now remove your general-purpose presser foot from your sewing machine.

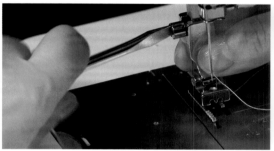

Step 6B

Then attach the invisible zipper foot to your sewing machine. Use a screwdriver to make sure the foot is on tight enough, so that it will not slide down while you are sewing.

Step 7A

Note that the upper thread is above the foot. However, we suggest that the upper thread should be under the foot with the bobbin thread. This helps to prevent the threads from tangling.

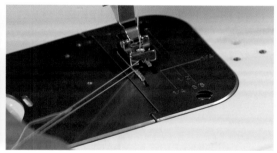

Step 7B

To achieve this, take a scrap of fabric and sew for a few inches. Then remove the work and, as you can see, the upper thread will now be under the invisible zipper foot.

Step 8A

Begin sewing the left half of the invisible zipper by inserting the zipper coil into the right groove on the invisible zipper foot. This places the needle on the left of the zipper coil.

Step 8B

Lower your invisible zipper foot, insert the needle, hold the threads taut behind the zipper foot, and begin sewing. Remember to backstitch at the beginning.

Step 8C

Sometimes the zipper top stop will not pass through the groove easily. Try leaving your needle in the work, raise the zipper foot slightly, then use your fingers to move the zipper coil to a lifted position. This will allow you to place the zipper top stop manually inside the groove. Then lower the foot to continue.

Step 8D
Hold the zipper coil in a lifted position, and remove the pins as you sew. By doing this, the needle will be kept as close as possible to the zipper coil, resulting in a perfectly set invisible zipper.

Step 8E
Stop sewing when the invisible zipper foot touches the top of the zipper pull, and then backstitch.

Step 8F
Clip the end threads, and then remove your work from the sewing machine.

Module 3:

Setting the Zipper—
Right Side

Step 1A
To sew the right side of the invisible zipper, position the right half of the zipper face down on the left fabric piece, with right sides together.

Step 1B
Make sure the zipper tape is not twisted when bringing it over to the left fabric piece.

Step 1C
Holding the zipper tape to the fabric, lay it down flat, with the invisible zipper face up. Make sure the top edges of the zipper and fabric meet, and that the edge of the zipper tape is facing right, toward the long pinked edge of the fabric.

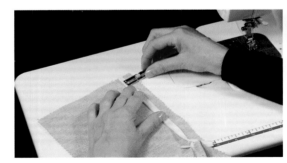

Step 2
Again, use the guideline you have drawn on the wrong side. Or, as we are doing, measure the ¾" (2cm) seam allowance for the zipper placement using your sewing gauge. Measure from the zipper coil to the pinked edge of the fabric.

Step 3
Pin this half of the zipper to the fabric. Insert the pins parallel to the zipper coil, so they are easy to remove as you sew.

Step 4A
Begin sewing the right half of the invisible zipper by inserting the zipper coil into the groove on the left half of the foot. This places the needle to the right of the zipper coil.

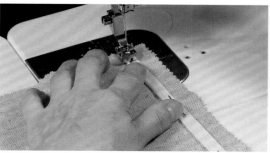

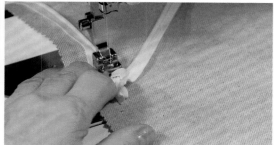

Step 4B
Again, if the zipper top stop does not pass through the groove easily, follow the advice on page 317.

Step 4C
Now finish sewing the right half of the invisible zipper following the same steps used for the left half, stopping when you reach the zipper pull.

Module 4:

Final Steps

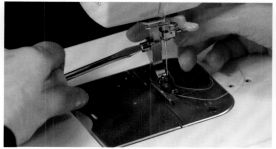

Step 1
To complete the invisible zipper setting, you will need a right-side zipper foot to sew the seam below the zipper.

Step 2
Remove the invisible zipper foot from your sewing machine, and replace it with a right-side zipper foot.

Step 3A
Close the zipper.

Step 3B
Have the two right sides facing each other, so that the wrong side of one half is facing up.

Step 3C
Insert a pin temporarily in the fabric where the zipper stitch ends. This makes it easy to see where to begin sewing.

Step 3D
Line up the right-side zipper foot and the machine needle at the pin on the zipper stitching line.

Step 3E
Once the machine needle is in the correct position, you can remove the pin in preparation for sewing.

Step 4A
Sew the seam closed, backstitching at the beginning and at the end of the seam.

Step 4B
Clip the end threads, and then remove your work from the sewing machine.

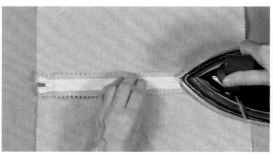

Step 4C
Press the seam open below the zipper.

Step 4D
Give the right side of the fabric a final pressing using an organza pressing cloth.

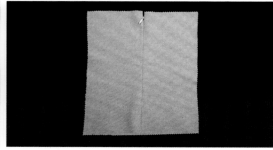

Step 5
You have now finished setting an invisible zipper.

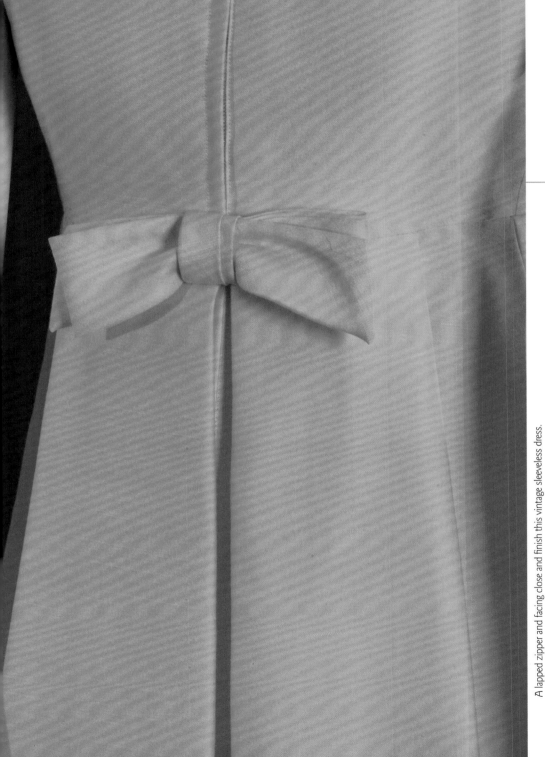

Lapped Zipper with Facing

Learning objectives

☐ Cut the pieces and set the zipper into the right body side, folding the seam allowance on the left body piece and sewing the other side of the zipper in place

☐ Add the facing, positioning it correctly and pinning it in place, sew the facing, and trim the seam allowance

☐ Use techniques to finish the zipper: clipping into a curved neckline, understitching, and hand-stitching the facings to the zipper tape

A lapped zipper and facing close and finish this vintage sleeveless dress.

Tools and supplies:

- Medium-weight cotton fabric
- Matching cotton thread
- All-purpose zipper
- Left-side and right-side zipper feet

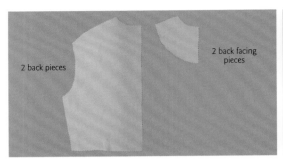

Step 1

For this lesson you will need to prepare two back body pieces and two back facing pieces. However, if this were not a sampler but an actual garment, you would need to interface the facings.

Step 2

Stitch the zipper to the right body piece, following the method provided in our Lapped Zipper lesson.

Step 3

Press back the ¾" (2cm) seam allowance of the left body piece to form a crease, and position the zipper ¼" (6mm) away from the crease on the seam allowance.

Stitch down the middle of the zipper tape.

Step 4

Now fold and press the ½" (1.3cm) seam allowance on the left back facing. Then position the left facing ¼" (6mm) away from the crease of the left body piece.

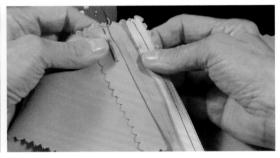

Step 5

Pin the left facing in place.

Step 6A

The next step will be to fold the back seam allowance over at the back crease of the body.

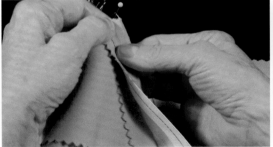

Fold this over, reversing the original direction of the crease—the zipper side folds forward and overlaps the left back facing.

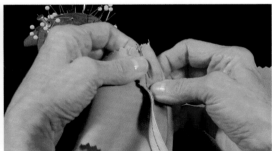

Step 6B

Secure the layers together with a pin, making sure that you have folded the seam allowance over exactly on the crease line. Make adjustments if necessary.

Step 6C
Add another pin at the neckline, midway between the center back and the shoulder, to hold the layers in place.

Module 2:

Sewing the Left Facing & Zipper

Step 1
Now sew the left facing to the body, starting from the shoulder, squaring off at center back, and ending with a backstitch.

Step 2
Trim the end threads and remove the pins.

Step 3A
Now turn the facing right side out to get an idea of how it looks. Note how the facing is now recessed in from the crease.

Step 3B
Note, too, how the folded edge of the facing aligns nicely with the zipper coil.

Step 4A
Now that you know that your left facing is perfectly stitched, you can trim the neck seam allowance. To do this, turn your facing back to the wrong side and trim the corner at an angle.

Step 4B
Then reduce the seam allowance to ¼" (6mm) along the back neckline.

Step 5A
Turn the facing back to the right side to sew the lap side of the zipper.

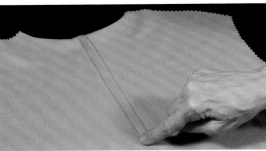

Step 5B
Following the instructions from our Lapped Zipper lesson, stitch the left side of the zipper.

Step 5C
For the facings on both sides, be sure to always clip into the curved portions of your neck seam allowance.

Tip
An understitch is a stitch made close to the seam edge of a facing to help keep the facing from rolling over onto the right side of a garment.

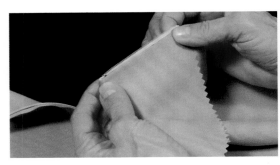

Step 5D
You will now be hand-stitching both facings to the zipper tape, lining up the folded edge of each facing with the stitching line of the zipper, as shown here with the right facing.

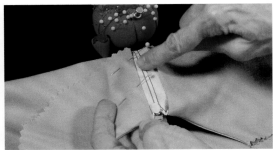

Step 5E
Pin each facing in place, as shown here with the left facing.

Step 6A
Before you sew the facings to the zipper, you may want to understitch ⅛" (3mm) away from the neckline's edge, all around the front and back facing.

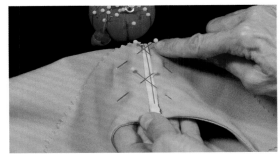

Step 6B
Once both facings are pinned in place along the zipper tape stitching line, hand-stitch both in place with a blind stitch.

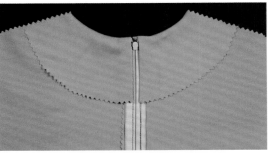

Step 6C
You have now completed a lapped zipper with a back facing.

Exposed Separating Zipper

Learning objectives

☐ Add interfacing to support the zipper, mark the center front and stitching line, and pin the two halves of the zipper in place

☐ Use both a right-side zipper foot and a left-side zipper foot to set the zipper

☐ Check that your topstitching is even, using a magnetic seam guide

☐ Topstitch the left front with a left-side zipper foot and the right front with a right-side zipper foot

Tools and supplies:

- Wool flannel fabric
- Fusible woven interfacing
- Size 5 (12"/30.5cm) nylon separating zipper
- Left-side and right-side zipper feet
- Pinking shears
- Magnetic seam guide
- Sewing gauge

Step 1A
For this lesson prepare a left and right jacket front, cut out of wool flannel. The center front length is 14" (35.5cm) and the edges have been pinked to prevent them from unraveling.

Step 1B
Interface the center front facing with a 1¾" (4.5cm)-wide piece of fusible interfacing to support the zipper stitching.

Step 2
On the right side of your jacket fronts, mark a white pencil dot, both top and bottom, to indicate the jacket's center front, which for this jacket is 1¼" (3cm) from the facing's edge.

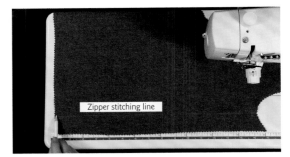

Step 3
Also mark a white pencil line ⅛" (3mm) away from the dot marks, to indicate the zipper stitching line. This measurement is half the width of the 12" (30.5cm) separating zipper coil.

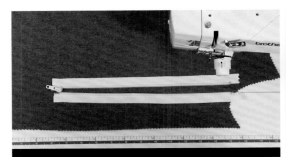

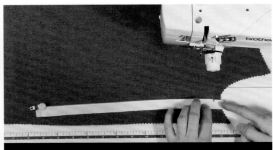

Step 1A
To begin, open the separating zipper and lay it face up on the right jacket front.

Step 1B
Remove the left side of the zipper from the table.

Turn the right zipper over, so that the zipper pull is now facing downward.

Step 2A

Position the zipper at the top of the jacket, along the white pencil stitching line. The zipper coil will be to the left of the stitching line.

Step 2B

The actual stitching will be done as close as possible to where the zipper coil meets the zipper tape.

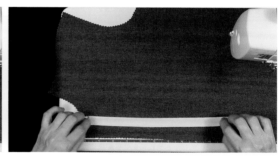

Step 2C

Once the zipper is in position, pin the layers together, placing your pins at a right angle to the zipper coil. Continue to check that you are pinning along the white chalk mark and that the zipper coil is to the left of the stitch line.

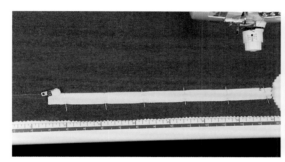

Step 2D

Place your last pin just above the zipper pull.

Step 3A

Now, move to the left jacket front and repeat the same steps to pin the zipper to the right side of the left jacket front.

This time you will turn the left zipper over, right side down, and position it to the right of the white chalk line.

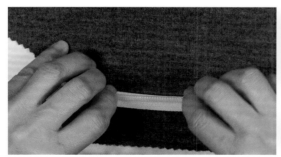

Step 3B

Pin the top edges together, then continue to check that you are pinning along the white chalk mark and that the zipper coil is to the right of the stitching line.

Step 3C

Place your last pin slightly above the zipper stop.

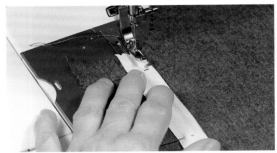

Step 1A
Before you can stitch the left side of the jacket zipper, you will need to replace your regular sewing machine foot with a right-side zipper foot.

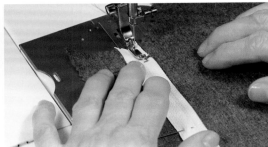

Step 1B
Position the left jacket front and zipper under the presser foot. The needle will be inserted very close to the left side of the zipper coil and in line with the white stitching line.

Step 1C
With your start threads positioned to the back, begin stitching with a backstitch and then guide the fabric through the machine. Be sure that your machine can stitch over the pins; otherwise you will either need to baste first or remove the pins as you sew.

Step 1D
Sew a backstitch when you reach the end to secure the zipper in place.

Step 1E
Remove your work from the machine, clip the end threads, and then remove the pins.

Step 2A
To sew the right-side zipper to the right jacket front, you must first remove the right-side zipper foot and replace it with a left-side zipper foot. Tighten the foot with your screwdriver, or with the side of a bobbin if a screwdriver is not available.

Step 2B
Position the right jacket front and zipper under the presser foot, with the needle inserted very close to the right side of the zipper coil and in line with the white stitching line. Grab your start threads and begin sewing, starting with a backstitch.

Step 2C
When you are about 2" (5cm) from the end of the zipper, stop sewing and lift the presser foot.

Step 2D
Now carefully raise the needle up and out of the work.

Step 3A
Lift the zipper pull up and move it past the zipper foot.

Step 3B
Once the zipper pull is out of the way, lower the needle back into the same stitch, lower the foot, and then sew to the end of the zipper tape.

Step 3C
Sew a backstitch when you reach the end, then clip the end threads and remove the pins.

Module 4:

Topstitching the Zipper—
Left & Right Sides

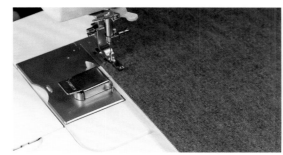

Step 1
With the center-front seam allowance folded under, exposing the zipper teeth, insert your machine needle ½" (1.3cm) away from the zipper coil. Here we are demonstrating the use of a magnetic seam guide, which will help keep your topstitching even.

Step 2
We are using our sewing gauge here to establish a topstitch that will sit ½" (1.3cm) from the fabric edge, and then positioning the magnetic guide accordingly. However, you could choose to stitch at ¼" (6mm), or even use an edgestitch instead.

Tip
Make sure that you have enough thread on top of the machine and in the bobbin before you start sewing. Zippers must be sewn in one continuous line for strength and visual appeal. If you run out of thread while topstitching, you will have to start again.

Step 3A
With the presser foot down and the threads to the back, sew a backstitch. For topstitching, set your machine to 8 to 9 stitches per inch (spi; 2.8–3.2mm stitch length). We are using a matching single cotton thread, but you could use two threads, contrast thread, or even a silk thread on top for decorative effect.

Step 3B
As you sew, continue to hold the fabric taut both in front of the zipper foot and behind it. This will help keep the fabric smooth while stitching.

Step 3C
For this sample we will stitch to the end of the jacket and then backstitch. However, you could also choose to hem the jacket first, in which case you would stitch to the end of the zipper.

Step 4A

To topstitch the right jacket front, remove the left-side zipper foot and replace it with the right-side zipper foot. You will now be repeating the topstitching steps on the right side of the jacket.

Step 4B

Just as you did for the left side, turn the seam allowance under on the right jacket front, exposing the zipper teeth. Insert your machine needle at ½" (1.3cm) from the fabric edge, with your magnetic seam guide aligned on the right side of the zipper coil.

Step 4C

Use your sewing gauge to check that your measurements are correct and that your magnetic gauge is positioned correctly.

Step 4D

Start with a backstitch, and with the start threads behind the presser foot and out of your way. Then, as before, hold the fabric as you guide it through the machine.

Step 4E

When you reach the zipper pull, remove the magnetic gauge from the machine so that you can raise the zipper pull and move it away.

Step 5A

Continue your topstitching to the end of the jacket, then clip the threads.

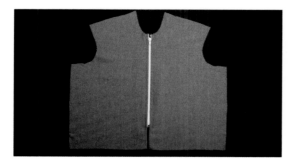

Step 5B

Place the right and left jacket fronts side by side and close the zipper to check your work. You have now finished sewing an exposed separating zipper.

Fly Front Zipper

Learning objectives

☐ Make a paper fly template

☐ Add interfacing to the self-facing of the right pant front; fold and press the facing and fly shield

☐ Attach the zipper to the left pant front, add the fly shield, and sew the zipper to the right pant front

☐ Mark a topstitching line using the paper template, topstitch the right fly, sew the self-facing to the fly shield

A fly front zipper adds a menswear touch to this women's trouser by Barbara Casasola, Fall/Winter 2014.

Tools and supplies:

- Muslin
- Fusible woven interfacing
- 7" (18cm) nylon coil pant (trouser) zipper
- Left-side zipper foot

Module 1:

Lesson Prep

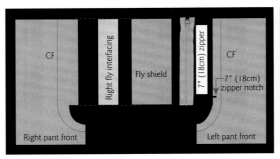

Step 1A
For this lesson you will need: a left pant front with a 7" (18cm) zipper notch, a right pant front with a 1½" (3.8cm) wide by 7¾" (19.7cm) long extension, a fly shield 3" (7.5cm) wide by 7¾" (19.7cm) long, a right fly interfacing 1½" (3.8cm) wide by 7¾" (19.7cm) long, and a 7" (18cm) zipper.

Step 1B
Begin by pressing your interfacing onto the wrong side of the right pant front's self-facing.

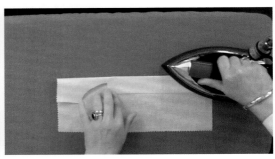

Step 2
Fold the self-facing along the center front line and lightly press.

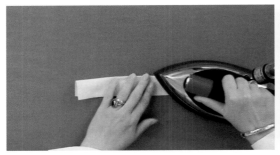

Step 3
Then fold the fly shield in half lengthwise and press.

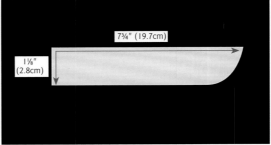

Step 4
Finally, make a paper fly template, measuring 1⅛" (2.8cm) wide by 7¾" (19.7cm) long, rounded out at the bottom on one end.

Step 1
Measure 7" (8cm) down from the top along the center front line and mark the zipper notch. Join the two pant fronts at the crotch, right sides together, starting at the zipper notch. Sew until you reach the inseam.

Step 2
In preparation for setting your zipper, you will need to change your machine foot to a left-side zipper foot.

Step 3
With the pant front face up, position the zipper face down along center front on the left piece, with the zipper stop aligned with the zipper notch.

Step 4A
With the pant front wrong side up, attach the zipper to the left pant front, stitching close to the coil.

Step 4B
Make sure that you reposition the zipper pull as you sew.

Step 5A
Open the seam as you reach the end of the stopper.

Step 5B
Your zipper should now look like this.

Step 6A
With the left pant front wrong side up, place the fly shield underneath so that the zipper is sandwiched between the two pieces, with the raw edges of the fly shield aligned with the raw edge of the left pant front.

Sew the fly shield in place along the same stitching line used to attach the zipper.

Step 6B
Make sure that you reposition the zipper pull as you sew.

Step 6C
Sew down to the end of the zipper stopper to secure the fly shield.

Step 7A
Fold the left pant front over to expose the zipper with the fly shield underneath. With the zipper open, begin topstitching the edge.

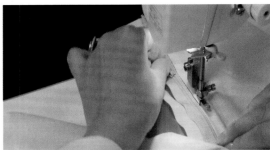

Step 7B
When you are a few inches from the zipper stopper, raise the zipper foot, leaving the needle in the fabric. Move the zipper pull up past the zipper foot.

Step 7C
Lower the zipper foot again and continue topstitching the edge down to the level of the stopper.

Module 3:

Attaching the Zipper to the Right Pant Front Self-facing

Step 1A
Place your folded right front self-facing on top of the zipper, matching the center front notches at the waistline.

Step 1B
Make sure the fold overlaps by the same distance all the way up to the top.

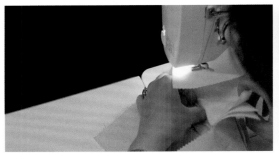

Step 2
Then pin along center front to hold the zipper in place.

Step 3

Turn your work to the wrong side and pin the zipper, face down, to the right self-facing only.

Step 4

Turn the work back to the right side and remove the top pins.

Step 5A

Turn to the wrong side again and stitch. Before you begin, pull the zipper down midway so that you will be able to stitch the zipper close to the coil on the right fly self-facing.

Step 5B

When you reach the midway point, lift the zipper foot to close the zipper before continuing down to the stopper.

Step 6A

Now place a second row of stitching on the edge of the zipper tape. Begin with your zipper closed and stitch up to a few inches below the top.

Step 6B

When you reach this point, raise the zipper foot with the needle still inserted, and move the zipper pull down to complete your stitching.

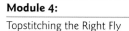

Module 4:

Topstitching the Right Fly

Step 1

Press the fly front area. Avoid pressing the zipper coil and pull.

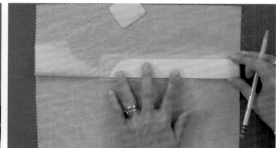

Step 2

Align the fly template along center front. It should be positioned at least ¼" (6mm) below the zipper stopper so that your needle does not hit the stopper. Mark the position with chalk or pencil.

Step 3

Change your zipper foot back to a regular foot and fold back the fly shield.

Step 4A
Keeping the fly shield folded back to the right-hand side out of the way, begin topstitching down from the waistline through the right pant front and its self-facing only. Follow the marking and stitch down parallel to the zipper.

Step 4B
Stop when the line starts to curve.

Lift up your work and fold the end of the fly shield up and out of the way of the needle.

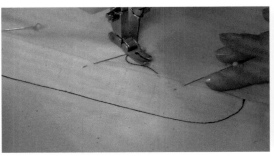

Then continue topstitching until you reach the center front line, finishing with a backstitch.

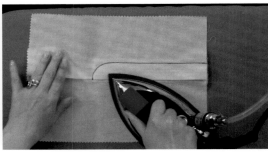

Step 5
Now press the fly area, but avoid contact with the zipper pull and coil.

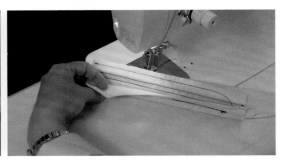

Step 6A
Now line up the right front self-facing and the front fly shield.

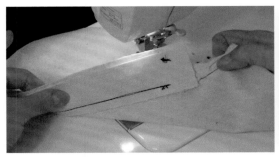

Stitch both pieces together by hand at the end, close to the topstitching line.

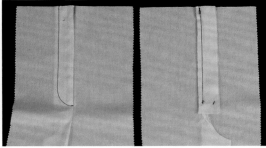

Step 6B
And this is your finished fly front zipper, shown from the right side and the wrong side.

An embellishment technique decorates the back of this evening dress.

Embellished Prick-stitched Zipper

Learning objectives

☐ Add interfacing to the fabric pieces, mark the zipper position, mark and baste a stitching line on either side of the opening

☐ Use Tiger Tape as a stitching guide, position the zipper, and baste in place

☐ Prepare beads and use beaded prick stitches as a decorative finish

Tools and supplies:

- Silk shantung fabric
- Fusible weft interfacing
- 7" (18cm) all-purpose zipper
- Size 10 beading needle
- 6-strand embroidery floss (thread)
- Silk thread
- Thread Heaven
- Tiger Tape
- 3.5mm pearl seed beads
- Open-top thimble
- Embroidery scissors
- Tweezers

Tip
This hand-sewn method is also useful when working with velvet. A machine zipper foot would crush the nap of the fabric.

Step 1
For this lesson you will need to prepare two pieces of fabric, each measuring 4½" (11.5cm) in the width grain, by 10" (25.5cm) in the length grain. (Here, we are using silk shantung.)

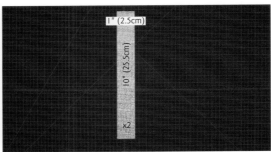

Step 2
You will also need to prepare two pieces of fusible weft interfacing, measuring 1" (2.5cm) wide by 10" (25.5cm) long.

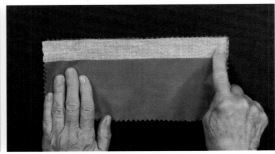

Step 3A
Press your fusible interfacing strip onto the wrong side of the first piece of fabric, along the length edge.

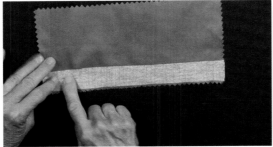

Step 3B
Repeat this process on the wrong side of the second fabric piece.

Step 4A
With your fabric pieces right sides together, line up your zipper along the length edge of the fabric. Then place a chalk mark at the end of the zipper stopper.

Step 4B
With your sewing machine, sew a seam ½" (1.3cm) away from the length edge. Sew from the zipper mark down to the bottom of the fabric.

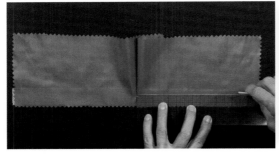

Step 5A
Lay the pieces flat on the table, right side up, then chalk a line ¾" (2cm) away from the edge on the right-hand piece, as demonstrated.

Step 5B
Repeat this step on the other side.

Step 6A
For basting (tacking), we will be using an open-top thimble and some DMC embroidery cotton.

Step 6B

Cut an 18″ (46cm) length of embroidery cotton, separate a single strand, then thread and knot a sewing needle.

Step 7A

Run a ½″ (1.3cm)-long basting (tacking) stitch along the stitching line on one side of the chalked zipper opening.

Step 7B

Clip the basting thread when you reach the zipper mark seam.

Step 7C

Knot the thread and repeat the step of basting along the stitching line on the other side of the chalked zipper opening. Do not catch the seam allowance as you stitch. Trim the end thread when you reach the end.

Step 8A

Fold the seam allowance of the zipper opening under and finger-press it.

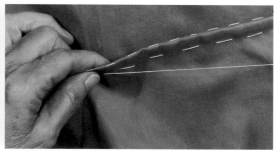

Step 8B

Now run a basting stitch ½″ (1.3cm) away from the folded seam allowance edge from the top to the end of the zipper opening. Sew your stitches ½″ (1.3cm) apart.

Step 8C

Sew a backstitch when you reach the end and then clip your end thread.

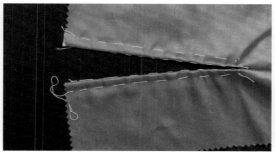

Step 8D

Now repeat this step on the other side of the zipper opening, as illustrated.

Step 9

Use your iron to steam and lightly press the wrong side of the zipper opening and the seam allowance.

Step 1A
For sewing the prick stitch, we will be using 100 percent silk thread.

We will also coat the thread with Thread Heaven conditioner to help keep it from tangling. (You could also use beeswax.)

Step 1B
Thread an 18" (46cm) length of silk thread through your needle, knot it, then pass it across the Thread Heaven, as shown.

Step 2A
Now position Tiger Tape along one folded edge of the zipper opening, from the top to approximately ½" (1.3cm) beyond the end of the zipper opening.

Step 2B
Repeat this step on the other side of the zipper opening.

Step 2C
Trim the top ends of the Tiger Tape on both sides.

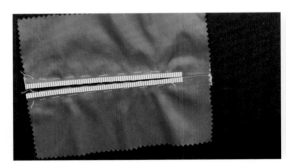

Step 2D
Trim the bottom ends of the Tiger Tape so that they are even.

Step 3A
Open the zipper and position it inside the zipper opening of the fabric, lining it up at the top.

Step 3B
The folded edge of the fabric must line up with the coil edge of the zipper.

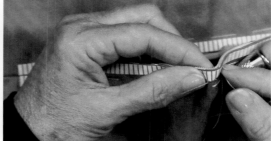

Step 4A

Now baste the zipper into the zipper opening, 1/16" (2mm) away from the edge of the Tiger Tape. You may be tempted to pin the zipper in place first. However, pinning may cause the fabric to pucker. Just take care that your zipper stays in place as you sew.

Step 4B

Hold the zipper in place with your thumb as you sew, using a 1/2" (1.3cm) basting stitch length.

Step 4C

Sew a backstitch when you reach the bottom of the zipper opening. Then trim the end thread. Repeat this process on the other side of the zipper opening.

Module 3:

Prick Stitching the Zipper & Adding Beads

Step 1

Take your strand of beads and release a few dozen beads into a small bowl. You will be using your silk thread to set the zipper with a prick stitch, adding beads at the same time.

Step 2A

Insert your threaded and knotted needle from underneath the fabric, right below the top zipper stopper and close to the edge of the Tiger Tape. Pull the thread through to the right side.

Step 2B

Insert the point of your needle into the opening of your first bead, and then slide the bead down the thread.

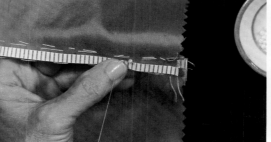

Step 2C

Lock the bead in place by taking your next stitch 1/16" (2mm) behind the first, coming up two marks past the bead stitch on the Tiger Tape.

Step 2D

Pull the thread through to the top. The spacing between the stitches will be 1/4" (6mm).

Step 3A

Now add another bead in the same way, taking a 1/16" (2mm) backstitch, then coming up two marks away on the Tiger Tape.

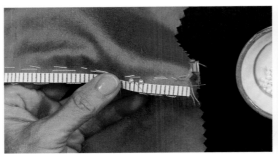

Step 3B

Pull the thread to the top, locking in the bead. Repeat these steps to continue adding beads.

Step 4

Guide the beads into place with your fingers as you stitch so that they align with the Tiger Tape.

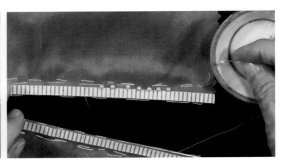

Step 5

Using a small bowl or cup makes it easier to insert the needle into each bead opening.

Step 6

When you reach the end of the zipper and you have sewn the last bead, secure it in place by going back into the bead opening and then passing the needle to the underside.

Step 7

Flip the fabric over to the wrong side and sew a triple knot. Then clip the end thread. Repeat these steps to sew the other side of the zipper.

Step 8

Once you have finished prick-stitching the other side of the zipper, carefully peel away the Tiger Tape from the fabric.

Step 9A

Now, using the tip of your embroidery scissors, snip the basting threads and remove them. Be very careful not to clip the actual bead threads.

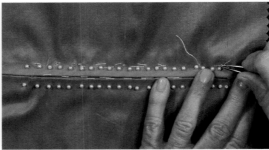

Step 9B

You may find that using tweezers to remove the basting threads is more efficient.

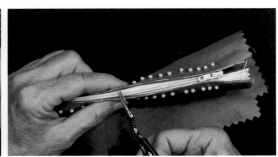

Step 9C

Do not forget to clip and remove the basting thread from the fold of the zipper seam allowance.

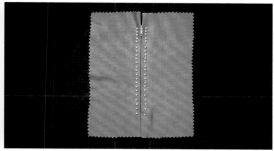

Step 10A
And lastly, trim the threads at the top of the zipper, as shown.

Step 10B
You have now finished your embellished prick-stitched zipper.

Self-evaluation

- ☐ Can I make a sample of every zipper application in the chapter?
- ☐ Did I use the correct zipper foot attachment for each zipper application?
- ☐ Did I use a pressing cloth to press my finished zipper?
- ☐ Did I use interfacing to stabilize my seam allowances before setting my zipper?

Glossary

A

All-in-One Facing A one-piece front and two-piece back facing that clean finishes both the neckline and armhole of a sleeveless and collarless garment.

All-purpose Thread Thread used for basic garment construction. Both 100 percent mercerized cotton and 100 percent polyester thread are suitable for linen, cotton, silk, wool, blends, and manufactured fibers.

All-purpose Zipper The zipper most often used on skirts, pants (trousers), and dresses. Available in various lengths, colors, and zipper teeth types.

Appliqué Fabric or trim that is applied to a garment, either by hand or machine stitching.

B

Backing Material used to add support to the underside of a fabric or other material. Can be fused or stitched in place.

Backstitch Reverse sewing stitch used to reinforce a seam or other area of a garment.

Ballpoint Needle Needle with a rounded ball-tip point, for working with knits.

Bar Tack Stitch that reinforces areas of stress, such as the end of a pocket or belt loop.

Basting Temporary stitches made either by hand or machine until they can be sewn permanently.

Besom Pocket A double-welt inset slit pocket used on tailored garments.

Bespoke Refers to a made-to-measure garment.

Betweens Needles Needles shorter than sharps, with a small rounded eye for making fine stitches. Especially used in tailoring, including pad stitching. Also known as quilting needles.

Bias Binding Fabric that is cut on the true bias for clean finishing a garment edge.

Bias Facing Facing cut on a 45° diagonal grain.

Bias Grain Diagonal direction of a fabric that yields the most stretch. "True bias" is at a 45-degree angle; "garment bias" is not.

Bias Strip Fabric strip cut on the bias grain that can be used to make loops or straps, reinforce a seam, or encase a raw edge.

Bias Tape A by-the-yard tape used to bind areas of a garment where a clean finish is desired. Available in a variety of widths, either single-fold or double-fold.

Blanket Stitch Hand stitch used as a decorative embellishment.

Bleeding When dye migrates from one material onto another.

Blind Stitch Small machine or hand stitch used on hems. The thread is hidden in the fold so that the stitches are not visible.

Blocking Process of manipulating muslin or other fabric so that the length and cross grains are at right angles to each other.

Bodice A fitted upper body silhouette used as a foundation sloper (block) from which stylizations are created.

Bonded Thread Finish Very strong thread with an applied resin finish.

Bound Seam A seam that is encased with either a fabric strip, tape, or a bias binding.

Break Point/Break line Point on a garment where the lapel turns back and the closure is placed, such as on a notched collar jacket.

Button Decorative ornament used as a trimming or as a functional fastener.

Button Extension Amount of space that is needed when planning a button closure.

Button Gauge Device used to measure the button size/diameter in ligne and metric.

Button Loop Closure made of thread, cord, bias, or non-bias fabric tubing.

Button Reinforcement Very small flat buttons or pieces of felt used to secure sewn buttons on the underside and to prevent the fabric tearing.

Buttonhole Hole through which a button passes to close a garment.

C

Cashmere A soft, fine, downy fabric produced from the wool of the cashmere goat.

Casing Tunnel made of fabric, in which a belt or elastic is encased.

Catch Stitch Hand-hemming stitch that alternates between the body and the hem. It is most often used on bulky materials and knit hems due to its ability to stretch.

Centered Zipper Zipper set with an even amount of fabric on each side of the zipper and where the zipper teeth are not exposed.

Centerline A line that denotes the center of a pattern or drape.

CF Center front of the body/dress form.

Chainstitch Hem/Seam A finish consisting of a series of looped stitches that form a chain-like pattern on one side of the fabric and a straight stitch effect on the other side. Most often used on knit fabrics or on the hem of jeans.

Check Fabric Fabric with vertical and horizontal lines that cross each other to form squares.

Chevron A pattern in the form of an inverted V-shape.

Chiffon A very light, sheer, plain-weave fabric in a fine, hard spun yarn of silk or manufactured fibers, with a dull finish and somewhat stiff hand.

Circular Knitting Machine Knitting machine that creates a seamless tube of weft-knit fabric.

Circumference Distance around a particular area, such as the waistline, bicep, wrist, or hip.

Clapper A wooden block tool with an open handle that is used to flatten seams and other bulky areas of a garment.

Clean Finish Refers to any method used to finish a garment edge, such as facings, hems, etc.

Clip To snip notches or release seam allowances, especially on curves and at waistlines.

Closures Any garment fastening such as buttons, frogs, snaps, clips, toggles, or buckles.

Cone A cone-shaped spool on which thread is cross-wound, forming an "X" pattern. Cross-wound thread cones are used on a sewing machine's vertical spindle.

Cop A spindle of thread that is cross-wound, forming an "X" pattern. Cop thread can be used on a sewing machine's vertical spindle or on a horizontal spindle using a spool cap.

Core Spun Thread A thread with a core of polyester filament covered with cotton or polyester staple fibers. Used on fabrics that have a finish or a tendency to pucker.

Cotton Canvas A medium- to heavyweight, durable plain-weave cotton fabric. Often used for making jacket and coat toiles.

Cotton Count System Part of the thread sizing "fixed-weight system," referring to the amount of thread required to weigh one pound.

Cotton Fabrics Fabric made from cotton bolls derived from the cotton plant and spun into yarn. Available in plain, twill, and satin weaves.

Course Describes the crosswise row of stitches on a plain stitch or basic knit fabric.

Couture Made-to-measure high-end clothing.

Coverstitch Type of hem or seam finish consisting of a series of looped stitches forming a chain-like pattern on one side of the fabric and a 2-needle lockstitch effect on the other side. A coverstitch finish is primarily used on knit fabrics.

Crack Stitch A machine stitch sewn as close to the seam as possible, to hold down another area of the garment such as a binding or when making a Hong Kong bound finish. Also known as "stitch-in-the-ditch."

Creaseline Line formed when folding a pattern over to form a crease.

Crêpe de Chine A lightweight, densely woven, plain-weave silk fabric, woven with a silk warp and a crêpe twist filling.

Crewel Needles Identical to sharps needles, but with a longer eye for threading multiple strands of thread. Also known as embroidery needles.

Cross/Crosswise Grain Fabric grain that goes from selvage to selvage, also known as the weft.

Cross-Wound Thread that is wound on a spindle, forming an "X" pattern such as on cop, cone, or vicone thread "put-ups."

Cuff Band that ends the bottom of a sleeve, or a detail on the bottom of pants or shorts that turns up over itself.

Cut-Away Armhole A stylized sleeveless armhole recessed in from the natural armhole.

D

Darning Needles Hand-sewing needles primarily used for mending and for basting layered fabrics together.

Dart A V-shaped stitched tuck that is used to create shape in a garment. Darts can be concave, convex, fisheye, French, straight, or curved.

Dart Intake Amount of dart material inside a dart's stitching lines.

Dart Legs The stitching line of a dart, from start to vanishing point.

Dart Pickup/Size The amount of dart material or dart intake.

Denier System A system for measuring the weight of density of thread. For example, a single strand of silk is approximately one denier.

Diagonal Basting Hand-basting stitch, stitched on a diagonal, used to control fabric layers during garment construction and pressing.

Diagonal Pinning Pinning seams at a 45-degree angle when sewing, to help the seams lay flat.

Double Overcast Stitch Hand stitch that creates an "X" effect, and is used on the raw edges of fabric to prevent fraying.

Double-face Wool Wool fabric made of two layers bonded together, usually in contrasting colors, which is made to be reversible.

Double-faced Seam Seam finish used on double-faced fabrics, and a technique used to create reversible garments.

Double-stitched Seam Seam finish used on sheer fabrics, where there may be some stress on the seams, while keeping the seam allowances minimally visible.

Double-welt Pocket A double-welt inset slit pocket used on tailored pants, jackets, coats, and dresses. Also known as a besom pocket.

Dressmaker's Pins Pins made of nickel-plated steel, in different sizes to suit fabric weights.

Drill A strong, warp-faced, medium- to heavyweight cotton fabric in a left-hand twill construction. Also used as interfacing for coats.

Duck Strong, medium- to heavyweight plain-weave fabric usually made of cotton or cotton blend. Also used as interfacing for coats.

E

Ease Slightly gathering an area into another area, such as easing extra fabric on a bodice side panel into the front panel. Also, allowing extra fabric to a pattern or drape for wearing comfort.

Elastic Stretch material sold by the yard, in various types, colors, and widths.

Elastic Thread Thread with an elastic core, used in the bobbin to create gathers, shirring, crimping, and smocking.

Embellishment Any type of ornamention on a garment, such as appliqué, beading, decorative stiching, embroidery, eyelets, or studs.

Embroidery Floss (Thread) A 6-strand hand-sewing thread, loosely twisted and slightly glossy.

Embroidery Needles see Crewel Needles.

Embroidery Scissors Scissors with small, very sharp blades, used for any precision cutting.

Even Basting Simple hand stitch approximately 4–6 stitches per inch (2.5cm), used to hold one or more layers of fabric together temporarily.

Exposed Separating Zipper See Separating Zipper. This zipper is the same, but the zipper teeth/coil are meant to be visible on the garment.

F

Fabric Cloth made of woven, knitted, felted, braided, netted, or bonded yarns.

Fabric Hand see Hand.

Fabric Weight The thickness or thinness of a particular fabric.

Face The right side of a fabric.

Facing Fabric added to the reverse of a garment to clean finish an area, for example on a neckline, armhole, sleeve, waistline, or pocket top.

Fell Stitch A hand stitch used to attach a raw or folded edge to a garment.

Fiber The strands or filaments from which threads and fabrics are made.

Filament A length of yarn that is one continuous length of fiber, such as silk, rayon, polyester, and nylon.

Fine Cotton Thread Thread such as a tex size 24 or a thread weight of 60 (60Wt.) used for stitching fine fabrics or for topstitching.

Finger-press Using your fingers to press flat an area such as a dart or seam allowance.

Fisheye Dart Curved, almond- or eye-shaped dart that adds shape to a garment.

Fitted When a garment sits close to the body with little to no wearing ease.

Flare Extending out from a straight or natural line, such as on a sleeve.

Flat Fell Seam Seam finish with one seam allowance covering the other. Often used on jeans or seams where extra strength is required.

Flat Seam A seam created by abutting two pieces of fabric edge to edge with no overlap, and sewing them together to enclose the raw edges.

Flat-bed Knitting Machine Machine producing weft or warp flat knit yardage.

Flex Curve A flexible device that can be molded to any contour, used for measuring curves, such as around necklines.

Fly Shield Separate extension piece sewn into the zipper opening of a fly front zipper.

Fly-Front Zipper A zipper topstitched in the form of a reversed letter J, commonly used on the front of jeans, pants (trousers), and skirts.

Fold Line Pattern position indicating where to turn up or under, such as on the hem of a garment.

Four-way Stretch A term given to knit fabric that has at least 100 percent stretch in both the cross and length directions.

Fray When raw edges of a fabric start to unravel.

French Dart Bust dart that emanates from the side seam and is positioned close to the waistline, resulting in a semi-fitted shape.

French Loop A hand-made thread chain that connects layers of fabric together loosely. Also known as French tacks.

French Piping Double-folded bias binding used to finish the edge of a sheer or lightweight garment, such as on a neckline, armhole, or hem.

French Seam Couture seam finish for sheer and other lightweight fabrics.

French Tack see French Loop.

Fusible Interfacing Support material with a press-on adhesive backing that adds structure. Available in various weights and colors and offered as woven, non-woven, and knitted.

G

Garment Bias Any bias grain that is not at 45 degrees. A 45-degree angled bias is "true bias."

Gather Pull threads to compress fabric, such as when shirring fabric into a waistline to create a gathered skirt.

Georgette A sheer, lightweight plain-weave fabric with a fine crepe surface and a dull finish.

Glazed Thread Finish Thread with a surface coating of wax and starches to reduce abrasion and increase durability, perfect for button sewing.

Glover's Needle A hand sewing needle with a triangular point for penetrating leather and leatherlike materials.

Grain The yarn direction of a fabric: crossgrain (weft), length grain (warp), or diagonal (bias). Also the smooth side of leather after tanning.

Grainline The direction of yarns in a fabric weave: crossgrain (weft), length grain (warp), diagonal (bias).

Grommets Circular rings with center holes to pass ties or laces through.

H

Hair Canvas Support material used as an interfacing or interlining in jackets and coats.

Ham Ironing tool used when pressing curved areas of a garment.

Hand The feel of a fabric: smooth, stiff, soft, drapey, rigid, crisp, or pliable.

Hand Baste Simple hand stitch approximately 4–6 stitches per inch (2.5cm), used to hold layers of fabric together temporarily.

Hand Pick Stitch A hand stitch with a small stitch pick-up. It is used as a decorative holding stitch, such as around a lapel edge, or in place of a machine stitch to hold a zipper securely.

Hand-Knit A garment knitted by hand using knitting needles.

Hand-Rolled Hem A labor-intensive, narrow hem finish used on sheer and lightweight fabrics.

Heavy-duty Thread A core-spun thread used to sew gathers and shirring, by hand or machine.

Heavyweight Cotton Drill Fabric A durable cotton fabric with a pronounced diagonal twill weave. Often used to press heavyweight fabrics.

Hem Finished edge of a garment, or the act of finishing the bottom portion of a sleeve, blouse, skirt, dress, or pant (trouser).

Hem Allowance The amount of fabric allocated to a hem.

Hem Binding A binding that finishes a hem or other raw edge. Available as sew-on tape, can be hand-made, or cut on the bias.

Hem Tape A by-the-yard sew-on tape used to finish a hem or other raw edge. Also known as seam binding.

Hem Tape Hem A hem finish that utilizes hem tape; the most common hem finish in the fashion industry.

Hemline Line that denotes the fold line of the hem before it is turned up and finished.

Hemming Stitch A running stitch that holds the hem in place before it is sewn permanently.

Holding Stitch A machine or hand stitch used to hold gathers, pleats, interfacing, or other areas of a garment in place, before permanent stitching.

Hong Kong Hem A hem finish used on wools, or any light- to-medium-weight fabric, whereby the raw edge of hem is bound with bias binding to create a clean finish.

Hong Kong Seam Seam finish whereby each opened raw edge of the seam allowance is bound with either a bias fabric strip or a by-the-yard single- or double-folded bias binding.

Hook and Eye Two-part metal closure that consists of a hook and a loop, positioned at the top of a zipper.

Horsehair Stiffening material used to add structure to areas such as hems and collars.

Horsehair Canvas A blend of wool or cotton and horse mane and tail. The horse hair is woven into the weft, resulting in a "springy" hand that is perfect for tailored jacket collars and lapels.

Horsehair Hem A hem technique utilizing horsehair material to create a hem on sheer and lightweight fabrics, when extra shape and structure is needed.

I J K

Inseam Inside length of a seam, such as the inside of a pant leg or sleeve. Men's pant sizes are measured from this length.

Inseam Pocket Pocket that is hidden or inset into a section of a garment such as in a seam.

Inset Pocket Pocket that is cut into a garment, such as a welt pocket on a jacket.

Interfacing Material used on areas of a garment to give it shape, body, and support. Available woven, non-woven, fusible, and non-fusible.

Interlining Material used inside coats and jackets for warmth and insulation.

Interlock A rib-knit variation made on a two-bed circular weft knitting machine. Also called double knit or double jersey.

Invisible Zipper Zipper with hidden coil teeth, inserted so that no machine stitching is visible from the right side of the garment. Often used on women's skirts, pants, and dresses.

Jacquard System of weaving or knitting that produces a patterned fabric or knit. Used to create brocade, damask, and tapestry and often used as lining material.

Keyhole Buttonhole Buttonhole in the shape of an elongated keyhole. Easy for a shank button to pass through, and often used on coats.

Knit Fabrics Fabric created using needles to form yarn loops that allow the fabric to stretch. See also Weft Knits and Warp Knits.

Knit Stitch Right side of the most basic knit stitch. Reverse side is known as a purl stitch.

Knitted Interfacing Interfacing made on knit machinery, used to add shape and support to a knit garment as well as on leather, faux leather, vinyl, and woven fabrics for a softer end result.

L

Lace Edge Binding Type of lace binding used to finish hem edges or as a decorative detail.

Lacing Cord, ribbon, or fabric strips used to close a garment, as on the front of corsets.

Lapel The portion immediately below the collar of a blouse, coat, or jacket that is folded back on either side of the front opening.

Lapped Seam Seam finish where one raw edge overlaps the other raw edge and is then stitched together on top of the seam. Can only be done in material that does not fray.

Lapped Zipper Zipper setting where one side of the fabric "laps" over the zipper, covering the teeth. It is most often used on dresses and on pants (trousers) and skirts that have a waistband.

Lapped Zipper with Facing A center-back lapped zipper with a neckline facing, most commonly found on tailored dresses.

Leather A material created by tanning animal skins. "Leather" refers to the grainy outside or fur-bearing part of a skin, also known as nappa, while the inside of the skin is the "suede" side.

Left-Side Zipper Foot A sewing-machine foot attachment with a left side notch, used for zipper-setting and when sewing close to a particular section of a garment.

Length Grain In a plain-weave textile the lengthwise grain, also known as the warp, is the strongest grain.

Lining A material used in a garment to add shape, provide comfort, and to cover the inner construction seams of a garment. Linings are generally smooth fabrics that enable the wearer to slip in and out of the garment with ease.

Lockstitch Machine The most commonly used sewing machine, with a single needle that interlocks two threads, one in the needle and the other in a bobbin. Industrial double-needle machines use twin needles.

Loop Turner Metal tool with a latch and hook end used to turn fabric tubings inside out, such as when making spaghetti straps.

M

Machine Basting Long, temporary machine stitches sewn at approximately 4–6 stitches per inch (2.5cm).

Machine Needle Points The point shape and tip of a sewing machine needle determine its performance. Round points are used for sewing wovens, ballpoint needles for knits, and sharp points for non-wovens such as leather.

Machine-foot Baby Hem Very small baby-like hem finish used on sheer and lightweight fabrics, made on a sewing machine with a ⅛" (3mm) hemming foot attachment.

Magnetic Seam Guide Magnetized gauge device used on a sewing machine to assist in the sewing of seams and topstitching.

Man-Made Fiber Any manufactured fiber such as acetate, rayon, acrylic, nylon, polyester, spandex, or those made from fibers derived from materials such as glass, metal, carbon, or ceramic.

Match To line up, as in matching notches or a plaid or stripe, at the side seam.

Matte Jersey A warp-knitted fabric made with tricot construction using fine crepe yarn, producing a dry, textured hand and dull finish.

Mercerized Cotton Thread Cotton thread that is treated to enhance its strength, luster, and durability. Sometimes called a "silk finish."

Microfiber A very fine synthetic filament or staple fiber, generally less than 0.01 denier per filament, producing a soft, lightweight fabric.

Milliners/Straw Needles The longest hand-sewing needle, with a small, round eye. Used for smocking, pleating, basting, and millinery.

Miter/Mitre To join two edges of fabric, cut at a 45-degree angle, to form a corner. Mitered corners are used on jacket and sleeve hems and skirt vents. Mitering also occurs when a plaid or stripe fabric seam comes together at a 45-degree angle, such as on a skirt front.

Mock French Seam Finish A seam finish used on sheer fabrics to clean the edge without the labor involved in creating a French seam.

Momme The unit of weight for silk fabrics. The higher the mommes, the heavier the weight. 8 mommes is approximately 1 ounce per square yard or 35 grams per square meter.

Monofilament Thread A single strand of filament fiber. These threads are finer and stronger than spun thread and less costly.

Multifilament Thread A thread consisting of several strands of filament. Since filament threads are made from continuous manufactured fibers, they require only a slight twist to hold them together.

Muslin Plain-weave, unbleached, and unsized fabric used in draping and available in a variety of weights, from fine to heavy.

N

Nap The direction of the pile on a fabric such as velvet or corduroy. Patterns must be laid out in one direction, usually nap smoothed up, before cutting.

Natural Fibers Fibers derived from animal, vegetable, or mineral resources, such as silk from the silkworm or linen from the flax plant.

Neckband On a garment, a neckband finishes the neckline. On a dress form (tailor's dummy) the neckband is located above the neckline.

Neckline The contour of the neck opening of a garment, from front to back.

Netting An open-mesh fabric available in varying degrees of stiffness. Often used as an interfacing for lightweight fabrics.

Nonfusible Interfacing Interfacing, either woven or knitted, without adhesive backing.

Nonwoven Fabric that is made by bonding or fusing fibers together. Examples are non-woven interfacing and felt material.

Nonwoven Interfacing Interfacing made by bonding or fusing fibers together. Available either fusible or nonfusible.

Notches Marks made on patterns to indicate where seams align, where hems are turned, and other key matching points.

Nylon A manufactured fiber that is strong and quick drying, and resistant to chemicals. Often blended with other fibers, especially when used as lining material.

O

Off-grain Garment that is not draped or cut on the proper fabric grain, resulting in a poor fit and a garment that is unbalanced.

One-Way Print A printed fabric with a distinct motif that must be cut in a one-way direction.

One-Way Stretch A knit fabric that stretches only one way, usually in the cross direction. This can also apply to stretch-woven fabrics.

Organza A lightweight sheer fabric with a somewhat firm hand. It is used for garment making, interfacing, underlining, and as a pressing cloth.

Outseam The pant (trouser) side seam from waist to ankle, or any out-facing seam, such as the center seam on a 2-piece raglan sleeve.

Overcast Seam A seam finish where the raw edges are slightly covered with either a hand-stitched overcast stitch or a sewing-machine zigzag stitch, to prevent fraying.

Overcast Stitch A diagonal hand stitch used to partially cover raw seam edges to prevent fraying.

Overlock & Open Seam A popular seam finish for light- to medium-weight fabrics, using an overlock machine/serger and a lockstitch machine. The seams are joined with a lockstitch, then the edges are overlocked and pressed open.

Overlock with Catchstitch Hem A hem finish using an overlock machine stitch to clean the raw edge and then a hand-sewn catchstitch

to stitch the hem. A catchstitch allows the hem to stretch.

Overlock/Chainstitch Neckline A knit neckline finish using an overlock machine to finish the raw edge and then a chainstitch machine to secure the folded seam allowance edge of the fabric to the body.

Overlocked Hem A hem finish created using an overlock machine to clean the raw edge. The hem is turned and stitched by hand or by machine. It is commonly used in the industry.

Overlocker see Serger.

P Q

Pad Stitch Small, diagonal running stitches that add shape and structure to areas such as the underside of a tailored jacket collar and lapel.

Parallel Darts Darts that are positioned side by side.

Parallel Pinning Pinning seams in the same direction of a seam or hemline that goes around the body/dress form. For example, the parallel pinning of a seam joining a bodice to a skirt.

Patch Pocket Pocket that is positioned on top of a garment.

Pick Stitch Very small hand stitch, also known as a stab stitch. It is used in tailoring around a lapel edge, for hems, in embroidery, and to sew a zipper securely on pile and napped fabrics.

Pin Basting Using pins to hold fabric layers together before sewing or during a fitting.

Pink To use pinking shears.

Pinked & Open Seam A seam finish in which the raw edge of the seam allowance is trimmed with pinking shears, 1/4" (6mm) away from the raw edge, and the seam pressed open.

Pinked & Stitched Hem A hem finish with the raw hem edge pinked and a line of machine stitching sewn 1/4" (6mm) away from the pinking. Popular for fabrics that do not fray easily.

Pinking Shears Scissors with a serrated blade, used to finish the edges of seams to keep them from fraying or as a decorative touch.

Piping Folded strip of cloth, sometimes with a cord insert, sewn into a seam or on a garment edge as a trim.

Placket An opening on a garment, such as the end of a sleeve or the front of a shirt, finished with a separate fabric band or facing.

Plaid A yarn-dyed woven or printed check fabric.

Plain Seam The most basic seam type, placing one layer of fabric over another and stitching them together.

Ply To lay one fabric piece on top of another.

Pocket Garment detail that can be applied in different ways: as a patch pocket; as a bag inset into a garment, as in a welt pocket; or sewn into a seam, as in an inseam pocket.

Pocketing Fabric used for garment pocket bags. Usually a tightly woven cotton or cotton blend.

Pointer A wooden or plastic tool with a sharp point on one end. It is used for turning areas that have to end in a point, such as collar tips.

Polyester A manufactured fiber that is strong, durable, wrinkle resistant, resistant to stretching and shrinking, and easily washed and dried.

Power Mesh A micro-fine 4-way stretch knit mesh fabric used in activewear, swimwear, lingerie, and as a lining for lace garments.

Preshrink To steam press and/or clean a test swatch before a fabric or trim is cut. This checks for shrinkage caused by certain treatments such as washing, drycleaning, or pressing.

Press Iron a garment or fabric to smooth it. It is best to iron in the direction of the grain.

Pressing Cloth Cloth used to cover a fabric or garment when pressing, to avoid damaging the fabric or creating shine marks.

Pressing (Tailor's) Ham A device shaped like a ham and used when pressing any curved area of a garment.

Pressing Mitt Padded glove used to press areas of a garment where an iron cannot easily reach.

Prewaxed/Precut Thread A 2-ply waxed nylon silamide thread. It is strong and smooth and used for hems, pad stitching, attaching zippers, buttons, hooks and eyes, and beading.

Prick Stitch A hand sewing stitch made up of very tiny backstitches, 1/16" (2mm) long, followed by 1/4" (6mm) spaces between each stitch. Useful when setting a zipper into pile fabrics, such as velvet, that a machine zipper foot would crush.

Purl Reverse side of a knit stitch (plain or basic stitch). The top side of the stitch is known as a knit stitch.

Put-up How a thread is packaged according to the type of thread, the machine being used, and

the sewing requirements. The most common "put-ups" are spool, cup, cone, and vicone.

Quilted Two fabrics stitched together either by machine or by hand with a layer of batting in between to create a raised effect.

Quilting Needles see Betweens Needles.

R

Rayon A manufactured fiber with high absorbency, a bright or dull luster, and a drapey hand, originally known as artifical silk.

Recovery The degree of resiliency of a knit fabric; how a knit fabric returns to its original shape after being stretched.

Rib Knit A knit stitch created using a series of alternating knit and purl stitches, or various combinations of these stitches.

Ribbed Knit A knit fabric composed of vertical dimensional rows achieved by alternating stockinette (stocking) stitch with reverse stockinette stitch.

Ribbon-Edge Hem A decorative hem finish for a sheer garment.

Right-Side Zipper Foot A sewing machine foot attachment with a right side notch, used for zipper setting and when sewing close to a particular section of a garment.

Roll Line The line at which a collar turns over, as in a roll collar.

Rotary Blade Cutter Device used with a cutting mat to cut fabric and paper.

Ruching A French term meaning to gather, ruffle, or pleat fabric into tight folds.

Running Stitch Small, even stitches, made either by hand or machine, that run in and out of fabric without overlapping.

S

Safety Stitch Seam An overlock or serger seam that uses five threads to join two seams with a chainstitch, while also overlocking the edge.

Satin Fabric formed almost completely of warp or filler floating in the repeat of the weave. The result is a smooth, lustrous surface.

Satin Organza A semi-sheer, organza-like, lightweight, fine satin-weave fabric with a firm hand and a somewhat glossy surface.

Scalloped Edge Decorative edge mimicking the edges of a seashell.

Seam Allowance Amount of material that extends beyond the stitching line. Seam allowances range from ⅛" (3mm) to 1" (2.5cm) and vary depending on the type of seam.

Seam Binding see Hem Tape.

Seam Finish A machine- or hand-stitched treatment used to keep the raw edges of the seam allowance from fraying. It is important to choose an appropriate seam finish for a particular fabric.

Seam Gauge Ruler with an adjustable tab used to mark areas of a garment such as buttonholes, pocket placement, and hems.

Seam Grading Trimming seam allowances at different widths to eliminate bulk on a seam.

Seam Guide Sewing-machine device used to measure the distance from the machine needle to the stitching line while sewing.

Seam Ripper Tool used to open sewn seams, rip out stitches, and open buttonholes.

Seam Roll A pressing aid, used for pressing straight and curved seams, or tubular shapes.

Seamline The stitching line of a garment.

Seamline Pocket see Inseam Pocket.

Self-lined Sheer garments are either unlined or self-lined with the same fabric as the garment.

Self-threading Needle A type of hand sewing needle that is designed for easy threading. Not recommended for fine fabrics, as they can snag.

Selvage Finished edges on fabric in the length/warp grain.

Separating Zipper A zipper where both sides separate at the bottom. Separating zippers are one-way, which open from the bottom, and two-way, which can open and close from either end.

Serger A type of sewing machine, also known as an overlocker, that uses 2–5 threads to sew an overlocking stitch finish over one or more raw edges on seams and hems.

Serging Thread Polyester thread used for serging, available in a cone or a vicone.

Set-in Interfacing Any non-fusible interfacing that is stitched into the garment seams, as compared to fusible interfacings that are pressed or fused to a garment.

Set-in Sleeve Sleeve that sits within a natural armhole as compared to a sleeve that sits in a drop shoulder or stylized armhole.

Sewing Gauge A 6" (15cm) ruler used for measuring hems and other areas.

Sew-through Button A button that is stitched through its surface holes to a garment.

Shank An extra piece under a button cap that makes it easier to pass through a buttonhole.

Sharps Needle General-purpose hand-sewing needle with a round eye and a very sharp point.

Shears Large scissors with sharp blades for cutting fabric. Fabric shears are generally long, heavy, and with one handle bigger than the other, for better balance when cutting layers of fabric.

Shell Fabric The outside of a garment, also known as the outer shell.

Shirring Running one or more parallel lines of stitches to form gathers, as in a skirt waistline.

Shirring Stitch A hand or machine stitch used to gather or shirr areas of a garment. Stitch length for machine or hand gathering is 7–9 stitches per inch (2.5cm), and longer for heavier fabrics.

Shirring Thread Heavier thread used for gathering or shirring fabric areas of a garment.

Side Seam On the dress form, a straight line down from the middle of the underarm.

Silhouette The line or shape of a design.

Silk Organza A lightweight, sheer silk fabric used for garment making, and also as an interfacing and underlining.

Silk Pins Thin steel pins that easily glide into silk and other fine, lightweight fabrics.

Silk Thread One hundred percent silk thread. Too strong for garment construction, but used for pad stitching fine wools and for embroidery.

Single Edgestitch Seam Seam finish used for sheer seams where there is little to no stress, such as on very full skirts. It is also used to keep seam allowances minimally visible on sheer fabrics.

Single-Fold Bias Binding with Crackstitch A bias binding used anywhere a clean finished edge is needed. The stitching of binding to garment is almost invisible on the right side.

Single-Fold Bias Binding with Edgestitch A bias binding used anywhere a clean finished edge is needed. The stitches that connect the binding to the garment are visible on the right side.

Single-Fold Neck/Armhole Binding A bias binding used anywhere a clean finished edge is

needed. The stitching of binding to garment is completely invisible on the right side.

Single-Welt Pocket A single-welted inset slit pocket used on tailored clothing. Often positioned horizontally on tailored suit jackets, or vertically on pants (trousers), skirts, casual jackets, and coats. Also known as a jetted pocket.

Sizing A finish or coating given to a fabric to provide added body.

Slash To cut into material to release it, for example slashing into the waist when dropping a flare for a skirt.

Sleeve Board A small, narrow ironing board used to press sleeves and other areas.

Slip Stitch A hand stitch that is used on hems and appliqué work. For a hem, the stitch takes up one thread from the underside of the body fabric, then is hidden in the folded hem edge.

Slit Opening on a garment that adds movement, such as on the side seam of a skirt or jacket.

Sloper/Block Basic foundation garment or toile, without seam allowances, from which designs are created. Slopers can be developed through the flat pattern process, using body measurements, or by draping on a dress form.

Slot Seam A decorative technique created by placing a strip of fabric underneath a seam to add dimension or contrast.

Snaps Prong and socket closure made of metal or plastic and used in place of a button.

Soft Thread Finish Refers to natural cotton thread or spun thread with only a small amount of lubrication. This thread has a fuzzy surface.

Spaghetti Straps Narrow tubular straps made from fabric bias strips.

Spandex A synthetic fiber with exceptional elasticity. Also known as elastomeric yarn, Lycra®, and elastane.

Spool A cyclindrical device on which thread is wound. Thread spools are stack wound, with one row of thread parallel to the next.

Spun Thread Staple fibers that are twisted together to make a single yarn. Two single yarns twisted together create a ply yarn or a plied yarn. Ply yarns are used for basic seam construction.

Stabilizer Material used to prevent areas such as seams from stretching, or used as interfacing to add support to larger areas.

Staple Fiber A length of yarn that consists of many short fibers twisted together, such as cotton, linen, and wool.

Staystitch Machine or hand stitch used to control an area and keep it from stretching.

Stitch A single looping of thread or yarn made by hand or machine.

Stitch Length see Stitches Per Inch.

Stitch-in-the-Ditch see Crackstitch.

Stitches Per Inch (SPI) The number of stitches per inch for a seam or fabric tells you the recommended stitch length. The tighter the fabric weave, the shorter the stitch length.

Stitching Line The part that will be sewn on a garment, such as a seam.

Straight Buttonhole The most common buttonhole, a rectangular opening made by hand or by machine.

Straight Grain In the natural direction of the weave, such as in line with the cross-grain yarns or in line with the length-grain yarns.

Stretch Lace A knitted lace fabric on a mesh ground, and with either 2- or 4-way stretch.

Stretch Linings Linings knitted or woven with stretch yarns, to offer the wearer most comfort.

Stretch Ratio The degree of stretch of a particular knit fabric, determined both by its knit structure and the type of stretch fiber used.

Synthetic Fibers Any fiber derived from synthetic polymers. Examples include acrylic, nylon, polyester, and spandex.

T

Taffeta A fine, crisp, plain-weave fabric with either a lustrous or a dull face. The fabric is smooth, sometimes with a fine cross rib.

Tailor's Chalk Removable chalk used for marking fabric.

Tailor's Knot Knot formed when looping two threads together at the same time and then pulling them with your fingers to form a knot.

Tailor's Tacks Temporary hand basting stitches used to mark sheer or fine fabrics, which a tracing wheel would damage. When cut apart, they leave threads that serve as outlines for stitching lines.

Tailored Edge Baby Hem Narrow hem finish, ⅛–¼" (3–6mm) wide, made by machine and used on sheer and lightweight fabrics.

Taped Seam A ¼" (6mm) wide twill tape used on seams to prevent stretching, particularly in key areas of knit garments.

Template A shape or form used as a pattern or guide to be traced off and copied.

Textured Thread A soft, textured thread manufactured with applied heat to increase its bulk. Used to finish raw edge seams and rolled hems, and for use in active- and swimwear.

Thimble Metal or plastic tool used when hand sewing, to help protect the fingers and assist in pushing the sewing needle through the material.

Thinsulate® A polyester or manufactured fiber blend used as an interlining in quilted coats.

Thread Thin, twisted yarns, available in different fibers, weights, and colors, that are wound on a spool and used for sewing. Choosing the correct type of thread for a particular project is important.

Thread Bar A hand-made thread chain used as a loop for buttons, hooks, or lacings.

Thread Count Number of warp and weft threads per square inch in a woven fabric.

Thread Shank A hand-made thread extension technique used when attaching a sew-through button to a garment, achieving the same effect as a shank button.

Thread Tracing A hand-basting stitch to mark a garment in place of a tracing wheel and paper.

Three-Needle Coverstitch Hem A hem finish with looped stitches on one side of the fabric and a 3-needle lockstitch effect on the other side, denser than a 2-needle coverstitch hem. Primarily used on knit fabrics and best sewn using a coverstitch machine. Can also be used on seams and necklines.

Tiger Tape A brand of adhesive tape used as a guide to ensure evenly spaced stitches.

Toggle Button A 2-holed elongated fastener used to close jackets and coats, sewn to a garment with either a cord or leather strip.

Toile A full muslin drape of a garment design that is ready for fitting. Cotton canvas is used for jacket and coat toiles.

Topstitching A hand or machine stitch, usually longer than a regular stitch, often sewn in contrast color thread or as decorative edging.

Tracing Marks Markings made on fabric using tracing paper and a tracing wheel, to indicate stitching lines. For fine and sheer fabrics, tracing marks are made with tailor's tacks.

Triangular Chalk Marker A metal roller that draws chalk onto fabric, making extra-fine lines. Also known as a chalk wheel.

Tricot Interfacing A warp-knit interfacing used to interface knit, woven, and leather garments.

Trim To cut away an area of a garment. Also a decorative detail, such as ribbon, braid, or piping.

True Bias Of a fabric, the diagonal direction, at a 45-degree angle, that yields the most stretch.

Tulle A soft, fine machine-made netting fabric with a hexagonal mesh, available in silk, cotton, or manufactured fiber. Also called English tulle.

Twill A strong and durable woven fabric with a diagonal rib or twill line, usually running from left to right. Woven in cotton or cotton blends, or in manufactured fibers for use as linings.

Two-Needle Coverstitch Hem A hem finish with looped stitches on one side of the fabric and a 2-needle lockstitch effect on the other side. Primarily used on knit fabrics and best sewn using a coverstitch machine. A 2-needle coverstitch can also be used on seams and necklines.

Two-Way Stretch Of a knit fabric, one that stretches 50 percent or more in the crosswise direction and 50–70 percent lengthwise.

U

Under Collar Bottom or under collar patterned smaller than the top collar, depending on the thickness of the fabric, so that it won't show once the collar is set into the neckline.

Underlining A layer of fabric used on the underside of a garment's outer fabric. It can give a lightweight fabric additional body; stabilize a loosely woven fabric; hide construction details; reduce transparency on a sheer fabric; or add structure to certain parts of a garment.

Understitch A machine stitch that holds seam allowances together on the underside of a garment and keeps it from showing on the right side, such as on a facing or under collar.

Uneven Basting Simple hand stitch that starts with one small stitch approximately ¼" (6mm) long followed by another stitch ¾" (2cm) long, then repeated. The stitch is used to mark areas of a garment temporarily.

Universal Needles A type of lockstitch sewing machine needle. It is the most common needle type, has a slightly rounded point, and can be used on knits and wovens.

V

Vanishing Point Where a dart ends.

Velcro A tape fastener consisting of two parts, one covered with tiny loops and the other with tiny flexible hooks, that adhere when pressed together and can be pulled apart.

Velvet A warp pile fabric with short, thick, closely woven cut pile on one side, available in silk, cotton, nylon, or blends.

Velvet Board A flat bed of tiny needles used for pressing napped fabrics to prevent damaging the pile. Also known as a needle board.

Vent see Slit.

Voile A lightweight, sheer fabric made of hard twist yarns in low-count plain weave. It is often used for interfacing lightweight fabrics.

W

Waist Dart Dart that emanates from the waist and vanishes in the direction of the bust on a bodice or dress, and in the direction of the hip on a pant, skirt, or dress.

Waistband A band that is attached to the waistline of a skirt or pant (trouser) and provides a clean finish at the waist.

Waistline Horizontal line around a body or dress form, indicating the narrowest portion.

Wale The lengthwise row of stitches on a plain stitch or basic knit fabric. Also describes a row on corduroy fabric.

Warp The lengthwise grain of a woven fabric or, in a knit, one that is produced on a flat-bed knitting machine.

Warp Knit A knit fabric that is produced on a flat-bed knitting machine in which the yarn zigzags in a vertical orientation.

Weave Refers to the three most common fabric weaves: plain weave, twill weave, and satin weave.

Weft The crosswise grain of a woven fabric.

Weft Interfacing A soft, weft-knit interfacing, stable both lengthwise and crosswise, and used to interface softly tailored woven garments.

Weft Knit A hand or machine knit with horizontal rows of loops known as knit and purl stitches. Most knitted fabrics are produced by weft knitting.

Welt A fabric inset strip or band used in the construction of a slit pocket.

Whipstitch A hand stitch used to piece together fabric with a limited seam allowance, or used as a decorative stitch when sewing together two separate pieces of fabric with flat edges, such as on the edge of a jacket lapel and collar.

Wide Straight-Grain Hem A hem finish used on sheer fabrics where the bottom of the fabric is folded over itself three times, and then hemmed using a blind stitch. This gives a weighty hem finish that can also be used on sleeves.

Wool Fabrics Fabrics made from the hair of animals, such as sheep, angora goats, or alpaca, among others. A wide range of wool fabrics and weaves is available, from featherweight wool gauze to heavyweight wool melton.

Wool Flannel A light- to medium-weight wool fabric of plain or twill weave with a slightly napped surface, popular for suits.

Wool Melton A medium- to heavyweight twill-weave, woolen fabric with a close-cut nap and a felt-like smooth surface. Used for outerwear.

Worsted Wool Wool fabric manufactured using the worsted spinning system, producing a yarn that is compact, smooth, even, and strong.

Woven Fabric that is made through the interlacing of yarns, either at a right angle to each other to create a plain weave, or in a combination diagonal weave to create a twill and satin weave.

Y Z

Yarn A continuous strand of fiber that is either composed of short fibers twisted together (as in cotton and wool fibers) or composed of endless filaments (as in synthetic fibers).

Zigzag Seam A machine-stitched seam sewn using a narrow zigzag setting. The stitch is perfect when joining knits seams together, in the absence of a chainstitch machine, as the zigzag stitch allows for "give" as the seam is stretched.

Zipper Closure device with metal, plastic, or nylon-coiled teeth and a metal pull. Available in various lengths, colors, and styles.

Zipper Foot Sewing machine attachment for setting zippers. Available for both left- and right-side zipper stitching, and in adjustable versions.

Zipper Notch Single or double notch at the side seam, center front, or back of a garment, to indicate the opening position of the zipper.

Index

Picture credits

Laurence King Publishing Ltd, the authors, and the picture researcher wish to thank the institutions and individuals who have kindly provided photographic material for use in this book. Every effort has been made to trace the present copyright holders; if there are any unintentional omissions or errors, we will be pleased to insert the appropriate acknowledgment in any subsequent edition.

All images except those listed below are courtesy the University of Fashion, with thanks to Berenstein Textiles, Fairfield, and 3M Thinsulate for samples shown in Chapter 3.

Page 13 t From *Great Inventors and Their Inventions* by Frank P. Bachman, 1918; **13 b** The New York Historical Society / Getty Images; **14 l** Chaloner Woods / Getty Images; **14 r** Roberto Westbrook / Blend Images / Getty Images; **15** Harry Myers; **17** Michel Arnaud / Corbis via Getty Images; **23** Ruth Jenkinson / Dorling Kindersley / Getty Images; **35 tr** William Gee; **42 c** (flax) © SeDMi / Shutterstock; **55** Reiner Rodriguez / age fotostock / Getty Images; **77** Kathrin Ziegler / Getty Images; **103** Thomas Barwick / Iconica / Getty Images; **113 t** Maarigard / Dorling Kindersley / Getty Images; **113 cl** Maarigard / Dorling Kindersley / Getty Images; **113 c** Andy Crawford, Steve Gorton / Dorling Kindersley / Getty Images; **113 cr** Deepak Aggarwal / Dorling Kindersley / Getty Images; **113 b** Maarigard / Dorling Kindersley / Getty Images; **137** Richard Bord / Getty Images; **145** VCG via Getty Images; **147 t** Michael Zwahlen / EyeEm / Getty Images; **147 bl** Deepak Aggarwal / Dorling Kindersley / Getty Images; **147 bc** Maarigard / Dorling Kindersley / Getty Images; **147 br** Deepak Aggarwal / Dorling Kindersley / Getty Images; **169** Image Source / Getty Images; **183** Julio Donoso / Sygma via Getty Images; **195** Victor Boyko / Getty Images; **197** Edward James / FilmMagic / Getty Images; **205** Peter Michael Dills / Getty Images; **209** George Pimentel / Getty Images for IMG; **211** Giovanni Giannoni / WWD / REX / Shutterstock; **215** Alexander Koerner / Getty Images for Bread & Butter by Zalando; **221** George Pimentel / Getty Images for IMG; **235** John Parra / WireImage; **241, 249** Peter White / Getty Images; **257** Brian Ach / Getty Images for NYFW: The Shows; **259** Edward James / FilmMagic; **263** Thomas Concordia / WireImage; **267** Attila Kisbenrdek / AFP / Getty Images; **273** John Phillips / Getty Images; **283** Jeoffrey Maitem / Getty Images; **287** Antonio de Moraes Barros Filho / WireImage; **293** Anthony Kwan / Getty Images; **301** Estrop / Getty Images; **307** Eri Kouguchi / EyeEm / Getty Images; **311** Peter White / Getty Images; **315** Broadimage / REX / Shutterstock; **321** Chicago History Museum / Getty Images; **325** Giovanni Giannoni / Penske Media / REX / Shutterstock; **331** Tim P. Whitby / Getty Images; **337** John B. Mueller Photography / Getty Images.

Chapter 4 answers (in *italics*)
The correct seam to use for the following:

- [ ] an unlined velvet jacket *Hong Kong*
- [ ] a full chiffon skirt *mock French*
- [ ] a fitted organdy blouse *French*
- [ ] jeans *flat-felled*
- [ ] a wool skirt *pinked & open*
- [ ] a cotton dress *overlocked*
- [ ] a reversible jacket *double-faced*

Chapter 5 answers (in *italics*)
The correct hem to use for the following:

- [ ] a silk scarf edge *hand-rolled*
- [ ] a full chiffon skirt *machine-foot baby hem*
- [ ] a decorative sheer skirt *ribbon-edge or wide straight-grain*
- [ ] a wool skirt with finished edge *hem-tape or Hong Kong*
- [ ] when the least expensive hem finish is needed *pinked or overlocked*